GOING BARMY

GOING BARMY

Despatches From a Cricketing Foot Soldier

Paul Winslow

Published in Great Britain by
SportsBooks Limited
1 Evelyn Court
Malvern Road
Cheltenham
GL50 2JR

First Published October 2012

Cover by Patrick Latham
www.3rdmancartoons.co.uk

A catalogue record for this book is available from the British Library.

ISBN 9781907524301

Printed and bound in England by TJ International Ltd,
Padstow, Cornwall

Dedication

To everyone I've ever watched cricket with. You made it so much fun it became addictive and cost me a bloody fortune.

Acknowledgements

My biggest thanks go to Rae, for supporting me during the writing, for reading a book about cricket despite not understanding half of the content, for amusing me with her random comments while I watched more cricket in the name of 'research' and for all her advice and invaluable feedback. Thanks also to Randall, for deciding to publish a book about a bloke getting drunk and watching sport. My gratitude goes to Graeme Swann for taking the time to show his love and writing the foreword. And to my family and friends who kept saying 'you should write a book about this'. I got round to it eventually.

Contents

Foreword

GETTING YOUR OWN Barmy Army song is a badge of honour. When you first start touring for England you usually find yourself ferrying drinks for those guys who are actually in the team. With the sun beating down it's not unusual to find the five or so subs sat under an umbrella bored out of their tree but knowing that the management team are watching at all times, and so the pressure is on to service the eleven prima donnas out on the field.

It was back in my days in this very position that I yearned to have my own Barmy Army song. I would hear the sometimes great, sometimes shite but often hilarious anthems start up and wish I could be either on the field or in the Army itself.

My time came in India. With a rearranged schedule and hence a small Barmy Army travelling support I made my Test debut in Chennai. I took a couple of wickets in my first over in what was a Roy of the Rovers kind of start. I was absolutely buzzing. It wasn't until the next morning as we were in the field that I noticed a new song emanating from the Barmies. My ears immediately pricked up because it was to the tune of *Champagne Supernova* by Oasis and I absolutely love Oasis…

'What lucky bastard has got this as their song?' I thought to myself.

And then as I listened closer I had the shock of my life.

'…in a Swanny super over in Chennaiiiii…' rang out across the ground.

I was spellbound. I had only taken those wickets late the night before, and already there was a full Barmy Army song to the tune of one of Mr Gallagher's finest numbers. Even though I still didn't know all the words I was pissing myself with excitement.

'You heard your song Swanny?' shouted Jimmy Anderson from square leg.

'I know mate, fucking brilliant isn't it?' I shouted back eagerly.

'It's better than mine' he replied. 'Mine's a pile of shit!'

The players have always held the Barmy Army in great esteem. Those hardy souls who travel the globe are especially favoured. You always know the same hardcore faces will be there from Barbados to Chittagong, from Dunedin to Delhi and from Sydney to Cape Town. These are the real Army members. The guys who write the songs, strictly administer the famous Dawn Patrol and more importantly support the team through thick and thin. Paul Winslow is definitely one of these.

My favourite memories of the epic tour down under in 2010–2011 have to be the two nights that followed the victories at Melbourne and Sydney with Winslow and the rest of the hardcore. I am a firm believer in celebrating in the 'clubhouses' that the Army take over for the week, and those two nights especially will forever be etched in my memory. Beer in hand, arm round the shoulders being egged on (and refusing I think) to sing Mitchell Johnson's new song. Brilliant, brilliant memories.

I'm glad that Winslow has written this book. Hopefully it will give you an insight into the life of the 'real', and often misunderstood Barmy Army. They are not hooligans, they are not troublemakers, they are just cricket nuts who fly the flag for this brilliant country we live in. They are the very heartbeat of our Test team abroad. And I love them for it.

Graeme Swann

Introduction

And did those feet in ancient time.
Walk upon England's mountains green:
And was the holy Lamb of God,
On England's pleasant pastures seen!

And did the Countenance Divine,
Shine forth upon our clouded hills?
And was Jerusalem builded here,
Among these dark Satanic Mills?

Bring me my Bow of burning gold;
Bring me my Arrows of desire:
Bring me my Spear: O clouds unfold!
Bring me my Chariot of fire!

I will not cease from Mental Fight,
Nor shall my Sword sleep in my hand:
Till we have built Jerusalem,
In England's green & pleasant Land

IT'S A BARMY ARMY tradition to sing *Jerusalem* at the start of every day's play so it seems only apt to repeat it at the start of this tome. It doesn't have anything to do with cricket, but it's England's unofficial national anthem to match *Flower of Scotland, Hymns and Arias* for the Welsh or *Fields of Athenry* for the Irish.

You could argue that we cheapen it a bit with the hand movements that go with it. 'Bring me my Bow' sees us pulling an imaginary bow. 'Bring me my Arrows' is met with imaginary darts throwing. A spear is thrown, the clouds are parted with our hands and the Chariot of Fire is enacted by pretend charioteering. For Mental Fight we point to our brains, before drawing our imaginary non-sleeping swords. Our hands rise to the heavens as we belt out the culmination. I'm not sure where the hand movements originated, but I've never seen them used by anyone other than us.

For many of us cricket is our religion and we sing this song with as much gusto as any church choir, although considerably less tunefully.

I couldn't even begin to guess how many times I have sung *Jerusalem* around the world now but it still sends a shiver down my spine when a good crowd sings it backed by our resident trumpeter, Bill Cooper. And it's not only the song I love. It's what it represents. As we sing *Jerusalem* another day of Test cricket is about to unfold before us. Another day watching the most complex and endearing of sports. And another day with a group of people who make watching that game fun even when the sport itself provides little in the way of entertainment.

Every day with the Army is the same, as a group of like-minded people gather to watch the sport they love and get behind their team. And yet every day is different as events on and off the pitch conspire to give each day its own personality. There's always a new story to tell so I thought I'd tell mine all in one place.

Paul Winslow

One

My recruitment

It's fun being in the Barmy Army

CRICKET WAS LIKE THE girl next door with whom I played occasionally as a child but largely ignored without knowing that later in life I would realise she was the most captivating, beautiful, engaging and encapsulating thing I would ever lay eyes on. I was to fall hopelessly, madly in love with something that had been under my nose since I was born.

Cricket has always been in my life. My Dad played a lot, my brother played a bit and in a household where sport was the predominant passion (of the three males anyway; my poor mother was more than apathetic) I always had at the very least a vague interest in the game. But while I loved sport as a kid, cricket never really grabbed my attention and imagination in the same way football did.

My first real memory of the sport dates back to 1986 when I was 11. We were on a family holiday in the UK and I remember sitting in the car listening to the radio as the rain poured down outside and the windows steamed up. A then stereotypical English summer day was lightened by an unstereotypical English cricketer as Ian Botham returned from his drugs ban, took two wickets in his first 12 balls and became the greatest wicket taker in Test history. But short of that, recollections of cricket from my early years are thin on the ground. I have generic memories of cricket being on television, but when I try to dredge particulars out of the deepest and darkest recesses of my brain all I come up with is a picture of Tony Lewis and Jack Bannister sitting in front of a window with raindrops pouring down it as they chatted during rain breaks. Hardly inspiring stuff.

I went to the occasional cricket match as a kid, mainly because my home town of Cleethorpes attracted some big games and became one of Nottinghamshire CCC's homes away from home. Looking back now I was privileged to watch some of the greats performing without realising how lucky I was. Richard Hadlee brought Nottinghamshire and New Zealand teams to play in his testimonial match. David Gower also turned up one year with a star-studded side. I recently discovered the programmes for these games in my Mum's loft. At the time they meant very little, but now my love of the game has developed these possessions have gained the precursor of 'cherished'.

What interest I did have in the game was largely because my Dad liked it and as I hero-worshipped him, whatever he did was cool with me. It's hard to be honest in retrospect, but I'm fairly sure that I did try to like cricket purely because he did without it ever engendering a huge amount of excitement in me. To put that into some kind of perspective he also liked trainspotting and I even tried to enjoy that despite finding it tediously dull. Trainspotting didn't turn out to be the girl next door.

One of the issues with cricket may have been that I never showed an aptitude for playing it. In family games I would need about ten outs to my brother's one to make my stay at the crease anything other than cursory. But then I wasn't any great shakes at football as a child either and that didn't stop me becoming a huge fan and a player of that sport.

So, as the subject matter of this book is watching cricket, we may as well skip through my childhood and fast-forward to July 1993. I had just finished school and was, assuming my A Level results were of sufficient standard, about to head off to university. As my group of friends contemplated going our separate ways on new adventures we decided a good day out was on the cards and we settled on the idea of a trip to Headingley to watch a Test match. I'm sure I went through many changes during puberty and beyond, but a deepening love of cricket hadn't been one of them. A love of beer had though and the two do go hand-in-hand.

The Ashes would be the consistent theme in my cricket-supporting life, so it's only prescient that my first glimpse of England playing international cricket would be against the oldest of enemies, Australia. Like any good sports fan I can reel off the team-sheets, scores and result from that first day of contact with the sport at that level. That's not because the day had such a profound effect on me that I remember every detail, but because *Cricinfo* is a stunningly good website and offers all that information to me at the behest of a few mouse-clicks. The only things I really remember are some blonde-haired surf dude called Shane Warne bowling and Graham Thorpe playing his second Test, the latter mainly memorable because he had scored a ton on his debut a couple of weeks before. He followed it up with a duck and 13 this time round as England lost by an innings and a lot. (He did better than his three fellow debutants in the previous Test. Where Thorpe would become one of my first England heroes, Mark Lathwell, Mark Ilott and Martin McCague never really jostled for position in my affections.) When you consider some of the statistics and occurrences I can now reel off about the most random games, and look forward to regaling you with very soon, the fact that I remember the cube root of nothing about this one is evidence that the experience generally failed to sear itself on my memory in any detail.

So my first date with international cricket had left no real impression. No fires had been awakened in my soul and there was little sign that this was a relationship that had any future. To torture the 'girl-next-door' analogy a tad further, I was leaving home now and the next time I would bump into her would be in Australia five and a half years later.

That was the next time I remember seeing Test cricket again. If there were other instances in between then they were so instantly forgettable they don't even have a file name in my brain's memory archive. The opponents were the same as that first experience, the venue considerably different. I spent the year of 1998 in Australia fulfilling the role of archetypal English backpacker. I lived in a house in Sydney where six people shared three bedrooms. I did terminally dull clerical work for not much money. I spent that money on cheap wine and then jumped into a car with three like-minded souls to travel the country. Such was my cricketing antipathy, the fact that England were playing the Ashes in Australia at that time was almost irrelevant, although I do remember interrupting a hedonistic alcohol and marijuana filled seven weeks in Cairns long enough to go and watch a tour game. According to *Cricinfo* we won but I was too busy enjoying cold beer to really remember, although I'm fairly sure I have a picture of me with Michael Atherton stuck away somewhere.

The more geographically informed of you may realise that I was pretty close to Brisbane and so could have gone to watch the first Test but the thought never even crossed my mind. Instead I worked my way down Australia's eastern coast, enjoying the delights of Fraser Island, the Whitsundays, Noosa and Byron Bay, during which time England lost the Ashes. But I made it to Sydney for Christmas and New Year and as my time in the country was coming to an end, a trip to the Sydney Cricket Ground seemed a perfect way to spend the final day of a year-long odyssey and a good way to start 1999. I would hazard a guess that I arrived at this conclusion because it lent itself to all-day drinking rather than appreciating top-class sport. Little did I know it was to be the first of regular quadrennial visits to the ground.

Making my way onto what was then Yabba's Hill there was already an atmosphere that awakened something inside me. The previous evening Darren Gough had taken a hat-trick and as they replayed it on the big screen the massed English hordes celebrated as though it was a live event. The details of that day can wait, but I bought into the Barmy Army ethos straight away. I loved it. I left the people I was with to immerse myself in the rowdy congregation of Englishmen and women. I was buzzing. But not so much that it made any discernible difference to my life. It was another four years before I would act on that chance meeting and make any more of it.

In 2002 I was travelling again. You'll notice that this is a recurring theme in my life. My second leave-everything-behind-and-disappear-with-a-backpack trip was larger in scope than my first foray around the world and I'd spent three and half months in South America. While I was loath to leave that particular part of the world, I was determined to go to Australia with the express intent of watching cricket and to indulge again in watching the greatest series of them all. What had changed to make this a priority rather than an opportunistic thing I couldn't honestly tell you, but this was an intense period of experiential living. I had started to follow England's football team overseas and had been to my first football World Cup in Japan earlier that year. There was a desire in me that still festers today to go everywhere, see everything and do everything. Watching a significant amount of Ashes cricket had to come under that banner.

And this was when cricket really got its claws into me. Two things combined to gird my cricketing loins. Firstly the singing, banter and wit of the Barmy Army I had enjoyed so much on that first flirtatious engagement four years before turned out to be more than an initial encounter fascination. Secondly I was to see something that I would not see again for some time, an England victory in Australia. And on top of that I got to see an

England batsman, Michael Vaughan, playing so well he would end the tour at the top of the world rankings. That's something I'm still waiting to see again. I had such a great time at the Test matches in Melbourne and Sydney that I even indulged in a couple of one-dayers as well. By the time the series had finished a pact was made with one of my companions that we would go to South Africa for the 2004–05 series specifically to watch cricket and enjoy some more of this Barmy Army lark.

After that South Africa trip I would not miss an overseas England tour until Bangladesh in 2010. And the only reason I wasn't there was because, well, I was travelling again. In the intervening years not only would I become addicted to cricket, addicted to the Barmy Army, addicted to the songs, the camaraderie, the highs (not so many on the field, lots off it), the lows (not so many off the field, a few too many on it), but I would work for the Barmy Army for several years, eschewing more lucrative jobs to fuel my desire to watch cricket, more cricket and then some more.

All of which is very interesting for me, but why would it interest you enough to pick up this tome and live my life retrospectively and vicariously through the pages of this book? Well, hopefully for a few reasons. The most obvious one is that if you've even bothered to pick it up you're probably a cricket fan, and most people who like cricket REALLY like cricket; simply reading about past Test matches can be interesting. Just researching this and scrolling through scorecards of matches I have attended was enjoyable in a way that only cricket fans can understand. But anyone could do that. This book is about my memories, but it's also to give some genuine insight into the Barmy Army and what it's like to be part of it. Misjudged by a media who do very little to find out the truth, loved by the players, discussed endlessly by those inside it, what is the Barmy Army, who are the Barmy Army and how does the actual business run?

I went from being a guy looking at this crazy bunch of people thinking how much fun they were having, to a guy responsible for relaunching the Army's website, editing its magazine, appearing on television and radio as its representative and writing really awful, but strangely successful, ditties about Tim Ambrose. I've argued long into the night about what the Barmy Army is, was and should be; conversed endlessly with cricket traditionalists, trying to prove to them that we're not a bunch of nihilistic hooligans, and answered a million questions for my non-Barmy Army friends. Along the way I have had an immense amount of fun, met some brilliant people and had more good times than anyone could ever ask for.

Two

Touring Down Under

You all live in a convict colony

Touring experiences in Australia:

1998–99	*5th Test (Sydney) – 2nd day*
2002–03	*4th Test (Melbourne) – Three days*
	5th Test (Sydney) – Three days
2006–07	*4th Test (Melbourne)*
	5th Test (Sydney)
2010–11	*1st Test (Brisbane)*
	2nd Test (Adelaide)
	3rd Test (Perth)
	4th Test (Melbourne)
	5th Test (Sydney)

HINDSIGHT IS A WONDERFUL thing, but looking back now there were signs that would suggest this whole saga was somewhat inevitable. I arrived at the Sydney Cricket Ground on the first day of the rest of my life with a motley assortment of acquaintances made during a year backpacking around Australia. We had congregated in Sydney for a New Year party that had started before Christmas and still hadn't ended despite the fact it was now January 3.

Mornings are usually the quietest times at cricket matches as hangovers are dealt with, breakfast is consumed and people ease their way into the day. But on this occasion it was different. The England fans were still revelling in the excitement of witnessing a Darren Gough hat-trick the previous afternoon and a replay on the big screen got the pulses racing again. The atmosphere was charged and the first beer of the day was consumed with a chaser of anticipation.

Despite England's performance that day being the opposite of something to get excited about (England were bowled out for 220), the depreciation in that early morning excitement was cancelled out by the joy of being at cricket and drinking beer in the sun, and the net effect was that the atmosphere was sustained throughout the day. I would guess it was early in the afternoon session when some irresistible force led me to walk away from my friends and into the merry, dancing, singing throng that was the Barmy Army. I didn't know anyone there but I didn't care and it didn't seem to matter. I picked up some of the songs and immersed myself in this amorphous mass of people who seemed determined to have the best time possible even though their team was getting a bit of a hiding on the field. When I returned to see how my erstwhile companions were I was stimulated by the kind of excitement that you can only get from this kind of primeval tribal gathering. There was an unmistakable feeling that we were all in this together, all sharing the same awesome experience, and that made us friends even if we didn't know each other.

That much I do remember, although specifics are thin on the ground. I couldn't in all honesty recount the songs we sang (although I could guess) or what we were singing about; there's just a blanket memory of happiness and hedonism. Indeed my only strong memory of that day had nothing to do with the cricket or the Barmy Army. When I came back from my sortie into the Army stronghold one of my friends insisted there were some Grimsby Town fans around us. The more astute among you might guess that I am a Grimsby fan myself, otherwise such news would hardly have been relevant.

Keen to find my fellow codheads I shouted something about Grimsby only for two Aussie guys behind me to pipe up and proclaim their love for the Mariners. This was slightly confusing as they had the wrong accent for Grimsby fans, but they explained that a friend of theirs from England was a big Grimsby fan, which was why they supported them. We started singing 'we piss on your fish, yes we do' which is not a song you would confuse with any other team in England. Certainly the other guy from Grimsby, stood a few yards in front of us, didn't and he joined in lustily. So my first specific memory of singing in a cricket ground was singing a football song about my rubbish little team with three blokes I didn't know, two of whom were Australian. I never sang about my football team again and I've never sung with Australians again. Indeed I became fairly harsh in my criticism of people who sing football songs at cricket matches, insisting along with many of my friends that we are 'only here for the cricket'. But these were my salad days and I forgive myself that early faux pas.

I'm sure I wasn't the only Barmy Army virgin that day because Australia is where a large number of people lose their Barmy Army cherry. It is the ultimate 'Hollywood' or 'glory' tour for the one-offs, the newbies. If you're going to do one tour in your life, the chances are it will be this one. It's a spectacular holiday destination in its own right and the fact that the last two Test matches run over Christmas and New Year makes it feasible to have an extended break here without using up an entire year's holiday allowance. While it is now ridiculously expensive, back then it was almost as ridiculously cheap once you'd covered your airfare. Another reason the tour is so popular is that Australia has an immense amount of ex-pats for whom this away tour is, in fact, a home tour. Indeed I will be one of those when the next Ashes take place in the country I now call home. Then there are plenty of people like the 23-year-old me who just happened to be in the country anyway; at any one time the Australian backpacker trail is full of young English people drinking their way around the island continent. There's also the unique relationship we have with our old convict colony to take into account. We love to visit Australia; they love to visit the UK. We all love to drink and we all have a similar sense of humour. But when it comes to sporting rivalry the gloves come off, which makes this Test series the spiciest of all both on and off the pitch. If you enjoy rivalry, this is the contest you want to see.

Put simply, there are many reasons other than being a cricket fan why you might find yourself watching cricket in Australia rather than some of the more far-flung places in which we play the game. If you're going to have a casual encounter with international cricket, there's a high probability it will happen there.

In this context it would be easy to look at my increasing attendance at the cricket over the four occasions I have been in Australia (one day, six days, two Tests, five Tests) as some kind of statistical metaphor for my developing relationship with the game from one-night stand to casual relationship to full-blown love affair. But in reality touring Australia always ended up being a matter of convenience as much as a cricket-specific adventure. On that first day it just happened to be there. Four years later Australia was the halfway mark on a round-the-world trip. Another four years later I had a wedding to attend (although the bride and groom thoughtfully set a date near the Ashes as they knew I would be there anyway). And four years later I would again use Australia as a staging post on a long bout of travelling. That's not to say I wouldn't have ended up in Australia purely for the cricket – I would – but strangely I've never been there exclusively to watch cricket and how much cricket I have watched has been dictated by circumstances as much as desire, whereas every other tour I have undertaken has been purely motivated by cricket.

The idea that I would go on tour simply to watch cricket was far from my mind as I left Australia the day after my first Barmy Army experience to head back to the UK. The previous year had seen me visit Uluru (Ayers Rock), explore the amazing sand mass that is Fraser Island, sail round the Whitsundays and visit Cape Tribulation. I had lived in the spectacular city of Sydney, relaxed in Byron Bay and driven thousands of kilometres exploring the country that acts as a magnet for many English people with or without the involvement of cricket. Along the way I made many friends, drank too much beer, smoked too much weed and had such a perennially good time that the final day was merely an extension of it. I had been spoiled so rotten by events of that year that a day at the cricket was merely an incidental addition rather than something to get excited about in a wider context.

The same should really be true of my next cricketing experience overseas. It was preceded by three months in South America, during which I walked the Inca Trail to Machu Picchu, marvelled at the Iguazu Falls, drove across the Salar De Uyuni, watched chunks fall off the Perito Moreno Glacier and partied harder than I had ever partied before. Leaving all that behind was tough and again cricket was going to have to work hard to stand out as an experience when compared with that little lot. But something had happened in the intervening four years to make cricket an attractive destination in itself and not merely a part of the journey.

I'm not sure what it was that made cricket a reason to go somewhere rather than just something to do if you happened to be in the same place, but it must have a link to my developing love of attending live international sport. In 2000 I had visited Belgium to watch France v Czech Republic in the European Championship. It didn't matter that England weren't playing. This was the chance to be involved in a major tournament and to revel in the atmosphere it creates. Having followed that up with a trip to watch the World Cup in Japan, the next Ashes tour was a natural event upon which to focus. It helped that my travel companion was a cricket fan as well, probably no more so than myself in essence, but enough that as we planned our trip it became an essential staging post.

And so we arrived in Melbourne on December 23, 2002, although any hopes we had of watching our team achieve sporting glory had been shot to pieces already; Australia had already won The Ashes 3-0, steamrollering England by fairly terrifying margins. One of my Aussie friends had moved to Melbourne and insisted we stay with her, which was brilliant in that we were offered a warm welcome by friends and family alike. Unfortunately that warm welcome was usually laced with many leery comments about how rubbish our cricket team was. Indeed it became a daily routine that as we would go out of the door there would be smart-arsed comments along the lines of 'you're off to watch your boys get hammered again are ya?' What made it worse is that when we would arrive back after the day watching England 'get hammered again' they would smugly point out that they had warned us what was going to happen.

I would guess that it was about this time that my anti-Australianism started. Actually anti-Australianism is not the right word. I love many of its people, I love the country and I'm actually writing this sentence in it as I recently moved over there to live with my Australian girlfriend. But while the majority of experiences in Australia are happy and friendly, when it comes to cricket the Aussies just love to stick the boot in, and that grates after a while. In the face of such an onslaught from our Australian friends, and at the grounds, I started to store some ammo to fire back. It wasn't difficult as the Barmy Army had been doing it for years. The staple topics were, always have been, and always will be, that Australia has no culture, no history, is a convict colony and that they voted for the Queen when they had the chance to get rid of her as the head of state.

Oh and that we have all had carnal relations with a lady called Matilda who waltzes. It's pretty juvenile, but no more so than their continual chirping about us sending them to paradise, about us getting sunburned easily, about us inventing cricket but not being able to play it, about us having crap weather and all of the other stunning pieces of insight they come up with.

As we had absolutely no sporting success to take the piss out of them about we had to resort to non-cricketing banter and win that particular battle instead. As my relationship with the country and its inhabitants developed, many of my Australian friends struggled to match up my obvious affinity for the country with my continual baiting of it. But what they have never quite realised is that while we're all friends, the amount of grief an English cricket fan gets from Aussie cricket fans is voluminous and when you're used to referring to a group of Aussies as convicts in a cricket ground it's difficult not to use the same nomenclature in a social situation.

And besides, if there's one thing the Barmy Army is good at it's taking the piss out of Australians. After just a couple of days my friends and I had bought into the Barmy Army ethos quite heavily and had learned the following that represent our staple Australian singing, firstly this to the tune of *House of the Rising Sun*:

There is a house in New Orleans
They call the Rising Sun
It's been the ruin of many a poor boy
Oh Lord I know I'm one
One foot on the platform
One foot on the train (choo choo)
I'm going back to New Orleans
To wear my ball and chain
1,2,
Ball and chain
Ball and chain

We came here with backpacks
You with ball and chain
Ball and chain
Ball and chain
We came here with backpacks
You with ball and chain.

Then there's our variation on The Beatles classic *Yellow Submarine*

In the town where I was born
There lived a man who was a thief
And he told me of his life
Stealing bread and shagging sheep
So they put him in the nick
And then a magistrate he went to see
He said 'put him on a ship, to the convict colony'
You all live in a convict colony, a convict colony,
a convict colony
You all live in a convict colony, a convict colony, a convict colony

And then there's our precursor to the Australian national anthem:

The Aussies love the English
You might find it quite strange
Cos we sent them all down under
With only balls and chains
And when they see the English
They always shout and scream
But when they had the chance to vote they
voted for the Queen
God save your gracious Queen
Long live your noble Queen
God save your Queen (you're a convict)
Send her victorious

Happy and glorious
Long to reign over you
God save your Queen

And our quite delightful rendition of *Waltzing Matilda*:

I shagged Matilda, I shagged Matilda
I shagged Matilda and so did my mates
And she moaned and she groaned
And she took it up the billabong
I shagged Matilda and so did my mates
We all shagged Matilda, we all shagged Matilda
We all shagged Matilda and so did our mates
And she moaned and she groaned
And she took it up the billabong
We all shagged Matilda and so did our mates

We would arrive home from a day at the cricket and if our Australian hosts mentioned anything about the disastrous nature of our team's performance then we would just launch into a few renditions of these. They actually found them just as funny as we did and it got to a ridiculous stage where they would actually ask us to sing songs for them wherever we were. Although they liked all of the songs, their favourite was the finger song. There have been many variations over the years, but back then it went like this:

Leader: *Today is Monday*
Crowd: *Today is Monday*
Monday is a finger day
(Monday is a finger day)
Are we happy?
(Are we happy?)
You bet your life we are
De de de de de de de de

Today is Tuesday
(Today is Tuesday)
Tuesday is a wanking day
(Tuesday is a wanking day)
Monday is a finger day
(Monday is a finger day!)
Are we happy?
(Are we happy?)
You bet your life we are
De de de de de de de de

The song builds up day by day until the finale:

Today is Sunday
(Today is Sunday)
Sunday is a day of prayer
(Sunday is a day of prayer)
Saturday's for rugby
(Saturday's for rugby)
32-31
(32-31)
32-31
(32-31)
Friday is a drinking day
(Friday is a drinking day)
Thursday is for shagging
(Thursday is for shagging)
Wednesday uurgghh
(Wednesday uurgghh)
Tuesday is a wanking day
(Tuesday is a wanking day)
Monday is a finger day
(Monday is a finger day)
Are we happy?
(Are we happy?)
You bet your life we are
De de de de de de de de

The key to the song was that with a good leader there was no need for anyone to learn the words as everyone merely repeated what the leader said. And the bit that really made it stand out is that while everyone sang 'De de de de de de de de' they stood up with a hand or beer on their head and turned round 360 degrees. Watching a few thousand people standing up and doing this random little 'dance' was a bizarre and humorous sight. The tune is actually a rugby drinking song based on Scaffold's *Today's Monday* that we unceremoniously nicked. And the reference to 32-31 is the score by which England had just beaten Australia at rugby.

Over the years we evolved the lyrics to be less crude and more relevant to cricket. The days would refer to what had happened on the pitch during that tour. Thus when Matthew Hoggard took a hat-trick against the West Indies on April 3, 2004:

> *Saturday's for Hoggard*
> *(Sarwan, Hinds and Chanderpaul)*

Sometimes references were merely to a trait of the country we were in, so in Sri Lanka:

> *Wednesday is for tuk-tuks*

This made the song uniquely Barmy, more about sport than sex and also different every time we sang it. But while we would come up with a raft of variations dependent on what country we were in, for now we sang the original and sang it loud all across Australia. I remember three of us swimming in the sea at Glenelg near Adelaide doing a rendition of it and trying to do 360 degree spins while treading water, much to the bemusement of everyone around us.

There were a couple of incidents in that fourth Test in Melbourne that stand out more than the standard songs we sang and showed the Barmy Army's ability to respond to circumstances with banter and funny ditties. It all came out because of Brett Lee. At the time Brett Lee was prone to bowling a few no-balls and there had been questions asked about the legality of his bowling action. We were in no mood to let this go unnoticed and uncommented upon. As he ran in to bowl, the Barmy Army cheer would build to a crescendo before everyone would shout 'no-ball' while standing up and making the signal for a no-ball. It was a clear attempt to put him off his game, which may or may not be cricket, but for people brought up on watching football this was tame. This bantering turned into a song to the tune of *Oh My Darling, Clementine* along the lines of 'Keep your arm straight, keep your arm straight, keep your arm straight when you bowl.' He bowled 13 no-balls in that Test and each received a rapturous cheer.

But it wasn't this that I found really funny, albeit it was very amusing to us at the time. As you would expect the Australian skipper wasn't scared to send Lee down to field right in front of the mickey-taking masses. As Lee took his station four wags (that's wags as in the shortened version of scallywags and not the later acronym WAGs) stood up and chanted 'Brett Lee give us a wave, Brett Lee, Brett Lee give us a wave'. Lee happily obliged only for the four lads to start singing 'Keep your arm straight, keep your arm straight, keep your arm straight when you wave.' The whole crowd started laughing, but the biggest smile was on the face of Brett Lee who was pissing himself. That kind of reaction endears players to the Barmy Army. We had a huge respect for the Aussies as players anyway but when they proved to be of good bantering type they'd attain status as a good guy as well as good player. If you've got any brains you'll try to get on with us anyway – like anything in life it's easier to ride with piss-taking punches than fight against them, as Justin Langer found out to his cost.

Langer would eventually earn the respect of the Army, but when it came to the issue of us no-balling Lee he made an error of judgement. As we rocked up the next day we all read the same newspapers with quotes from the undersized opening batsman belittling the Barmy Army for its baiting of Lee. He was quoted as saying:

'I think they were a disgrace... These people standing behind the fence drinking beer, most of them are about 50 kilos overweight, making ridiculous comments. Gee whiz, as far as I'm concerned, it's easy for someone to say that from behind a fence. While they pay their money and all that sort of stuff, gee whiz, I reckon there's some sort of integrity in life.'

If he thought we were going to take that kind of thing lying down he had another think coming. To the tune of *He's Got The Whole World in his Hands* we started singing 'We're all ten kilos overweight, we're all ten kilos overweight etc etc' before moving on to being 20 kilos overweight, then 30 and up to 50 before ending up with a chorus of 'We're so fat it's unbelievable.' But we weren't finished there. It had not gone unnoticed that Langer was short of stature and so we had another version that insisted 'You're 10 centimetres underheight, you're ten centimetres underheight' etc etc until a chorus of 'You're so small it's unbelievable'. As far as I am aware that was the last time Langer said anything bad about us and a couple of days later his appearance in the paper consisted of him signing a portly Barmy Army member's beer gut. Having said that, the damage was already done and his song already written to the tune of *My Old Man's a Dustman:*

Langer is an Aussie
He wears the gold and green
He is the biggest whinger
That we have ever seen

He wasn't very happy
When we called Brett Lee's no ball
He's got a very big mouth
And he's only five feet tall

There's something that Langer overlooked when he made his comments. The Barmy Army doesn't usually sing about opposing players except in jest, but when it comes to Australia the rules are different. On the one hand there's the history and rivalry of the two countries but a bigger reason is the behaviour of Australian cricket crowds. The abuse faced by English cricketers playing in Australia over the years has been well documented and on occasions pretty vitriolic. So we play them by their own rules and their own standards. Australian crowds routinely no-balled Murali and Shoaib Akhtar, but at no point did Langer have words to say about his own fans. Where you draw the line about what represents acceptable behaviour is a matter for personal opinion but I would generally back England's fans to behave better than Australians have done in the past.

Langer did learn his lesson – he told the BBC so himself four years later when preparing for the 2006–07 Ashes:

'I am expecting to get both barrels from the Barmy Army, but like I keep saying to the Barmy Army, as loyal as they are to England, I'm as loyal to my team-mates. When you have two loyal groups there's always going to be a bit of heat there, so we'll see what happens. If I don't make any runs I'll be grumpy and I won't like them, if I make runs I'll be happy. I've learned my lesson, don't worry.'

As Australia won that series 5-0 he obviously had little reason to worry about us but then his original outburst in 2002 had come with Australia on their way to a 4-0 lead and he'd scored 250, so theoretically he should have been happy back then as well. That 250 was part of an Australia first innings total of 551 for six, a performance backed up by the bowlers who bowled us out for 270 and enforced the follow on. England's second innings wasn't so bad, with Michael Vaughan's 145 underpinning a decentish score of 387. Thanks to Vaughan we had something to celebrate and that's just one of the myriad great things about Test cricket. Even in the darkest moments there are always mini-moments of joy to get excited about, whether it's someone taking a wicket or one great innings among a sea of otherwise fairly mediocre ones. We even had reason to get a tad excited as Australia contrived to lose five wickets chasing the 107 they needed to win. Ultimately, though, we were still 4-0 down and facing an ignominious whitewash, which made what happened next all the more remarkable.

England won in Sydney. It's still hard to believe. Michael Vaughan scored yet another majestic century – his third of the series. When I think back now and consider the man love I had for Vaughany which would manifest itself over the next few years, this was the equivalent of snogging a girl at school and not realising quite how hot she was, only to see her subsequently and realise you had had a right result. (I realise that analogy is startlingly close to the one I used earlier on. I have my own concerns about my inability to compare cricket to anything other than teenage girls but I'm dealing with them so if we could just gloss over it I'd be grateful.) And Andy Caddick was awesome. But if I'm honest he was more like the girl who you were enraptured to have pulled at the time but who, in retrospect, didn't quite have everything. Despite getting smashed for 5.26 an over in the first innings he took 10-fer in the match as England won by 225 runs. We even had the temerity to declare our second innings. I'm guessing at that point we were singing (again to the tune of *Oh My Darling, Clementine*):

Andy Caddick
Andy Caddick

Must be worth a million pounds
He was too good for the Kiwis
So he plays for England

Here was a perfect example of why watching sport is so addictive. You endure the massive lows (and England have provided me with quite a few) because they make highs all the sweeter. When you have plumbed the depths you truly appreciate the peaks and after all the preceding misery this was both unexpected and joyous. We were witness to something truly brilliant, although one of our number didn't witness the very best part of it.

Day four had already been a decent one. We had seen Vaughan add another 70 runs to his overnight score before finally succumbing on 183, leaving England on 345-5 in their second innings, a lead of 344 after equal first innings showings. Bearing in mind our performance so far in the series, and that there was a day and a half still to go, we knew England were perfectly capable of losing their remaining wickets cheaply and succumbing to another defeat. As two more wickets went down before tea that was definitely feasible. The evening session looked set to be decisive.

Clearly we would need some sustenance to see us through this tense, final session and that, as it was with frightening regularity on that tour, would come in the form of a pie and a pint. Phil, my travelling companion throughout the South American trip, was dispatched to the bar and pie shop, leaving me and our friend Jim to relax and enjoy the start of the next session. And that session would be one of the most enjoyable I have ever seen. More precisely there was a period of 12 overs that were as good as any. England lost a couple of wickets quickly and at 408-9 were still not even guaranteed a draw, never mind a win. But remarkably the tenth wicket put on over 40 – in 6.3 overs. In years to come I would see Steve Harmison play many innings that sports journalists are contractually obliged to call cameos but this was the first. He hit 20 off 23 balls with Alec Stewart joining in the fun at the other end. The excitement in the stands was awesome, particularly during one Brett Lee over that went for 17, and there was an excitement when England declared. Could we really get among the Aussies and force a win? This was new ground for us after the misery of Melbourne and certainly for those in the crowd who had seen many defeats in Australia. It would have been new ground for Phil as well, but there was still no sign of him.

If those six overs had been fun then the next six saw the England fans going berserk as Caddick and Hoggard took three wickets between them to leave the Aussies in real trouble. But Phil missed all that as well. Jim and I were bemused on the one hand as to where the hell he had got to and upset on the other because we had no food or beer. We were also aware that he was going to be rather annoyed when he finally reappeared and worked out what he had missed. He eventually arrived back to impatient and completely selfish cries of 'Where the fuck have you been and where's my beer?'

He explained that the beer and pie shops were shut and that he had just spent ages queuing for tickets for day five as he had figured that with the game poised as it was he would get them in early. We felt quite bad that we had been bad-mouthing him for a lack of beer provision when he had been putting himself out to perform such a magnanimous gesture and rejoiced in the fact that we would be there to see the denouement the next day. Then Phil explained that having battled his way to the front of the ticket queue he realised he didn't have his credit card so had actually failed to bring back anything. He had just missed a dozen overs of more than exceptional cricket in order to achieve absolutely diddly squat, returning to find us hysterical with excitement but still unhappy that we were thirsty and hungry. Poor bastard.

But he did have the consolation that there was a real possibility England would win a Test match so we turned up excitedly for day five and duly saw it happen.

Amid the joyous celebrations there was time to show that the Barmy Army could be selfless; that they truly appreciated the game and those who played it. Steve Waugh was under tremendous pressure to be removed from the captaincy and had responded in typical Waugh fashion by hitting a century. As he went up to make his end-of-series speech the Barmy Army gave a huge cheer and shouted his name as though he was one of ours. He might have been belting us round for years but we respected him as a cricketer and if this was to be his goodbye then we wanted him to know that we'd appreciated watching him. I doubt if the Aussie fans had ever sung his name so loud.

It's perhaps one of the many reasons that the Australians actually like the Barmy Army more than the English. Certainly that's how it feels. I remember walking through a small town a few days later wearing my Barmy Army T-shirt and a mother and son coming up to us and asking if we were part of the Army. When we said yes she was full of praise, saying we were awesome and how much her son enjoyed us being in the country. And that's generally what you get over there. The majority of Aussies think we genuinely bring something new to the game and add to it as a package. They laugh at our songs, respect the fact that we support a team through thick and thin and genuinely respect us. At home there seems to be a fairly consistent dislike, especially from the press. You do get a few Aussies who think they can take on the Army and after one or two too many stubbies stand in front of us and get a bit abusive. Usually by the time we've quickly chanted 'You've had too many Milos' the police remove them and even the majority of the Aussies around agree that's a good thing.

But we didn't care what the Aussies thought that afternoon and evening because we were going to celebrate and celebrate hard. It's always difficult to make comparisons between particular occasions, but in my mind the celebrations of that win were, if anything, more tumultuous and enthusiastic than those that would follow our series victory in Australia eight years later. Maybe it was because it was the first time I had enjoyed such an occasion or maybe it was because it was so unexpected, or maybe it's all in my imagination. All I did know even then was that if that was how we would celebrate a single Test victory in a 4-1 series defeat then winning a series would be mind-blowing.

That celebration consisted of lots of drinking and lots of singing and somehow I ended up as the centre of attention in the pub we arrived at straight after the game, a pub where I achieved something every bit as dramatic and unexpected as England's win: I got the manager to change his mind about kicking me out. That's no mean feat in Australia I can tell you. Although in years to come I would become one of the more recognisable faces on cricket tours, at this point I was very much a nobody and I didn't know any of the Army regulars.

But back then there weren't too many regulars so most of the people in our pub were probably also enjoying their first taste of cricket touring. At the time I had rather dodgy blonde hair and owing to my physique didn't look dissimilar to Brett Lee. (I should perhaps point out in the interests of honesty I am tall and skinny, whereas Brett Lee is tall and slimly ripped, but it was close enough in those circumstances.) So when some people in the pub started singing 'Brett Lee give us a song' it was slightly surreal, but what the hell? I started a couple of the songs I knew and somehow became the ipso facto leader of that particular gang. My status was only interrupted when Jimmy Savile came in as part of his tour of pubs to lead us in a rendition of *Everywhere We Go*. (It wasn't the real Jimmy Savile; we have a guy who looks like him, and sings a song called *Everywhere We Go*... more about all that later.)

In between leading some singing I was chatting to a group of Aussies who were enjoying watching the Poms celebrate. One of them came up with a song and asked me if I could get everyone to be quiet so they could sing it for us. I stood on a barstool, got the pub quiet, they sang the song and everyone cheered. Except the bar manager who came over and told me to leave his establishment because he'd already told me repeatedly not to stand on the barstools. In fairness he'd done that once but as I pointed out that's not 'repeatedly', and I was only up there for a few seconds. The Australians were horrified that in doing them a favour I might have got myself kicked out and they also pleaded on my behalf. This had no noticeable effect on the manager, who insisted I leave, but as everyone in the bar's attention had been on us to start with they soon realised what was going on and came to my rescue. 'He goes, we go, he goes, we go' they chanted as the manager and I got into something of a Mexican stand-off. I rather smugly told him that I would be happy to leave his building but that if I did I was going to take everyone else in the pub with me. Now the amount of money being transferred from English pockets to Australian tills was rather substantial, so financial common sense won the day and I was reprieved. Those celebrations went on long into the night.

The next time an England performance would instigate such scenes of rapture would be on home soil and my celebrations got me into a different kind of trouble. So much has been written about the 2005 Ashes series I need not go into too much detail here, but it's worth a quick mention as that home series was the first in which the Barmy Army was allocated a specific area at each ground in an attempt to generate an atmosphere similar to that we managed overseas. That came in handy for me as it enabled me to wangle tickets, and when I was there to witness us finally win the Ashes the celebrations were akin to those in Sydney two and half years previously.

This time the bar staff of London had no issues with my behaviour but my girlfriend did because I was so excited I forgot to call her and tell her where we were. Although she was South African she had been a part of the Army on the recent tour of her homeland and did love the craic but when she called at midnight and (rightly) berated me for not calling her I pleaded with her 'not to ruin the best day of my life'. Mistake.

I remember her intimating that if this was the best day of my life then what chance would she have of competing with cricket. I hastily backtracked and said it was ONE of the best days in my life. I'm still struggling to think of many better, but the really interesting point was that winning at cricket had suddenly become so important to me that I would risk and incur the wrath of my girlfriend. By then the addiction was beginning to take a serious grip.

Indeed by the time the next visit to Australia came round touring had become a regular habit. Jim and I had fulfilled the promise we made to each other during that 2002–03 tour of Australia and been on the 2004–05 tour of South Africa. I followed that up with a trip to Pakistan following the home Ashes victory in 2005 and then a trip to India in early 2006. In the process I got to know the people who ran the Army, some of the regular tourists and the history behind the organisation. I had even started to work for the Barmy Army as a freelance journalist, having written and produced their entire Ashes magazine. Because of this, going on tour had changed somewhat. I could now expect to see a few faces I would recognise so was more than happy to go to games on my own. There were still far more faces I didn't recognise because while no one has ever done the maths the 2006 Australian tour was probably the biggest Barmy Army tour ever and probably the biggest there will ever be. I base that outrageously unscientific statement on the fact that the hype about cricket had never been as big as it was in the aftermath of the 2005 victory, that Australia was then still a cheap place to visit, that the UK was still on a pre-recession spending spree and that seeing England win in Australia was a holy grail that will rarely have the same allure among current Barmy Army members now it has been done.

The mass exodus in 2006 to see if England could back up the 2005 victory by winning in Australia for the first time in 20 years consisted of a travelling horde full of real hope; almost a hint of expectation. Prior to the 2010–11 Ashes pundits were declaring it England's best chance to win since Gatting's 1986–87 side, but that's pretty much what everyone was saying back in 2006–07 as well. It's a bloody stupid thing to say, as of course the next chance will be the best chance because all of the others have already gone begging. But looking back the optimism for the 2006–07 series seems misplaced. With no Michael Vaughan, no Marcus Trescothick and no Simon Jones, the 2005 team was weakened immensely. There were doubts about who should be behind the stumps, doubts about who should be the spinner and doubts about who should be skipper. And if we're honest probably none of that really mattered because that Australian team would have smashed us anyway.

As much as I was keen to visit some of the other Australian grounds rather than repeat Melbourne and Sydney, wedding and work commitments ensured that my itinerary would again consist of the final two Tests. And that meant that by the time I rocked up the series was, yet again, done and dusted. If the Ashes 2006–07 had been a boxing match the referee would already have stopped the fight. Even the normally happy-go-lucky Army had had the stuffing knocked out of it. Huge numbers of people had put their lives on hold and gone out for the entire series with high expectations and now it had almost become something to be endured. There was not much of anything to look forward to each day other than another few hours of torment. The Barmy Army business was also having major problems at the time, so smiles were not in abundance.

There was another problem and that was derived from the fact that I was well on the way to becoming a Barmy Army snob. Many people went to Australia, more than went anywhere else, to be a part of the Barmy Army as much as they did to watch the cricket. But they did so without necessarily knowing what the Barmy Army was and what it stood for. Many people think it's like going on a football tour, but while there are obvious similarities there are huge differences and we're very proud of them. To understand those differences requires more than a simple aside here so I will attempt to boil it down elsewhere.

But while the media and players always acknowledge the power of the support from the stands, the regular Barmy Army members often bemoan the insidious appearance of football-style chanting. We get annoyed that people don't attempt to learn more than the basic songs, leading to accusations (accurate ones) that as a group we merely repeat the same old things time and again. And it frustrates us that many of these people are merely jumping on a bandwagon without taking the time to appreciate the game.

The ultimate example of this would occur some four years later during the first Test in Brisbane in 2010. On day one a large section of England fans consistently sang the distasteful football song *Ten German Bombers* which is sung to the tune of *She'll Be Coming Round the Mountain*:

There were ten German bombers in the air
There were ten German bombers in the air
There were ten German bombers, ten German bombers
There were ten German bombers in the air
And the RAF from England shot one down
And the RAF from England shot one down

And the RAF from England, the RAF from England
The RAF from England shot one down

This is repeated until there are 'no German bombers in the air'. Quick research shows that this was first sung by schoolchildren during World War II, but while it may be have been acceptable in those trying times I can't help thinking it should have been consigned to the dustbin of history long ago. It first came to my attention during Euro 2004 in Portugal. Two years later I cringed and died a little inside as I stood in the main square of Stuttgart (a city heavily bombed during World War II) during the World Cup as thousands of England football fans serenaded their generous hosts with multiple renditions of the song. It was embarrassing. And yet at least then it was vaguely relevant, if repulsively so. But why on earth would you sing it in Brisbane? That's Brisbane, Australia. A country whose RAAF had done its fair share of shooting down Germans itself. It was nonsensical, stupid, embarrassing, pathetic and highly irrelevant.

But that nadir was still to come, although the signs were already there in 2006–07. During the Melbourne Test match the moronic chanting got so bad that Billy the Trumpet, another Army stalwart by the name of Simon Humphrey and I left the Barmy Army section at one point. Not only was the singing getting repetitive but the lack of appreciation of what was happening on the field was getting tedious.

Four years previously we had no-balled Brett Lee, and while we might then have been pushing the boundaries ourselves it was relevant. But the furore over Lee's action was now in the past, so for people to bring it up again smacked more of blind repetition than doing anything to utilise our brains and react to changed circumstances. Lee did bowl five no-balls in a match in which we scored only 320 runs so maybe they were right and I was wrong.

Of course people are entitled to behave and sing any way they want. But for cricket fans, who love the intricacies and sophistication of the game and enjoy being part of the Barmy Army because it offers a more thoughtful, respectful and insightful variation to football supporting, it gets annoying when we're hijacked by football supporters. There's a delicious irony here in that one of the things we're most falsely accused of is being loud idiots who don't appreciate the game, and yet we're the ones who complain the most when we're joined by people who are exactly that.

It was more of the same for the Sydney Test, both on and off the field, so all-in-all it was a fairly unedifying few days. We were actually in the game for the first two days, but after that it was the predictable pulverising. Despite that, one of the highlights of my time watching Test cricket occurred during that match. On day two an Aussie friend, Adrianne Sarkozy, called to ask what I was up to the following evening. I replied that I was shattered and had every intention of going back to our apartment to chill out and do not very much. 'Well look, (Allan) Lamby has invited me out to his boat for dinner and you can come if you want to,' she said. I don't care how tired you are, you don't turn down an invite like that.

We walked to the harbour and wondered which of the luxury yachts might be his. To give you an idea of just how luxurious the yachts were, one belonged to Sir Richard Branson. When we finally got hold of Lamby he said his boat wasn't at the harbour, but he would send a tender for us. His wasn't a boat, it was a bloody ship. As we walked in the cabin he was doing a schtick with Dennis Lillee, reminiscing about the old days.

As soon as they'd finished Lamby came over to see Adrianne and as I stood there minding my own business Lillee strolled up to me and said 'G'day mate, I'm Dennis.' I stopped short of saying that I knew perfectly well who he was and introduced myself. After a bit of chit-chat

Lamby told Adrianne to go and entertain his guests on another table before turning to me to insist I sat next to him. Ex-England wicketkeeper Paul Downton was also in attendance and the two England boys and the Australian legend quizzed me about the Barmy Army and how it worked. By the end of the night I seem to remember singing anti-Australian songs to Dennis Lillee... you don't get to do that every day. And it just goes to prove my maxim that following cricket can be awesome even when it's rubbish. You never know what might happen.

It was an interlude of happiness in an otherwise miserable Test match watching experience. I've experienced lower lows, but for consistent misery this took the biscuit and I only had to sit through two Test matches of it. When the time came for Australia to effectively read us the last rites the atmosphere in the crowd was mock funereal. We sat with Billy the Trumpet and encouraged him to play as many quasi-suicidal songs as we could think of. 'We'll win again, don't know where, don't know when' was one that sticks out. The funeral march was another. And *Always Look on the Bright Side of Life* had never been so apt.

At this stage we were resorting to anything to amuse ourselves and as Hayden and Langer came out to knock off the winning runs we decided we'd go round the entire England team asking them for a wave. We started at the top of the order with Strauss and Cook and went through them all. Having done that we figured we may as well ask the Aussie batsmen as well. Langer, who had perhaps learned his lesson from four years previously, graciously acceded and waved his bat in our direction. Hayden didn't. I'll give him the benefit of the doubt and assume he didn't realise what was going on. And then we figured maybe the umpires would acknowledge us. The Barmy Army singing 'Aleem give us a wave' to Aleem Dar and watching him respond was one of the funnier moments of that tour. But that only goes to show how little competition there was.

Although there was little enjoyment to be had on that tour, we were privileged to watch the last hurrah of one of the greatest Test cricket teams to ever take the field and to see the culmination of the careers of some truly great players. Where four years previously we had chanted Steve Waugh's name, this time we showed our appreciation for the greatness of Warne, McGrath and Langer. Warne was serenaded by a chant of 'We wish you were English'. Under our breaths we were also saying 'and good bloody riddance' as we would no longer have them putting paid to our hopes and dreams.

Both captains, as usual, acknowledged the magnificent away support. I'm sure being a part of that winning Australian team must have been awesome. But if you were going to be the team on the end of a 5-0 thrashing then I'm fairly sure we're the fans you would want behind you; never slagging you off, always trying to help, no matter how desperate the situation.

As we sat having a rather miserable beer after the end of play Billy the Trumpet, our mutual friend Adrian Raffill and I sat and declared that we couldn't be arsed touring Australia again. It wasn't just the result, we also felt that the Army had been invaded by those football fans who didn't love the game like we did. We couldn't get any new songs going because people were busy singing the same ones over and over again. We'd rather watch in silence than watch with non-cricket-lovers. We quickly realised we were talking absolute tosh and that we'd almost certainly be back next time because the lure of the game would win out. After so much misery we couldn't afford to miss out on the possibility of glory. It's the very essence of what makes watching England, or any other team, so addictive. If you've put yourself through the bad times you can't risk missing out on the good times. Sadly for Adrian he did stick to his word and so did miss out on the good times. Bill and I were there for all five Tests in 2010–11, which just goes to show you can't believe a word we say.

The postscript to the Ashes series was a Twenty20 game a few days later. Hope springs eternal in the Army so we declared ourselves available for selection to go and watch what was a relatively new phenomenon. Vaughan was back (the idea of Vaughan being a Twenty20 player seems strange now but nobody then had really worked out the vagaries of the format) and we were confident we could gain back a little bit of respect. We got hammered. Australia hit 14 sixes to England's one and that's about as much as you need to know.

Whereas those who had endured the whole tour had to go back to an English winter and a few weeks of poverty, I at least had the consolation of more holiday and a wedding to attend in Melbourne. I couldn't wait to get there and away from cricket. Whenever my Aussie friends brought up the subject of cricket I insisted it was Su and Tim's day and we should be talking about them, not some stupid ball game.

My memories of that Australian trip are fantastic, but they revolve around a great New Year, a stag do and a wedding. The cricket... it's all to be forgotten. It's not just the English media who pretend that series didn't happen. Most of us have wiped it from our minds as well.

Fortunately redemption was waiting, but that can wait a while...

Three

What is the Barmy Army?

We are the Army, the Barmy Army

I-oh, I-oh
We are the Barmy boys
I-oh, I-oh
We are the Barmy boys
We're England's famous cricket fans
We travel near and far
When we're not singing
You'll find us at the bar

Repeat verse one

I-oh, I-oh
You couldn't fill a fridge
I-oh, I-oh
You couldn't fill a fridge
Your mother's wearing Tupperware
Your father's wearing pants
We're all going to a disco dance

THE BARMY ARMY IS England's group of 'famous cricket fans' and it does travel 'near and far'. You can often find the Army 'at the bar', and more occasionally at a 'disco dance'. There's not much Tupperware around, so it's probably best to leave the relative accuracy of that song there and move on to a more considered appreciation of the fundamental question that has interrupted the relating of my hedonistic cricket tales – what is the Barmy Army? You might think it's a simple query to which you already know the answer and be tempted to skip this bit in order to get to more tales of derring do from around the world. But stick around, you might learn something and it's more complicated than you might think. The media regularly gets it wrong and seeing as most people get their information from the media it's time somebody put them right, although that's a battle we have been struggling to fight for a long time now.

There are many people in the Barmy Army who can't agree on exactly what the Barmy Army is or what it should be. On a very basic level the answer is that the Barmy Army is England's vocal, travelling cricket fans but if it were really that simple I wouldn't have chosen to dedicate hours of my time to writing about it. And besides, the Barmy Army exists in England as well so you could argue the 'travelling' part of that sentence is irrelevant. And while the majority are vocal, some enjoy being near the singing rather than joining in themselves, so 'vocal' could be redundant as well. But then that would leave you with 'England's cricket fans' and that's definitely not accurate.

The reason there is so much confusion is that from a small acorn a mighty, multi-branched oak has grown, so to get our head round what it's all about it's necessary to go back a long time ago to a colony far, far away.

The full history of the Barmy Army has been told by those who were integral to its formative years and the crux of its formation goes as follows. During the 1995–96 tour of Australia – not for the first time the England cricket team were getting their arses handed to them on a platter – a bunch of England fans continued to have a great time anyway. Dave Peacock, one of the founders of the Army, had some T-shirts designed with the legendary phrase: 'We came here with backpacks, you with ball and chain'.

These sold quickly and when the Australian press coined the term Barmy Army for this bunch of fun-loving, chanting fans, co-founder Paul Burnham produced the first official Barmy Army T-shirt emblazoned with the legend 'Michael Atherton's Barmy Army' plus a map of Australia with the Test venues. Thanks to an unlikely win in Adelaide the T-shirts became immensely popular, sold in their thousands and on returning home Paul, Dave and Gareth Evans trademarked 'Barmy Army' and set it up as a business.

From that moment the Barmy Army grew organically and could be described simply as England's vocal travelling support. Indeed the first time I interviewed Paul Burnham for a magazine feature he told me that anyone who has been to watch England overseas and got involved in the singing and vocal support could consider themselves a member of the Army. So far, so simple.

But whenever a business or organisation grows from being a small, niche operation to something bigger there is a tipping point when it loses its simplicity. And as the Barmy Army became more popular it faced a struggle to retain its identity. Through no fault of its own it became a catch-all title for England's overseas cricket fans. This had two consequences. There were those who disapproved of the vociferous support and were horrified to find themselves being lumped under the same banner, while the Army was equally horrified to find itself blamed for anything and everything that was done by any cricket fan regardless of whether they were 'one of us'. And the generic and flippant use of the name also started to be used to describe the support at home matches even though the Barmy Army never sat together at a home Test match until the Ashes series of 2005. England football fans are called England football fans, England rugby fans are called England rugby fans; slowly but surely England cricket fans became known exclusively as the Barmy Army.

This was an issue for the Army because it prided itself, and will continue to do so, on certain standards of behaviour. While a lot of the Army were football fans as well, there was a clear definition between how football fans behaved and how the Army did. The idea was to take the element of vocal support and apply it to cricket, but with less abuse, a more positive attitude to the team being followed and with an appreciation of the game they were watching that far exceeded what many football fans would manage (bear in mind football hooliganism was still very evident in the mid-90s, if not as rampant as it had been). England football fans had a bad reputation. England's vocal cricket fans were determined they would not be the same, despite the fact that some members of the press assumed immediately they would be. One, the late Ian Wooldridge of the *Daily Mail*, even went so far as to intimate he would like them gassed. As Paul Burnham says, 'The British media was pretty uneducated. They looked at us and said, "Well, they're football fans". But football fans don't go away in the middle of the football season to watch cricket, particularly if the team is losing heavily.'

No one in the Army is going to pretend that the Barmies never swear and never sing songs directed at opposition players (especially Australians), but generally the language is clean and the support is focussed on getting behind England's players with respect for both the game of cricket and the opposition. This behavioural standard was implicit until it was eventually codified into the following rules:

Have Fun – good, clean and entertaining fun
Be Passionate – about supporting cricket, win lose or draw
Show Respect – for all players, officials, fans and grounds' rules and regulations
Give Consideration – to people's views, beliefs and cultures
Mind – your language!

The issue the Army faced was that as it grew it inevitably started to attract those football fans from whom it was keen to differentiate itself. While numbers were still manageable it was fairly easy to introduce newcomers to the then unofficial codes of conduct the Army had in place, but as bigger numbers joined in it was difficult. At home it was nigh on impossible, so the unruly behaviour that can be found at places like Headingley would automatically be associated with the Army. There are a couple of specific examples that go to prove the difficulty the Barmy Army has experienced.

The most renowned was during the 2009 Ashes series when Ricky Ponting got booed at Edgbaston. Instantly the media was full of spluttering about how disrespectful the Barmy Army was to the great game of cricket and how our behaviour sullied the reputation of the sport. Leaving aside for the moment the fact that Ricky himself didn't seem to care one jot and came out publicly in defence of the Barmy Army, there is a slight problem with this theory in that the booing was not coming from the Barmy Army section. I'm not going to sit here and promise that every single one of the Barmy Army was quiet, but from my position at the back of the stand the majority of the booing was coming from elsewhere. But hey, 'English cricket fans boo Ricky Ponting' equals 'Barmy Army boos Ricky Ponting'. At least it does for headline purposes. So our reputation suffers by the actions of others.

Certain England fans continued to boo the Australian captain during the 2010–11 Ashes series and as the general grouping of all the fans under the Barmy Army banner is stronger abroad than at home the Army again got the blame. This is where the issue gets really confused. Most of those involved on this occasion would consider themselves part of the Barmy Army, while many in the Army wouldn't associate themselves with this behaviour. So whose Army is it anyway? The media tar us all with the same brush and yet even we can't always agree on things.

For those in the Army who think booing the opposition captain for no real reason is just not cricket, there's nothing they can do to stop others. The issue of whether booing opposition players is acceptable is irrelevant here (although it's interesting to note that the booing of Michael Clarke by his own fans during a 2011 ODI in Melbourne was louder), but it highlights the problems the Army faces.

During the tour of Sri Lanka in 2007 one of the England fans decided to take off all his clothes and streak at the Sinhalese Sports Club ground in Colombo. It was apparently the first instance of a cricket streaker in the country and there are no prizes for guessing who got the blame. The radio coverage instantly used the term 'Barmy Army' even though he wasn't from our stand. Ironically he came from closer to the press box. Not only did he not come from our section, it transpired when he was identified that he didn't like the Barmy Army. He must have been delighted when the Army was implicated and it's another example of how it gets the blame for everything.

So therein lies issue number one when it comes to defining the Barmy Army. Those who have been involved in shaping it, maintaining it, developing it and caring for it have a clear definition of what it is, but those who write about it, those who join it without realising what it stands for and even those who are not involved at all can both skew public opinion and have a damaging effect on its reputation.

But this is only the start of the Barmy Army's schizophrenic identity issues. While the term is used to describe England cricket fans it is also the name of the business set up back in 1995. The business has expanded over the years from merely selling T-shirts and merchandise to running tours, releasing music, publishing magazines and books, ticket reselling and a whole lot more. When people realise this they are generally surprised. Tell someone you work for the Barmy Army and the general reaction is one of amazement that it is a business venture and not just a group of crazy cricket fans.

The Barmy Army business does an extraordinary amount for England cricket fans behind the scenes and negotiates on their behalf, but the fact that it is a business militates against it. As long as it is seen as a business there will be a suspicion from outsiders that they are in it for money rather than the good of the fans. It's a battle it struggles to win. It inevitably causes friction between those who are a quintessential part of the Barmy Army in the stands and the people who own the brand. Paul Burnham is the man responsible for running the Barmy Army business and no one should ever doubt his commitment to English cricket and the England team. But some money has to be made in order to run the organisation that underpins everything, and when you have to make money sometimes you have to make unpopular decisions.

Not that Paul, by his own admission, has ever been that good at making money and that's because he has often put the interests of the fans ahead of the interests of the business. Indeed, as he told Penny Wark of *The Times* in 2009, 'Our sole objective is to maximise support for the team and do the right thing for cricket, not to make money. It's a supporters' club. The more people we've got, the more noise we make.'

This dichotomy between generating income and doing everything to facilitate a broad support became apparent to me when I produced the magazine for the 2006–07 Ashes series. Paul was adamant it should be free of charge so people would have access to the song lyrics in the back and therefore make the singing more varied and louder. It was admirable, but from a business point of view it made no sense to me. I saw the magazine as another piece of merchandise to be sold.

That example was a microcosm of the biggest issue he had at that time. The Army had grown so big and it was offering so much to so many people without charging a fee that often it would end up costing him money. If you wanted to know information about England tours the chances are you'd ring the Barmy Army rather than the ECB and therefore it became an unofficial England cricket information service. It had also become a ticket retailer, but one that didn't charge for its administrative services and would sit on piles of tickets until people rang up and asked for them. It gave magazines away for free and held Barmy Army events for fans. All of these 'services' were free to pretty much anyone who wanted to utilise them. Until you got involved with it you could be forgiven for not knowing just how much work went on behind the scenes, and all of this led to the issue of business v supporters coming to something of a head in 2007.

Until 2007 'membership' of the Barmy Army had been free. As Paul intimated you could consider yourself a member even if you had only joined us for one day. If you wanted to take that a step further there was a free email newsletter you could sign up to for information about what was happening, how to get tickets and other general English cricket information.

The decision to create a subscription-based membership scheme caused controversy, especially among the people who had been around the Army for years and had in large part been responsible for building its success. How could something so inclusive all of a sudden become a subscription-based service? In truth that wasn't what had happened, but the way it was designed and communicated to the old hands was flawed. On many occasions the motivation and requirements for the move had to be explained one-on-one over several beers. I was an advocate of the scheme, albeit with reservations, and involved in its implementation, but in Barmy Army terms I was a relatively new face and found myself involved in many of these conversations with people who had been touring years before I had even considered it. I remember one comment in particular from a friend who said he was used to being able to call the office a couple of days before a game and get ten tickets for him and his mates. When I pointed out that those tickets had been paid for months ago, that someone had to do all the admin and that if he didn't take those tickets they would be unused and thus become a financial burden on the company he looked perplexed.

The membership scheme was never meant to ostracise anyone, it was designed to create a better structure for the services the Barmy Army offered. There was a simple requirement for a revenue stream to facilitate those services. Someone had to be paid to sit and take all those phone calls asking about the next tour dates, someone had to be paid for negotiating ticket allocations home and away, someone had to be paid for working out seating plans, someone had to be paid for maintaining a decent website (no wonder I was an advocate – the last 'someone' was me). The real issue was not so much having a membership scheme but how much it would cost. I was firmly of the belief that there should be tiered membership. I figured that everyone would probably happily pay a fiver a year to be a member and access the website, get all the news, have access to tickets and generally feel part of the gang. However, the new businessman at the helm – more of him later – insisted on a one-in, all-in price of £40. The upshot was that many of the people who had made the Barmy Army what it was declined to become members. I couldn't blame them. I probably wouldn't have joined myself if I wasn't working for them. Indeed I am not a paid-up member now.

Conversely I know people who joined and paid a membership fee without getting anything out of it other than becoming a card-carrying member. Others joined only to get priority tickets without being an 'active' member. With around 3,000 people shelling out to be an official member we had the rather strange situation of having members who had never been in the stands with us while many of the familiar faces who sang and made up songs were not 'official' members. It was around this time that the internal discussions about what the Barmy Army should be became long-running and fierce.

By 2007 the Barmy Army had to some extent become a four-pronged monster. There was the Barmy Army as a business entity, then there were three different groups of people who represented the Barmy Army. There were the 'regulars' – the core group of people who toured most of the time and who were mainly responsible for writing new songs, instigating singing and trying to ensure everyone behaved themselves. Then there were the occasionals – the great group of everyone who watched cricket with the Army overseas. And in addition there were the official members, many of whom never travelled overseas, but wanted to be part of the Barmy Army for home games and lusted after the priority access to tickets that membership included. For some time the 'regulars' had a division within itself in that you had the hardcore who had been travelling for years and a new group, of which I was one, who picked up on it later but toured religiously afterwards. But while there may have been some mistrust between regular oldies and newbies those barriers were broken down eventually because the motivations of both groups were the same: love cricket, watch cricket, enjoy a beer, enjoy a song and enjoy each other's company.

All of which means that on any given day the Barmy Army could be a different entity. The hardcore group of people who made it to India in the aftermath of a terrorist attack is bound to be different from a group of members who may go to only one day of a Test match in the UK, which will again be different from a group of thousands who make it to Australia for a Test or two during the Ashes. There's no wonder we sometimes have a perception problem when even to us the Army can be a different beast every day, and some days we like it more than others.

Ultimately, the Barmy Army is anything you want it to be. For many it's something they join in with once every couple of years and fundamentally means going to cricket, getting pissed and singing songs. And who's to argue with that? But for many the Barmy Army is more than a supporting group; those who tour regularly have a close bond where the Barmy Army means something more than just a day out – it is an important part of life. People have met husbands, wives, friends and lovers and had life-changing experiences through it. Indeed it can often feel almost like family. It's a family anyone is free to join and it's a large family with different branches. The comparisons are obvious when you think about what a family is. Kendall Hailey, in her book *The Day I Became an Autodidact,* wrote: 'The great gift of family life is to be intimately acquainted with people you might never even introduce yourself to, had life not done it for you.'

This is relevant because one of the things which makes the Barmy Army special is that you do end up being friends with people you would never otherwise have met. But it's not just that you would never have met them, it's that you wouldn't usually associate with them. I have friends within the Barmy Army that I would have been friends with had I met them at work, through mutual friends or travelling in some far-flung place. And those people do tend to be among my best friends in the Army. But there are a lot of people with whom I happily socialise during a cricket tour that I perhaps wouldn't in any other setting. One of the greatest things about the Army is that there are no social barriers. We come from all over the country and from different financial and social backgrounds and yet mooch along quite nicely based on nothing more than a love of people hitting a ball with a bat.

Someone else who could equally have been describing the Barmy Army when she wrote about family was American humourist Erma Brombeck who said: 'The family. We were a strange little band of characters trudging through life sharing diseases and toothpaste, coveting one another's desserts, hiding shampoo, borrowing money, locking each other out of our rooms, inflicting pain and kissing to heal it in the same instant, loving, laughing, defending, and trying to figure out the common thread that bound us all together.'

Now I have never knowingly shared a disease with anyone in the Army and I'm not even going to speculate about whether others have, but while we obviously know what that 'common thread' is, the rest of that comment is scarily accurate. And HM The Queen, whom we sing about often, could also have been talking of the Army when she said of the Windsors: 'Like all the best families, we have our share of eccentricities, of impetuous and wayward youngsters and of family disagreements.' There's an unattributed quote about families that also sums up the Barmy Army. 'Families are like fudge – mostly sweet with a few nuts.'

So it's family to some, an occasional dalliance for others, but what is it to me? I was originally one of those casual Barmies who turned up on occasion, sang songs and got drunk and loved this crazy, new experience. I have also been involved on the business side, desperate to find ways to monetise the thing in order to provide better services for England cricket fans. But all of that is incidental compared to what I really love about the Army.

'My' Barmy Army is a group of like-minded people who follow England at home and abroad, when their wallets and lifestyles allow, but mainly concentrate their efforts on away matches. They like to sing and while they love nothing better than going through the oldies they're never more excited than when composing new songs. They generally love a beer or two and are welcoming and inclusive to anyone wanting to join in the fun, as long as they're well-behaved and respectful of the game we love. The majority of people I watch cricket with now I have met through the Barmy Army, which makes it a special and endearing part of my life. While many people I know are faces I encounter only on tour, there are others who are now firm friends away from cricket. Like any large congregation, people tend to create smaller groups of like-minded souls so I have a group of close friends. But I love the fact that the smaller social groups, an inevitable by-product of a larger group, will also mix together. Everyone talks to everyone in the Army, which is one of its great benefits. It hurts when people sometimes refer to my group of friends as a 'clique'. Our group is far from exclusive as its ever-expanding nature goes to prove.

So while the Barmy Army is whatever you want it to be, to me it is a close group of friends combined with other groups who all come together to have a great time, enjoy a great game and enjoy each other's company. And while I'm at it I'll outline some of the things in which this core group passionately believes.

We don't like beer snakes. We don't get the attraction. What is so fascinating about putting a bunch of empty cups inside each other? Yet go to many Test matches and the construction of such a thing can attract people's attention more than the cricket. Weird. We hate Mexican Waves. If you're watching a bunch of people stand up and sit down in order you're not watching the cricket and if you really find that entertaining you needn't spend money on a Test match ticket when an empty box would probably keep you amused for a day. They were mildly amusing for one tournament (the Mexico 1986 World Cup) and should have been left there. Plus the fact they can't help the cricketers' concentration on the field.

We believe that cricket is a game the tradition of which should be respected, as should opposition players. Yes we like to sing, which may not be traditional in English cricket, but not moving during an over, applauding opposition milestones, listening to the opposition's post-match comments, appreciating the opposition and being friendly to the locals when you visit their country are all essential.

We hate singing football chants at cricket matches. We're only here for the cricket. The fact that we support a different team from you in a different sport is irrelevant. We support England. We may not always agree with the selections made and we may not rate some of the players, but they are representing our nation so we will get behind them. We not going to say we never swear because sometimes we do but we try not to, especially if there are children around.

We like to come up with original songs so we can keep the repertoire fresh and not repeat the same things over and over again. Otherwise we do lay ourselves open to being boring, monotonous and repetitive. And we love Test cricket over and above any other format of the game. We will watch T20 and ODIs because they are a form of cricket but to us they are poor, unsophisticated relations.

We understand that not everyone will agree with us and that everyone is entitled to have their own version of the Barmy Army but that's ours for what it's worth. We can't impose those beliefs on everyone who ever joins us, but we don't think they're a bad set to try to instil.

Whatever your interpretation or perception of the Barmy Army, I truly believe they are the best sports fans on the planet. The amount of time, money and effort spent to follow England's cricket team is immense. No matter where England play, the Barmy Army is there, in its many thousands in Australia and the West Indies, in big numbers in South Africa, providing the huge majority of spectators in New Zealand and Sri Lanka, exploring India and even braving Pakistan when it was on the agenda. We even go to Edinburgh, Belfast and Dublin to watch one-dayers and we'll be desperate to experience Zimbabwe if England ever get round to playing there again.

I've often wondered what it is about the English – the British, and Irish, in general – that they seem to follow sport away from home more, and with more vitality, than anyone else. Yes the Australians get about a bit, the Dutch love to get behind their football team and the Kiwis their rugby, but we just follow everything. No one has a bigger football support, nothing comes close to matching our cricket support, and wherever the British Lions play or World Cup rugby is happening there's always a huge contingent of fans from the home nations.

Jim White touched on this in *The Telegraph* in 2010: 'This is the glorious point of the Barmies – indeed, of this nation more generally. Lovely as triumph might be, the purpose is not the pursuit of winning. The blokes pinking up in the Victoria sun represented a strain of sporting support that is gloriously, wonderfully and uniquely British. Only among our fans is there such stubborn insistence on maintaining loyalty in the face of defeat. Only our followers exhibit such levels of wilful masochism.'

But while that 'wilful masochism' is apparent across several sports, it's cricket that benefits the most. Take England's travelling fans away from cricket grounds around the world and the truth is there would be very little left. You only have to look at games between the likes of New Zealand and Pakistan, or West Indies and India, to realise that as a spectator sport Test cricket is dying on its arse and we're the generator that keeps it going. It's a point made by Dr Dominic Malcolm from Leicester University, who wrote the snappily titled *International Review for the Sociology of Sport*. 'The Army is hugely significant to the financial viability of cricket. A younger audience with disposable incomes is precisely what the game needs. The image of the old fogey has restricted it for a long time.'

The reality is that if we all stopped going tomorrow cricket would still survive as the money from Indian television deals is significantly more than we put into the game. But sport needs spectators; they are part of the packaging, part of the spectacle and part of the event. You only have to think about how often the Barmy Army is referred to on television to work that out. Without us cricket lacks atmosphere and vibrancy and surely we should be given some credit for that.

It's not just the numbers, but the style of support that makes me a proud Barmy Army member. Unlike England's often despicable football fans, who ruin matches so much that I can now no longer bear to be in the same stadium, the behaviour of cricket fans is for the most part exemplary. These days there might not be the level of football hooliganism that blighted the 80s and early 90s, but the language and vitriol spouted at an England football match is embarrassing. I'm not saying everyone in the Barmy Army is an angel and that butter wouldn't melt in our mouths, but we do watch our language when children are around, we concentrate largely on supporting our own players rather than abusing the opposition (or, for that matter, abusing our own players as many England football fans love to do), we are friendly with the locals, we are witty and inventive and passionate and knowledgeable about the sport we love. We do get behind the team however it is performing, we can sing our hearts out for five days solid and then turn up somewhere else and do it all over again and we do it all with smiles on our faces win, lose or draw.

And that, as far as I am concerned, is exactly what supporting a sports team should be about.

Four

Touring South Africa

We've got eleven South Africans in our team

Touring experiences in South Africa:

2004–05	*3rd Test (Durban)*
	4th Test (Cape Town) – Three days
2009–10	*1st Test (Pretoria)*
	2nd Test (Durban)
	3rd Test (Cape Town)
	4th Test (Johannesburg)

WHILE SOUTH AFRICA IS famous for its big five in wildlife terms, it is one of the big three in terms of overseas touring, taking its place alongside Australia and the West Indies as the most popular destinations. A tour of South Africa is about as close as you can get to touring Australia. They are the only tours that take place over Christmas and New Year, the countries share many similarities in terms of modernity, culture and climate and Cape Town and Sydney run each other close as two of the most beautiful cities in which to watch Test cricket. As, like Australia, South Africa has a surfeit of alternative tourist attractions, it is little surprise it is among the more popular tours.

All of which made it a very obvious place for me to extend my Barmy Army experience outside of Australia and makes it look suspiciously like I was in this for tourism as much as cricket. In truth there were three elements that came together perfectly to make this the ideal place in which to broaden my cricket-watching horizons. Firstly there was the tourism; secondly the 2002–03 tour of Australia had awakened a desire to experience cricket and the Barmy Army in a different environment. Finally, by the time I embarked upon it I was in a relationship with a South African girl, Sam, whose family still lived there. A joint trip for Christmas and New Year ticked more than one box. Sam and I had several discussions after that holiday about what came first, the desire to visit her family or the cricket. She was insistent it was family, but I clearly remember deciding when I was in Australia that this 2004–05 tour would be on my agenda anyway. That may mean I was a little bit more liberal with the truth than I should have been when we discussed it, or equally likely that she chose to think that we'd decided to go on holiday together and the cricket was just fortunate timing. The truth was probably somewhere in the middle, but either way it was a happy coincidence and Sam would enter fully into the Barmy Army spirit, so much so that somehow I would subsequently talk her into a trip to Pakistan.

We did indulge in some tourist attractions before we got to hear the sound of leather on willow. A trip to the Pilanesberg Nature Reserve led to up close and personal relationships with a variety of wildlife and the fact that they messed up our booking for the cheapest accommodation available, putting us instead in the most expensive, didn't harm the experience at all. Our five-star room was a far cry from the three-bed sweat pit dormitory we would later inhabit during the Durban Test match.

A family Christmas in Johannesburg followed and a very nice time was had by all, but come Boxing Day I was more than ready to watch some cricket and Sam's Dad very kindly dragged himself out of bed to drive to the airport at a particularly unsocial hour for my flight to Durban. I left Sam behind for a couple of days of extra family time. England were already 1-0 up in the series following a good win in Port Elizabeth so hopes were high.

Of course everything was overshadowed completely on Boxing Day 2004 by news of the tsunami that devastated parts of Asia and took so many lives. Except for me it didn't overshadow the cricket, not because I am a heartless sod who cares more about sport than truly shattering events, but because when I'm on tour news from the outside world rarely permeates into my consciousness. Although I knew there had been a tsunami, the magnitude of it was lost on me. When I first heard about it I was sitting next to a guy who lived in Sri Lanka and it barely registered with him even though his girlfriend was still there. The days were spent at the cricket, the nights were spent partying. I didn't see a newspaper, didn't watch television and didn't interact with anyone who wasn't a cricket fan. It's hard to believe that anyone could be so oblivious to such a huge news story and now, with ubiquitous internet access on mobile phones and laptops, it probably wouldn't happen. But even when I bought raffle tickets to support the Barmy Army fundraising effort on day five I didn't know much about what had happened. Not that I would escape the ramifications for long. A message from one of my best friends at university informed me that a mutual friend was missing. They never found his body and it's discomfiting to think that as we were indulging in an orgy of fun and partying there were parents, families and friends around the world worrying about their loved ones.

I was joined at lunchtime on Boxing Day by Jim, to whom I'd first mooted the idea of this trip as we were celebrating England's 2002 Test victory in Sydney. He had flown in from the UK after a family Christmas and knew even less about world events than I did so our priority was to busy ourselves getting stuck into plenty of Castle Lager. Unfortunately South Africa were gorging on English wickets with a similar enthusiasm. England were bowled out for just 139 and South Africa finished day one on 70-3. This was not why Jim had spent the previous 12 hours in the air and not what we had envisaged. But hey, we were in South Africa, watching cricket, it was roasting hot and we knew nothing of the world's tragedy. What we did know was that the Barmy Army had drunk more in the ground that day than the entire crowd had ploughed through in five days when the West Indies were in town the previous year. You could argue that such an 'achievement' is neither big nor clever, but we felt quite proud of ourselves nonetheless.

It helped that there were people walking round with kegs of beer on their backs and that they would pour a glass at your seat rather than putting you to the inconvenience of going to the bar. According to its website, Major Tom (for such is the name of the company that provides the service) 'utilises proprietary backpack systems to promote and serve all beverages from draught beer to hot soup. Often seen at events and venues where traditional, static bar facilities cannot reach or meet the potential demand.' Well the potential demand here was huge and when you've got a bunch of guys walking round with 'Major Tom' written on the side of the backpacks it's nigh on impossible not to shout 'Hey Major Tom, this is ground control and we need some more beer.' Or maybe that was just me.

It should not have been possible to consume as much beer as we did in such merciless heat without dehydration and fatigue setting in but it just seemed to give us more and more energy. And while the Durban ground is not one of aesthetic beauty it is of great practical use to the Barmy Army, with its combination of grass bank and seating, with more than enough space to allow us all to congregate where we wanted. After two days we had become friends with everyone in our section, most of whom were intrigued to see if my raucous behaviour would change with the arrival of Sam the following day.

It's a Barmy Army tradition to serenade pretty much every boy/girl combination walking past with Joe Jackson's *Is she really going out with him*? The more unlikely it is that the pair in question are in a relationship the funnier it becomes. A male/female police pairing tends to be the most amusing target, while female television presenters with male cameramen also tend to be on the receiving end. And it almost goes without saying that if a couple of lads walk past and decide to give the Army a bit of stick then they get 'Is he really going out with him?' Generally you try to avoid being the target of this song, whether you are in a relationship or not, but when Sam got to the pub after day two her drunken boyfriend welcomed her by singing 'Is she really going out with me?' Fortunately our relationship involved a lot of drinking anyway, and as she had an almost obsessive love of springboks (a quite delectable combination of amaretto and crème de menthe that slides down with ridiculous ease), she simply set about catching me up. The week wasn't going to get any quieter. Jim, Sam and I were a terrible trio at the time, sharing many party nights in the bars of London that almost always ended up back at the house Jim and I were sharing, so the three of us proceeded to tear it up for a few days in spectacular style. In Cape Town Jim would meet one of Sam's best friends and end up in a relationship still going strong to this day, far outlasting Sam and me. But then he never took her to the cricket.

Our good spirits were helped by the fact that the first disastrous day was as bad as it would get in a Test that would be forever dubbed the Bouncebackability Test. That word had been coined by football manager Iain Dowie in a TV interview and the Saturday morning television show *Soccer AM* was trying to get it into the *Oxford English Dictionary.* Daniel Finkelstein even wrote about it in *The Times*. But for us it would always be relevant to cricket more than football and why not? If scoring 570-7 declared after a first innings embarrassment didn't define bouncebackability then nothing would. Several guys behind us took it upon themselves to spell it out with a letter on each person's T-shirt. Having seen this trick fail miserably with much smaller words as people struggle to sit in the correct places for it to read properly, they gained respect for nearly always getting it right.

The compelling action on the field and some real bonding experiences in the crowd made this a great week. I was well and truly immersed in the whole experience, as was pointed out to me by Sam after I caught her looking at me in a slightly knowing way. 'This is you, isn't it?' she said. 'This is you in your element.' I couldn't argue with her. Sunshine, cricket, great people, singing, atmosphere, beer. If you were to make a list of the things that made me happy at that stage of my life then they would all be in the top ten. I was enthralled, in a happy place which transcended being drunk or being in a good mood. I had found in one package something that meant everything to me. I'm the kind of person who does things to extremes when I find something I like and it was obvious this was my new 'thing'. There was to be no going back.

The rollercoaster ride that would typify watching England was almost encapsulated in that one Test as we overturned a 200-run deficit after the first innings to set South Africa 378 to win. We then had them eight down before bad light intervened. This seemed like a particularly bad joke considering we had been sitting in roasting sunshine sweating our arses off for five days without so much as seeing a cloud. My memories of this Test are again of the macro rather than micro variety, so in my brain there is an overwhelming impression of the five days rather than a lot of specific memories. I can't really remember many of the different songs that were doing the rounds at the time other than the standard ditties, such as:

When I was six, I had no sense
I bought a flute for fifty pence
The only tune that I could play
Was Michael Vaughan's Barmy Army

However, I will always remember enjoying one of my all-time favourites that had been written in honour of South Africa's Shaun Pollock. He had lost the captaincy after an unsuccessful World Cup campaign in 2003 when he miscalculated the number of runs South Africa required on the Duckworth–Lewis method and was subsequently serenaded to the tune of *Da Doo Ron Ron*:

My name is Shaun Pollock and I cannot count
One more run run, one more run
I miscalculated and we got knocked out
One more run run, one more run

Oh I had a panic attack
Oh and I got the sack
Oh we needed one more run
One more run run, one more run

Why this song in particular took my fancy I don't know, but I still sing it to this day because it struck a chord (b'dum tish) with me. Everyone has their favourite Barmy Army songs but there is rarely a logical reason for it. Singing it was never more enjoyable than on the final afternoon when he ran himself out to leave South Africa eight down just as they had looked safe. As it turned out they were safe, so he had the last laugh. Rumour has it that Shaun liked the song so much he sang it to himself in the nets. I do hope that's true.

With only two days between the second and third Tests there wasn't a lot of time for sightseeing, indeed there was hardly enough time to sober up as one of those days was New Year's Eve. Thankfully there now has to be at least three days between Test matches and while I suspect the ICC introduced this rule to protect the players, I can safely say that the fans are every bit as grateful. A combination of Christmas Eve, Christmas Day, Boxing Day Test match, New Year's Eve and a Test starting on January 2 is a daunting prospect for those who wouldn't let any of these events go by without indulging in an ale or two, so a day off somewhere along the way is most welcome. But that wasn't the case back then, which was a shame as we'd decided to drive down the world-famous Garden Route that makes up much of the journey from Durban to Cape Town. Having to rush that was annoying and meant we didn't get to fully enjoy it. It also led to one of the weirder New Year experiences of my life.

We hadn't booked anywhere to stay on New Year's Eve, which was always going to be interesting, so when I discovered that Sam's parents were holidaying in Port Elizabeth, halfway to Cape Town, I suggested we might join them. I reasoned they would love to see their daughter again and as we had just come off the back of a five-day epic bender a quiet night on NYE wouldn't really go amiss. When every day is a great day there's no need to celebrate another as if it is anything special. As it turned out, Sam's parents had a spare room with three single beds. In retrospect that seems ridiculously fortuitous, but as we were in one of those phases when everything in the world was going our way it seemed entirely natural.

The evening's entertainment was a dinner-dance that felt like going back in time. Port Elizabeth is a lovely town, one of the nicer venues in South Africa, and we were all distraught when it was the casualty of the 2009–10 tour being cut to four Tests. It has some great establishments, but the hotel in which we spent the night wasn't one of them. It seemed they had gathered all the freaks from the surrounding area and put them in one place to see in the new year. I swear most of the people were married to or planning to marry members of their own family. The music was like something from a horror film and if Jack Nicholson had smashed an axe through the door and screamed 'Here's Johnny' I wouldn't have batted an eyelid.

We ordered a bottle of wine that was corked. The waiter didn't know what corked meant. We got a replacement. It was corked. He still didn't know what it meant. Jim went with him to see what was going on. The wine was stored in a dark, dank cupboard representative of a sommelier's nightmare and it wasn't going to be worth opening any more bottles. Ever. While Sam chatted amiably with her family friends, Jim and I wondered how we had ended up here. Thankfully Sam's Dad took pity on us.

Sam found the three of us an hour later in the hotel bar and when she asked what we were doing her father politely informed her that he was saving us from enduring any more of what was transpiring in the next room. We went to bed at about ten minutes past midnight and were on the road early to get to Cape Town. It was a sobering experience in more ways than one and about as diametrically far away from the Barmy Army experience as you could get.

While Sam had bought hugely into that experience, enjoying getting involved in the singing when she wasn't hiding from the sun reading a book, she had friends in Cape Town and so Jim and I were on our own when it came to watching cricket. Well, we were on our own except for the thousands of others who had turned up for the most glamorous Test of the tour. The majority were trying to collect their tickets at the same time before play on day one, but that was easier said than done. The ticket office consisted of a rickety old caravan that might well have been stolen from the people with whom we spent New Year's Eve and was utterly incapable of dealing with the masses. The number of times I have turned up to an international cricket ground only to find facilities akin to a summer fête is truly worrying. We got in eventually, only to find out that our seats were rubbish. Newlands is arguably the most beautiful cricket ground in the world. Certainly the backdrop of Table Mountain cannot be beaten and the ground itself, with its combination of stands and grass banks, is a thoroughly enjoyable place in which to watch a game of cricket. Unless, that is, you end up in the temporary stands which sit back from the ground and feel somehow disassociated from the rest of the ground. You can guess where we were. We blagged our way onto the grass bank on occasions but the experience couldn't have been more different from our Durban fantasy where we were immersed in everything that was going on. All of which, combined with the fact that England got smashed, led me to do something that I have never done since. I voluntarily missed a day of cricket while on tour. As I missed that day in order to go shark cage diving I will never regret it. If you're going to miss cricket, do something memorable with your day. Watching a few great whites swim past my nose was definitely memorable, but I never walked away from action on the field in favour of touristy activities again.

Something momentous happened during that Test match which would have a dramatic effect on my life, although I wasn't to know it at the time. It was the first time I talked to Paul Burnham, the co-founder and main man of the Barmy Army. It wasn't a particularly long or pleasant conversation, but in retrospect the moment he gave me his business card and told me to call him when back in England was something of a watershed moment in my life. Other than that it was memorable for being one of the worst Tests I have seen overseas in terms of result and lack of interaction with the Barmy Army, who were lording it up on the grass bank while I sat in the cheap seats. England would ultimately win the series 2-1, but I witnessed only a draw and a defeat, although this did nothing to dampen my enthusiasm for the experience as a whole.

Even with defeat there were memories to cherish as I ended up talking about the game to Andrew Flintoff. I'd met my first England cricketer when I interviewed Matthew Hoggard at the team hotel for a magazine feature. As a journalist you get used to meeting famous people, but this was the first time I'd interviewed one I'd paid to watch an hour or so previously. We had a good chat about various things and I was excited about the experience. But it was to get more exciting when I returned to the players' hotel the following day to pick up a disc with some images on. I sat down to wait in the foyer and realised I was next to Flintoff, busy nursing his baby daughter Holly. I said hello and we ended up having a natter for 15 minutes. I walked out on a high. As a fan, casual encounters with your sporting heroes aren't everyday experiences. And while I would discover that cricket is probably one of the best sports for interaction with the players, these first encounters had me giddy as a schoolboy.

By the time I returned to South Africa for the 2009–10 series interaction with cricketers was commonplace and I didn't have to worry about missing England victories because I didn't miss Test matches. I was at a stage where doing one or two Tests per tour made no sense, so it had to be all or nothing. The four Tests I attended on that second South Africa tour meant I had been to 18 consecutive away Test matches. This had been helped out by the fact that I had been working for the Barmy Army for much of this time, but I still had to give up a lot to make that possibility a reality. Eighteen Tests on the bounce is not that many compared to some stalwarts, but it seemed a lot to me.

That run came to an end after that tour, as did my professional association with the Barmy Army. I had been working for them for several years in one capacity or another, but wanderlust had got the better of me again so I decided to stop. My friends would point out that I was always travelling somewhere or other, but I hadn't slung on the backpack and left everything behind for about six years so it was time to do it all again. Tyler White, a fellow Barmy Army man and traveller, had suggested to me at a party a couple of years before that it could be fun to go to South Africa for the cricket series and then travel round the continent for a few months before heading back there for the football World Cup. He wasn't actively recruiting but he must have known subliminally that dangling a carrot like that in front of someone like me was only going to have one result. Before he'd even finished outlining his plan I had informed him that whether he liked it or not he now had a travel partner. I cancelled all my freelance journalism contracts, including the one I had with the Barmy Army, and embarked on a tour with no work responsibilities to fulfil.

As an incidental note I reckon I must have hit some kind of record in 2009 for watching one team play international cricket in different places as I watched England in eight countries. With a West Indies tour that took in Jamaica, Antigua, Barbados and Trinidad, a home series that saw us play Australia in England and Wales, an ODI against Ireland in Belfast and a series in South Africa, the chances of doing more have to be very slim.

My experience on a Barmy Army tour by this stage was dramatically different from my first tour of South Africa due to the fact that I now had a close group of Barmy Army friends and a wider group of acquaintances that came as a fairly obvious result of attending small tours and working for the business. This meant there was no such thing as going 'on your own', and finding people with whom to share accommodation and travel was easy. It was now almost as much a bunch of mates going on holiday together as a cricket tour.

A large number of my close group of friends constituted a fair proportion of the away support for the first Test in Centurion. It's not the most attractive place to play Test cricket and doesn't even have the innate crazy Asian atmosphere that some of the equally unattractive Indian venues benefit from so it really is unremarkable. My only memories of Pretoria (Centurion is just down the road from Pretoria so most people choose to stay there) are the lack of watering holes and the proliferation of posters stuck to lampposts offering cheap and safe abortions. It's hardly a selling point when it comes to tourism is it? And in a country that struggles to shrug off the legacy and enduring elements of racism it seemed more prevalent there than anywhere else we went. Certainly when one of our friends who lived in Johannesburg explained to a group of local lads that he was going out with a black South African girl the reaction was not what you would want of a progressive, egalitarian country.

There was one overwhelmingly positive experience in this regard though. Nelson Mandela had been quick to spot the role sport would need to play in reintegrating South African society and few men could have played a bigger role in that than Makhaya Ntini. He was the first black African cricketer to play for South Africa and we would have the privilege of seeing him play in his 100th Test, a great achievement for anyone, but particularly poignant in these circumstances. And while we may have found evidence of enduring racism elsewhere there was certainly none when it came to celebrating that achievement as the whole country seemed to revel in it as a sign of just how far South Africa had come.

On a more basic level it also meant that we all got free beer for a day thanks to a special offer to celebrate his achievement. As we walked into a pleasant, if uninspiring, ground on day one, we were handed vouchers that promised the bearer a free beer when Ntini took his first wicket. As South Africa batted first this didn't happen on day one, so on day two we received more vouchers and were quick to ensure that we picked up a handful each from the pretty girls doling them out. At the end of day two England had only lost one wicket and Ntini hadn't taken it. We repeated our voucher collection technique on day three and what do you know? In the first hour Ntini bowled Strauss, his 389th and penultimate Test wicket. We didn't actually think they would honour every voucher we had tucked away over the previous three days, but they did and seeing as he'd taken the wicket so early in the day there was plenty of time to redeem them. Cheers Makhaya – you made that a cheap day for us, so much so that a few of our number took to singing:

He bought us our beer
He bought us our beer
Makhaya Ntini
He bought us our beer

With so few people at the game we were able to take maximum advantage of that little offer, but the lack of numbers meant we struggled to generate much in the way of atmosphere no matter how well lubricated we were. Graeme Swann's innings of 85 from 81 balls in the first innings did give rise to the chant 'Swann, Swann will tear you apart' to the tune of Joy Division's *Love Will Tear Us Apart* and that was about as noisy as we got for four days. It was just a handful of us singing that chant then but thousands would ensure it reverberated around Australian cricket grounds a year later. We also wrote another song for him that didn't become as popular because it was a song rather than a chant and because not a lot of people knew the context for it. During a warm-up game Matt Prior had a bit of fun with an opposition batsman by warning him that there are 'two things you should never do in life, cut a spinner or pat a burning dog'. Such random musings were not to be ignored by us, so on day one a group of us were singing, to the tune of *My Old Man's A Dustman*:

Oh Graeme Swann is bowling
He's going to get you out
Whenever it is turning
He'll always have a shout
And when he takes a wicket
He'll tweet it on his blog
So never cut a spinner or pat a burning dog

The song got a lot of airing during South Africa's first innings when Swann took five wickets, but it was his batting that proved more important than we could have guessed at the time as England only just escaped defeat. There was an outside chance of an England victory on day five, but with 353 needed to win it would take something special and with the loss of two quick wickets there was a need to consolidate rather than attack. With Kevin Pietersen in dominant form and no more wickets going down until tea the draw seemed imminent and we all sat relaxing and basking in the sunshine to watch the game play itself out. Then KP ran himself out and when Trott went it was 205-5 but there was still no reason for major alarm. Then three wickets fell for four more runs, the ninth for not much more and we were staring a really shitty defeat in the face.

This dramatic turn of events led to the crowd suddenly going mental. As the ground was so sparsely populated, it was easy for home and away fans to inhabit the same space and on this occasion there were so few of us that we could take that to extremes. The last few overs saw South African fans and England fans standing on the grass bank, mixing together and getting behind their teams in a scene unlike any other I had ever seen at a cricket match. We celebrated every run or dot ball; they cheered on their bowlers, exhorting them to take wickets. We chatted, shared beers and displayed a general love of the game, together enjoying the excitement at what was transpiring in front of us.

At the end there was mutual respect and congratulations with regard to the sporting event we had witnessed and the part we had played in it.

The South Africans had not been slow to point out to us that England's team consisted of a high proportion of players born in their homeland. The fact that Andrew Strauss and Matt Prior were born in South Africa would never usually have been brought up (especially not with

Strauss's accent), but because we also had Jonathan Trott and KP, who could easily have played for South Africa, then it became a big point of discussion. There's no point arguing against something like that, so it's best to do the opposite and embrace it. That was definitely our tactic as we came up with a song that celebrated the South African influence on the England cricket team over the years. To the tune of *Ten Green Bottles* we sang:

We've got Andrew Strauss in our cricket team
Andrew Strauss in our cricket team
We've got one South African in the England team
We've got Andrew Strauss in our cricket team

We've got Jonny Trott in our cricket team
Jonny Trott in our cricket team
We've got two South Africans in the England team
We've got Jonny Trott in our cricket team
We've got Kevin Pietersen in our cricket team...
We've got Matty Prior in our cricket team...
We've got Robin Smith in our cricket team...
We've got Allan Lamb in our cricket team...
We've got Tony Greig in our cricket team...
We've got Ian Greig in our cricket team...
We've got Robin Jackman in our cricket team...
We've got Chris Smith in our cricket team...

We've got Basil D'Oliveira in our cricket team
Basil D'Oliveira in our cricket team
We've got 11 South Africans in the England team
We've got Basil D'Oliveira in our cricket team

The last verse was sung with particular gusto, firstly because it was the last verse, but more importantly because D'Oliveira's inclusion in the England team had led to the beginning of sporting sanctions against apartheid South Africa, the watershed for so many South Africans playing for us. The first time we sang it we were making it up as we went along so even as we were singing a verse we all had to look round and agree which name would come next. I doubt I have them here in the order we sang them that day, but I remember whoever came up with Chris Smith saved our bacon as we struggled to make a full team.

Our South African influence was also apparent in another song for one of those imports, Jonny Trott, who came to this series on the back of a debut hundred against the Aussies in the decisive Ashes Test in England. Songwriter extraordinaire Giles Wellington, ubiquitously known as Gilo, had penned the following in his honour to the tune of *When Jonny Comes Marching Home*:

He left the Cape to wear three lions
Trotty, Trotty
He hit a ton to win the urn
Trotty, Trotty
He hits the ball, it goes for four,
He plays the shots we all adore
Jonny Trott is England's number three

Na na na na na na na na na na na na na
Jonny Trott is England's number three

There was more of the same in a little used, but excellent ditty by Huw Davies that played on the fact his name was a little bit like Del Boy's from *Only Fools and Horses*:

Stick your passport in your pocket
And your kitbag in the van
Cos if you want the Ashes
And you don't mind Saffers
Then brother, he's your man
Cos where he comes from is no mystery
But he's gonna lead us home to an Ashes victory

A song for him was driving us berserk
But then we thought that Jonny Trotter works

La-la-la-la-la la-la-la-la-la-la

Trott wouldn't give us any reason to sing those songs during the second Test as he accrued just 18 runs, but that really didn't matter as England raced to an emphatic win, during which Swann's 'pat a burning dog' song was again in evidence thanks to his nine wickets. We pretty much had the ground to ourselves on day five as we watched England take the five wickets they needed to win by more than an innings and while we'd partied with South African fans at the end of the first Test, this time we shared our celebrations with the England players.

With a largely empty ground it was easy to head down to the area underneath the players' dressing room for the presentations. What followed was extraordinary. The players hung out of every window available as we serenaded them through pretty much every song in the repertoire. They were drinking it in and joining in the singing and it was further proof that the bond between us was growing stronger. Collingwood relived his attempts at singing the high-pitched bit from *The Lion Sleeps Tonight* that he had first tried in New Zealand. Deco, more of whom later, continued his wooing of Matt Prior by reeling off about four different songs for him. Neither fans nor players seemed ready to end the impromptu singalong, but eventually we went our separate ways to carry on the celebrations all over the city. It was one of those remarkable moments that cricket can throw up where players and fans are all in the same headspace.

There was another privilege to come. As we decamped to the nearby Hilton hotel bar (one of the more salubrious cricketing drinking holes we inhabit), umpire Steve Davis was in attendance. If he was hoping to wind down he didn't get much chance as we quizzed him for over an hour on the vagaries of the Decision Review System, new laws referring to light, how the technology works and more. He was accompanied by one of the guys responsible for some of that technology and they answered each of the many questions we fired at them without ever making it feel like we were bothering them. Again it's rare you can get that close to finding out what's actually happening in the engine room of the sport you love.

That was a happy victory, but our next celebration was of a different nature. Watching your team try to eke out a draw while batting is a stressful experience. The knowledge that any ball can mean a wicket and edge you that much closer to defeat is nerve-wracking. Fortunately in cricket it's rare that games are that close, so you don't have to go through it too often, but in this series we'd go through it twice. We'd already endured it once at Centurion and we did it again in the Third Test. We were back in Cape Town, one of the few grounds to attract good crowds throughout an entire Test match. There was no ticket office caravan involved and this time I was safely ensconced on the grass bank where I belonged.

This is perhaps the best grass bank in cricket from a Barmy Army point of view. There's a bar at the back, which means you don't need to miss any of the action while you're queuing for a beer; it's one of the most populated, which means it is conducive to a great atmosphere and the angle of the bank, while it could be a bit steeper, is generally good enough for people to get a good view of the game.

The game in question started off unremarkably with honours more or less even after the first innings. But by the end of day three South Africa were well on top as they built up a big second innings and as we went into day five England had only seven wickets left as they tried to bat out the draw. Saving the match was going to be a tough ask. Generally you can depend on England to take you agonisingly close to glory before a final failure or to save the match but only after putting everyone through the wringer. And what a wringer that last day was to be.

It was the kind of day when you need sustenance. After far too many days of drinking substandard lager Huw Davies suggested to me that we should dedicate our imbibing that day to Brutal Fruits. What's in a name? Had he suggested a day drinking Bacardi Breezers I'd have questioned his masculinity. However, in South Africa Bacardi Breezers are called Brutal Fruits, which sounds a much more acceptable beverage for a man to consume. And consume them we did on the day that we will forever remember as Brutal Thursday. By the time we'd had our first double Brutal (two bottles conveniently filled a pint glass) England were four down as the players had their morning session drinks. Another round had been dispatched by lunch and England were five down and in brutal trouble. Those of you who know what happened next may think that England's afternoon resistance was due to Collingwood and Bell, who were at the crease at the time. But that would be to underestimate the role played by about a dozen of us who pulled a favourite cricket watchers' trick after heading to a pub for lunchtime refreshment. 'We're not going back in the ground until we lose another wicket,' came the call and we all agreed solemnly, safe in the knowledge that our decision would have a direct and incontrovertible effect on what would happen a few hundred yards away.

There can no going back from such a decision. If you make it and return to the ground before another wicket falls superstitious logic dictates that any wicket that does fall is your fault. Bell and Collingwood might have been feeling some pressure, but we had our own to deal with. We dealt with it by drinking lots of Brutal Fruits and liberally interspersing them with Jägerbombs and Springboks. We made it to tea with no cause to go back as South Africa strived unsuccessfully for another wicket. And it was a good afternoon to watch on TV as we could appreciate fully a phenomenal spell of bowling from Dale Steyn. As much as being there live is unbeatable, there's no denying that you do miss out on a lot of the intricacies of the game when watching it at the ground.

Having made it to the tea break we decided to head back. I know that we broke our own rule by doing that, but there's another unwritten rule that states you can't miss the end of a game, so something had to give. Besides, there was a team to cheer on now there was hope of a draw, so it was time to go in and see how many Brutal Fruits they still had available. Stocks got a hammering in that final couple of hours as nervousness had its usual effect of increasing drinking speed. You have to do something between balls, and lifting a glass to your lips is the obvious thing.

With an hour to go England still had five wickets left. They had done all the hard work and we could relax, couldn't we? Could we hell. What followed was the most nerve-wracking cricketing experience of my life. Two quick wickets had us running for more Brutal refreshment as the nerves started jangling like a doorbell on a just opened door of a corner shop. No one on the grass bank was sitting. The whole crowd stood in a fidgety, nervous, twitchy mass of agitation. I'm not sure when I started turning 360 degrees after each ball, but I had to do something. We'd run out of Brutal Fruits and no one was willing to go to the bar and miss the drama. Once I noticed I was doing it I couldn't stop and I knew that if I failed to turn in a circle between balls it would inevitably lead to us losing a wicket. My mates understood the seriousness of that particular situation and they weren't alone. I clearly remember a guy I didn't know imploring me to 'keep turning mate, keep turning'. The good luck it brought obviously ran out with Broad's wicket though. It had got us close, but there were still 20 deliveries left and two wickets remaining. Bell was still there. Obviously the reason we had lost a wicket was actually because our glasses were empty, but more Brutality would have to wait.

Four runs. The boundary is irrelevant. Nineteen balls to go. Dot ball. Eighteen. Wicket. Bell had played an epic knock of 78 from 213 balls, but he was gone. Seventeen balls left. Swann and Onions with it all to do. Onions had been there at the end in Centurion. Surely he couldn't do it again? Sixteen, 15, 14, 13. Wicket maiden. Two overs left. Twelve, 11, 10, 9, 8, 7. Swann sees off Steyn, but can't retain strike. In Centurion Onions had survived 12 balls. Here he'd already done five and was facing up to the prospect of making it 11 if England were to survive. Admittedly South Africa had failed to get him out all series, but he'd faced only 40 balls. And here he was facing Morne Morkel. A leave. Five to go. Short one played safely. Four left. Full ball dug out. Three. Yorker repelled. Two. Beats the bat. South Africa appeal. Not given, but they use a review. We're certain it's not out, but we can't be sure and the tension is ratcheted up another notch and it means more time. No nails left, glasses are empty. We try to drink from them anyway. It's not out. One more ball. It's left outside off. England celebrate and we go mental. A draw in those circumstances is often better than a win. Most wins are seen coming a long way ahead. You know you're on top and it's just a matter of time. It's the big ebbs and flows, the tension and nerves that make a result in your favour so much more enjoyable.

Things were going to get even more brutal. The release of tension was followed by a party of epic proportions even by our standards and at one point I was being undressed to the theme tune of *The Full Monty*, leaving me wearing little but a newspaper billboard asking 'Who's Your Favourite Stud?' I don't know why that's relevant, but it's my strongest memory. I don't know how it's possible to drink that much booze and not die, and while everyone has big nights out there's nothing quite like one where everyone is in the same mood, all celebrating the same thing. This was our party and we were going to make the most of it. Sometimes we like to party with the players, but on this occasion it wouldn't have been right. It wasn't a win, but it felt like one and we were going to treat it like one. For me that remains the best post-match night out that didn't involve the players.

We moved on to Johannesburg. I've been to some seedy places in my time, but even then I usually feel OK walking around as long as I'm not in the dodgier suburbs. In Joburg no one walks anywhere (when I say no one what I obviously mean is no white people or rich black people) because it's too dangerous. You can't get a feel for a city when you have to get cabs everywhere. And even when you're in a car it's not like you're always safe, which is why it's perfectly acceptable in Johannesburg to run a red light if you feel in danger. Our taxi driver for the week had a gun in his glove box which he'd kept there since the last time he got robbed. Our friend's cousin had been carjacked the year before when the criminals held a gun to her three-year-old's head. And even when you wanted to run this gauntlet it wasn't always easy to get a cab because of local taxi wars. Lovely place.

The ground is no great advert either, lacking a bit in character. There is a grass bank, but seeing as it was a family area with no alcohol it wasn't much use to us. So we ended up in a nondescript stand watching England get absolutely hammered while we failed to get an atmosphere going. All the highlights of that Test happened away from the ground. We went to an evening with Matthew Hoggard at the club he played for when he was in South Africa. Hoggy asked me to ask suitably daft questions during the Q and A and I was all too keen to remind him of his less than noteworthy contribution to the Barmy Army cricket team some years previously. The room was full of geeks with questions that rambled on longer than most of his overs. 'So Matthew, having seen you play for a Yorkshire Second XI in 1990 and following your career closely ever since, I would be interested to know your feelings on the matter of the Umpire Decision Review System and whether you think that, if you were playing today, the third ball of your fifth over while playing South Africa in 2005 on a Saturday would actually have led to a wicket considering that video replays of the incident showed that there was a slight change in the revolution of the ball and with that in mind is your favourite colour red?' was not one of the questions, but they felt a bit like that. Mine was not of that ilk. 'Could Hoggy please talk us through his debut for the Barmy Army Cricket Club?' I asked. He took one look at me and said, 'Could Paul Winslow please talk us through his facial hair?' Suffice to say I had a beard at the time and Hoggy had got a duck on his debut. More about that (the duck, not the beard) later.

That night gave us the opportunity to relive a couple of great songs that had sadly been filed away under No Longer Required. The first goes to the tune of *The Jungle Book* which seems apt for Hoggy:

Now Hoggy's the king of the swingers
An England VIP
He has a bowl, the wickets roll
The Aussies out by tea
Oohh Oohh Oohh
I wanna bowl like you-ou-ou
Don't wanna bat like you, just bowl like you-ou-ou
Oh yeah it's true-ue-ue
I wanna bowl like you-ou-ou
Don't wanna bat like you, just bowl like you-ou-ou

The second is one of those great crowd participation songs that shows the Barmy Army at its most effective:

Leader: Oh how we love
Crowd: Oh how we love
Our Yorkshire boy

(Our Yorkshire boy)
Matty Hoggard, Matty Matty Hoggard
Matty Hoggard, Matty Matty Hoggard
Oh how we love
(Oh how we love)
Your floppy hat
(Your floppy hat)
Our Yorkshire boy
(Our Yorkshire boy)
Matty Hoggard, Matty Matty Hoggard
Matty Hoggard, Matty Matty Hoggard

The song builds up gradually until the final verse:

Oh how we love
(Oh how we love)
Your 12 wickets
(Your 12 wickets)
Our nightwatchman
(Our nightwatchman)
Our Hat-trick boy
(Our hat-trick boy)
Sarwan, Hinds and Chanderpaul. Sarwan, Hinds and Chanderpaul
Yours straggly hair
(Your straggly hair)
Your two cross-eyes
(Your two cross-eyes)
Your loping gait
(Your loping gait)
Your smelly farts
(Your smelly farts)
Your knobbly knees
(Your knobbly knees)
Your pigeon toes
(Your pigeon toes)
Your swing bowling

(Your swing bowling)
Your straight batting
(Your straight batting)
Your floppy hat
(Your floppy hat)
Our Yorkshire boy
(Our Yorkshire boy)
Matty Hoggard, Matty Matty Hoggard
Matty Hoggard, Matty Matty Hoggard

It's a brilliant song for a couple of reasons. Firstly it lasts a long time, always a good thing during a long day at the cricket. Secondly it involves repetition of every line so it doesn't require anyone to know the words. What it does require is that you have someone with the chutzpah to stand up and remember all the lines to sing them solo in the first place. You will meet Southgate later on and it is he who played this role with aplomb. Indeed the song was so good we also used it for Flintoff when he was our hero. That version went:

Your pedalo
Your gorgeous wife
Your ample girth
Your chain smoking
Your beer drinking
Your slip catching
Your seam bowling
Your six hitting
Our all-round man
Freddie Flintoff, Freddie Freddie Flintoff
Freddie Flintoff, Freddie Freddie Flintoff

On England's previous visit to Johannesburg in 2005, Hoggy and Freddie had taken 15 wickets between them in a famous victory, but in the 2010 clash the entire team would only take seven wickets in an ignominious defeat. I had envisaged a glorious series victory being sealed on the final day of the series, January 18, to celebrate my 35th birthday. Sadly the game didn't even go that far as South Africa wrapped it up in four days. The obvious problem was that England dropped Graham Onions, who had not been dismissed in the entire tour. But with team scores of 180 and 169 he would have had to bat for about three days to help get us out of that situation, probably too much even for his match-saving skills. A bad injury then interrupted Onions' Test career and while he did make a solitary appearance in the summer of 2012, the chances of him playing on another overseas tour are slim. That would be a shame as he looked excellent and I beg his apology for not coming up with a decent song for him, mainly because we struggled to find a rhyme for Onions. The best I could do was a *Hey Jude* remake that went:

Onions
You bowl it well
They've got Dale Steyn
But you're much better

Onions, when you peel the batsmen will cry
They'll wonder why
You're Graham Onions, Onions, Onions, Onions...

Na na na na na na na... Onions

A much simpler, more succinct and accurate chant was made in light of his performances with the bat in this series and that was that:

Onions
He's going to make you cry
He's going to make you cry
Onions

England never recovered from losing a wicket with the very first ball. It was only the 28th time it had happened in Test cricket, although Strauss can take comfort in being in good company – Sunil Gavaskar did it three times. He could also take comfort that he wasn't Jimmy Cook, who did it on debut, and that he wasn't Bangladesh's Hannan Sarkar, who managed it three times in four Tests against the West Indies between 2002 and 2004, dismissed by Pedro Collins on each occasion.

It seemed like no one was intent on hanging around much that day as England were four down after 50 balls. South Africa would only need to bat once, but then they did have some help thanks to further teething problems with the Decision Review System which has had such a profound effect on our cricket watching.

As travelling fans we'd had more exposure to the DRS than most and while players and commentators discussed its merits or otherwise from the point of view of those playing the game, as usual no one had asked the fans what they thought. When we first encountered it during the 2009 tour of the West Indies it was universally hated. It had a horrible effect on the game from a spectator point of view. The explosion of joy and happiness you get whenever the umpire's finger goes up is tempered when you know that it's not the end of the story. Yes, there's an element of brilliant tension building as you wait for the review, but it's not quite the same.

By the time we got to Australia for the Ashes in 2010–11 we would benefit from replay screens that showed us what the umpire was seeing and that made the whole thing more enjoyable as we had an idea what was happening. In the West Indies we didn't have such a luxury and the best clue was that you could gauge a reaction from the changing room, if you could see it. In South Africa there was a collective straining of necks to see into a corporate box to watch replays on the television. Graduating to playing the footage on the big screen at least gives the fans the same footage as the umpires and improves the spectator experience.

The other issue in the West Indies was the time taken for appeals to be made. On occasions it was patently obvious that the West Indians (and probably the English as well, but we're never so blinkered as when considering our own sports teams) were looking for a signal from the dressing room as to whether to appeal or not. It's simple. If you're given out and you think you were in, appeal. Don't ask your mates what the telly says. But teething problems aside, the system became a lot smoother and more accessible to the paying public over the years. Just as it seemed to be working, however, the Board of Control for Cricket in India had their two penn'orth and DRS was fudged to exclude Hawkeye unless both teams agreed to it. But it wasn't Hawkeye that was at fault when we were in Johannesburg, or the reason for this little digression.

We would probably have lost that Test anyway, but if you review a blatant nick from the South African skipper when he's on 15, it's fairly bloody annoying when it's turned down and he goes on to get a ton. Everyone in the ground who looked at it knew Graeme Smith was out so we were mystified how the third umpire could give him a reprieve. It transpired that the third umpire had said not out because there was no noise. It further transpired that there was no noise because the relevant microphone wasn't turned on. Technology has its limitations and some of them, ironically, are human.

It wasn't only technology that was not working in that stadium. On day four, when a glory-hunting home crowd threatened to actually put some bums on seats in a ground that had been otherwise largely deserted, the ticketing system broke down so no one could pay on the door. This wasn't an issue for me as I had a ticket, but annoyingly this was the day when my girlfriend, Klara, was willing to come and so we were stuck outside. (Sam and I had, by this time, gone our separate ways and I was inflicting my cricket love on someone else.) Eventually they just had to let everyone in for free, so at least I saved on the price of buying her a ticket. At least I assume it was me who would have had to buy her ticket – she would never have agreed to come had it meant her spending money on it. Unlike Sam she never bought into the idea of a day at the cricket as a good way of spending her precious seconds on this planet.

As the majority of people in the ground had no tickets, allocated seat numbers for those who did became redundant and it was a free-for-all. That led to some amusing arguments with locals who ostensibly had tickets for the area we had been inhabiting for the whole Test. We weren't slow to point out that not only were seat numbers invalid, but that we'd been sitting here supporting our team every day and didn't just turn up when there was a bit of glory in the offing so we were going to carry on sitting here. As it turned out we weren't sat down anywhere for long. The game was lost quickly and the series was over. For me this was not a disaster as I was about to go travelling, but for others another cricketing odyssey was over and domestic reality beckoned. Before we left the ground I snaffled myself an early birthday present. As the ECB had new shirt sponsors the players very kindly decided to give away some of their training kit. I have no idea whose training top I ended up with but it was a fantastic souvenir of the tour.

The post-series drink-up involved Stroh Rum (the 160% proof stuff) which is never clever. But we struggled on and the night ended at the players' hotel where Graeme Swann held court to a bunch of fans and a couple of the players' other halves. In retrospect, well even at the time if I am honest, it all seemed a tiny bit sycophantic. People hung on his every word but to be fair to him, and much as it pains me to say it, he is a funny bloke. While he was entertaining all-comers, Andrew Strauss and his wife Ruth were having a quiet drink with friends across the bar. I knew them to chat to by this stage and although I was aware the introduction of Stroh Rum into my system didn't make for the most entertaining or cerebral conversation I went to have a natter. As I told Ruth about my plans for the year ahead and all the travelling that would be involved she admitted to being extremely jealous. I stopped short of telling her that I would swap it for the life of the wife of an international cricketer, but I did point out that her life wasn't so bad. I guess the difference is I'm a cricket nut so travelling a lot to watch a family member play cricket would be awesome. Having to bring up kids when your husband is off to the four corners of the earth fulfilling his cricketing requirements would have its downsides I guess, but we agreed that life was pretty damn good anyway for both of us. I headed back over to Swanny's audience and as midnight ticked over figured there were a lot worse ways to spend the evening that heralds your birthday and the end of another tour of great memories.

Five

The characters who form the backbone of the Army

He joined the Army, now he's a part of it

WILLIAM COOPER IS a trumpet player who boasts such luminary bodies as the English National Ballet and the London Philharmonic Orchestra on his CV. He has an Honours degree from the Guildhall School of Music and a Postgraduate Diploma from the Royal Academy of Music. He makes a living from playing and teaching the trumpet. And he also plays it at cricket grounds around the world. When people let him.

Billy the Trumpet, as he is invariably known in cricketing circles, first got involved with the Barmy Army in 2004 on England's tour of the West Indies. 'I used to watch a day at the Oval every summer and I watched a lot of county games when I was at college, but then I decided to save up the pennies and go out to the Caribbean in 2004. I took my trumpet because if I don't play for three weeks the muscles go a bit and seeing as I had a big concert to play on my return I thought I'd better practise to make sure I didn't play like a muppet. I had no intention of unleashing it on innocent cricket watchers,' he explained when I asked him how he got started.

'Having said that I did take it to the game one day with half a mind to play it, but the atmosphere never seemed right. I wasn't in a quiet section, but then I wasn't in the nutters' section either. I remember that was the day I first met Jimmy (Savile – an introduction to him coming up) and he said I should come and play it, but it didn't feel right. That night I got drunk and left my trumpet in a taxi and figured I'd never see it again.

'A couple of weeks later, it was the fourth day of the Antigua Test, I heard something that sounded a bit like a trumpet. I borrowed some binoculars and I could see this guy playing my trumpet; it was bright blue so it had to be mine. Quite a lot of the kids I teach now have coloured trumpets, but back then you couldn't really get them. Anyway, I went over and the bloke asked me to play a tune to prove it was mine so I played *The Great Escape* and everyone started singing along to it. Leafy (Barmy Army co-founder Paul Burnham) came up and asked me if I would come and play the next day. I didn't have a ticket but he managed to find me one and that was the start of it. I've done a bit of pretty much every tour since.'

Billy's repertoire of songs is seemingly endless as he reels off favourites such as the aforementioned *Great Escape*, the *Rocky* theme tune and pretty much anything else that occurs to him or the many people who ask him for a tune. '*Jerusalem* is my favourite song and if you get a whole load of people singing it it's incredibly powerful. But I can play umpteen number of tunes and when you get the fifth bloke in a row pissed up wanting you to play *Jerusalem* it can get a bit monotonous,' he says.

It's not just cricket fans who recognise Bill now, the players do as well. Hoggy has been known to have a go at playing his trumpet – without much success it has to be said – and Bill has been lucky enough to meet a few of the other players over the years, culminating with the highlight of his Barmy Army 'career' when he appeared on stage with the team at the Trafalgar Square celebrations which took place after England won the Ashes in 2005.

'I nearly didn't go because I was so exhausted after a long summer, but Leafy rang me and he told me to get down. I remember a couple of guys in McDonald's asking me if I was the Barmy Army trumpeter and then asking to have their photo taken with me, which was bizarre. I was very nervous to go up on stage but a couple of the lads chucked me over the barriers and Tres and Fletcher said it was fine for me to be there. The security guards came over and Fletcher just said "no, no it's alright he's with us" so I stayed up there.'

Since that zenith his cricketing career has been something of a rollercoaster ride, particularly in England. In the majority of Test playing nations he never has a problem. In India, Pakistan, Bangladesh and Sri Lanka noise is an integral part of a cricket match so no one is likely to complain about a classically trained trumpeter serenading everyone. Sadly Bill missed the last Caribbean tour because of work commitments, but it's fair to say that there wouldn't have been any issues with him playing there either. Neither the Kiwis nor the South Africans have issues with him. And that leaves only two nations – Australia and England. While he is now largely welcomed in both, he did go through a period of being *persona non grata* for a while.

As England got ready for the 2006–07 Ashes in Australia, the Barmy Army was doing its own preparations. Discussions with Cricket Australia had been positive and the Trumpet was given the green light to do what he does best (that's possibly a little bit harsh – he probably plays classical music better than cricket anthems, but live with it for now).

So it came as something of a surprise to him when he was thrown out of the first Test at the Gabba in Brisbane for, erm, playing his trumpet. Now as we shall see, getting thrown out of cricket grounds would become an occupational hazard, but this threatened to be a bigger issue, especially seeing as an agreement about his attendance had been brokered. Things got no better for the second Test in Adelaide where again Bill was mute.

This was causing headlines at home and consternation in Australia where Leafy was, well, quite upset is an understatement. There was even talk of the Barmy Army boycotting the rest of the series. That seemed overly dramatic, and anyway impossible to enforce, although by the fifth Test people might have enjoyed an excuse to not watch the humiliation.

After numerous discussions and negotiations he was reprieved and by the third Test in Perth the trumpet was back. Trumpetgate, as almost no one was calling it, was over. He played for the rest of the series and while the more cynical may say that the Aussies were more than happy for him to play as it was so obvious that England were getting hammered on the field, it was nonetheless a successful outcome and by the time Bill returned to Australia in 2010–11 he was welcomed at all grounds.

That has not always been the case in the UK, where he was banned from all grounds even after the joys of 2005. He wasn't unwelcome personally but musical instruments in general were prohibited and no one was willing to make an exception for him. The ruling was made presumably to end the incessant droning of plastic trumpets similar to that provided by vuvuzelas at the 2010 World Cup, but Bill hardly came into that category.

As the Barmy Army wrestled with this issue it did provide for some genuinely funny moments. At Trent Bridge in 2006 he played from the roof of the Trent Bridge Tavern. For the uninitiated the Trent Bridge Tavern is in the corner of the ground and can be accessed from the back of the stands or from the street. As it is not strictly speaking in the ground, the powers that be couldn't do much about him playing. So come the tea break he was whisked up to the roof and we stood a few floors down singing along. All we could see was the edge of his trumpet but we could hear well enough.

The Oval also provided a couple of amusing memories. We had begun to calculate how long it would take between him starting to play and a security guard telling him not to. Not that he was anxious to get thrown out, but if he was only in attendance for a day or two and was preparing to leave the ground he figured that entertaining the crowd was his duty. At the Oval we hit upon a cunning ruse to protect him. There had been some discussion with the security people at the ground about him possibly being allowed to play, but no hard and fast decision was made so he figured the only way to find out was to just play the thing. It didn't go well and he was on the verge of being thrown out although he managed to stay in the ground on condition that he didn't play his trumpet.

By the time he was due to leave he figured he would give it another blast and a couple of us worked out that if he sat in the furthest corner from the walkway and the fairly sparse crowd filled up all the seats around him the security guards wouldn't be able to do much about it. We slowly moved everyone to fill the spaces and had people sitting in the aisles as well. When he piped up there was nothing the poor security guys could do about it without manhandling us out of the way.

I looked down and saw the head of security, with whom we'd been dealing earlier in the day, laughing his head off. He found the whole enterprise genuinely funny. When Bill finally departed I figured I'd better go and smooth the waters, but I hardly needed to bother. I apologised and said we weren't meaning to take the piss but that it was ridiculous that he wasn't allowed to play when it was so obvious most people wanted him to. He agreed with me that it was a stupid rule and that we'd saved him hassle as he wasn't in a position to do anything about it.

The other story that springs to mind with regard to the Oval was a game I didn't attend, watching it on TV instead. I heard the familiar refrain and instantly had texts, emails and IMs asking if I had heard that Bill was playing. The playing didn't last long so I called him that night to see what had happened. It turned out he had been invited up to one of the hospitality boxes and they had asked him to play a few tunes. He started belting them out from the balcony and the security guys immediately went on the chase.

Bill's tactic was to get the trumpet hidden away somewhere before they got in and use the 'who, me?' excuse. It worked but only because Alec Stewart, of all people, held the door shut to give him time to hide his instrument.

It may sound like he was deliberately flouting authority just for the sake of it, but to us there was a principle at stake. Players and fans alike love Bill and what he brings to cricket overwhelmingly. He adds something to the day and in other sports he would be embraced and encouraged. The band which plays at England football matches doesn't have as much musical talent or as big a repertoire but the FA pays them to play although they were initially banned from playing at Euro 2012, a punishment which pleased a lot of England fans. When Bill starts to play there is genuine excitement and if he gets asked to a corporate box and requested to play what's he supposed to do?

Bill is also a form of crowd control like no other. If something starts kicking off in the crowd, if people are making beer snakes or someone is chanting something unsavoury then what would you rather have – a bunch of security guards steaming in to deal with something they don't understand and almost certainly exacerbating the situation with heavy-handedness or a trumpet player piping up thereby diverting everyone's attention to him and defusing the tension?

Thankfully the issue was gradually resolved. Old Trafford was the first to let him in tentatively and, shock horror, the ground didn't fall down because of it. Headingley also eased off on the draconian measures and Cardiff not only let him play during the 2009 Ashes, the authorities embraced the idea of his being there. Amazing what a difference it makes when the ground in question is hosting its first Test match, an opening Ashes Test at that, and wants to put on a spectacle.

At a meeting I attended in a Barmy Army capacity with the ECB earlier that year they insisted that each ground had autonomy on the decision about whether Bill was allowed to play. All I can say is that the grounds didn't give that impression and if I was to guess I would think the message was something along the lines of 'it's up to you whether he plays or not but we'd rather he didn't'. Some grounds still don't want him around, but generally he's managed to ease his way back into most, which is the way it should be. It's kind of ironic and kind of sad that he's welcome everywhere around the world, but not in his own country.

I've been lucky enough to sit next to Bill throughout many of his exploits. Among my friends there are those who believe I do it only because it's a sure and certain way of being on television, but the opposite is true. If he chirps up and I'm filling my face with a sandwich or picking my nose then it's not ideal. It was a natural thing that happened because we enjoyed watching cricket together as much as anything.

Bill likes people he knows and trusts to form a barrier around him. There's a very practical element to this in terms of creating a forcefield around his trumpet. Hitting a trumpet while it is being played is not good for the player, but that's not always at the forefront of people's minds when they're singing and dancing after a few beers. Also the incessant demands on him to play this tune or that tune can be filtered if the people around him are not doing the asking. Not that we don't badger him on occasions but we do try to give him a break at times.

One person who rarely gets a break and is arguably more famous as an international sports fan than Bill is Victor Flowers, aka Jimmy Savile. His tight white jeans, St George singlet and hat, England flag and mane of white hair have become synonymous with the Barmy Army. He's had his picture taken with people more times than any player and is the true icon of England's travelling army.

Vic first came to real prominence during the millennium tour of South Africa where he got excited about the whole idea of being a part of the Army, the way so many others had. It was during that tour that he first got involved singing the 'one song' he has in his repertoire. Not that he was particularly good at it at first and Leafy has told me many times that he had to go over and tell Jim that while he was doing a great job it would be even better if he could learn the correct words. That might explain why he never bothered to learn another song in the ten intervening years, although, to be fair, after enough coaching and cajoling he did finally pick up the words to *Jerusalem*. It doesn't help when people accuse us of having a limited repertoire that our main choirmaster has just one song to his bow, but that's the one the majority want him to sing. And because everyone only has to repeat what he says it means everyone can get involved. The song goes as follows:

Jimmy: Everywhere we go
Crowd: Everywhere we go
The people want to know
(The people want to know)
Who we are
(Who we are)
Where we come from
(Where we come from)
Shall we tell them
(Shall we tell them)
Who we are
(Who we are)
Where we come from
(Where we come from)
We are the England
(We are the England)

The characters who form the backbone of the Army

The Mighty Mighty England
(The Mighty Mighty England)
We are the Army
(We are the Army)
The Barmy Barmy Army
(The Barmy Barmy Army)
Andrew Strauss's Barmy Army
Etc Etc

Because of his persona as Jimmy Savile his song is usually prefaced by Billy the Trumpet playing the theme tune to *Jim'll Fix It* and there is a song that goes with that tune, although not many people know the words.

He came to South Africa
And that was the start of it
He joined the Army
And now he's a part of it
Now then, now then
Jim'll fix it for you

This is inevitably followed up with chants of 'one song, he's only got one song' before Vic will generally preface his singing with the waving around of a cigar and a Jimmy Savile impression along the lines of 'Now then, now then, what we need now is a Barmy Army wicket. Can Jim fix it?' It's probably the first song most people will sing with the Barmy Army and while for those of us who attend the majority of Test matches it can get repetitive it's important and forms a core part of the Army's identity. Vic is a celebrity in his own right and never seems to get tired of having his photograph taken with fans.

'I'm just one of the boys, not a celebrity,' he once told me. 'But if you're in the spotlight you are representing the Barmy Army and you have to make a good show of yourself and keep up the good name of the Army. After all, people enjoy seeing us lot as much as they look forward to seeing the players. I think it's good because kids see us having a great time on television and they'll ask their dads to get them a ticket and they will get hooked. So it's good for the game.'

Any army needs more than one leader, however, and the pressure is often taken off Vic's shoulders by some other not-so-shrinking violets. Chief among these is Neil Rowe, aka Southgate. He has something of a split personality. A British Airways pilot in real life, he is a doppelganger for ex-footballer Gareth Southgate and can often be seen walking around in an HM The Queen outfit. A load of his mates decided to go to a game once dressed as Her Majesty and he never lost the habit. His pink skirt and jacket outfit is to be seen regularly at grounds where he is serenaded by the National Anthem (he claims to have retired the outfit but we're not convinced). Southgate is a self-confessed media whore who would pretend to get upset with me when I started working for the Army and subsequently ended up on television more than he did. He's a great man to have in the ground though because he's not shy about getting up in front of everyone and taking the heat off Vic. His *pièces de rèsistance* were the homages to Hoggy and Freddy as outlined in the chapter on South Africa. But he's also the first person to go to if you've written a new song and don't want to stand up and sing it yourself or at least want someone to share the workload.

While I have joked that I would never fly on a plane if I found out he was the pilot, he has flown the England team on occasions and made jokes about jettisoning Darrell Hair over the ocean after some particularly dodgy decisions during the 2009–10 tour of South Africa. It's a shame he wasn't around when Gower was playing – give the two of them a Tiger Moth and who knows what might have happened. Although he does confess to his love of fame and media exposure (he has been serenaded by the Army to the song of 'he's a media whore, he's a media whore, Gareth Southgate's a media whore') he claims that his 'fame' was not sought after.

'I've always liked a sing-song and being part of the Army we've all got to do our bit. With deference to our esteemed leader (Jimmy), it was never intentional that I'd start a few, but once the lads spotted my penalty-missing likeness, and then you've got 2,000 singing "Southgate, give us a song" there's nowhere to hide. My favourite was the Hoggy song and while I can't lay claim to writing the original, I tweaked and added a few lines as his legend grew.'

Neil's own legend also grew thanks to myriad appearances on the documentary *An Aussie Goes Barmy*, filmed during the 2006–07 Ashes series. 'It was a shame they couldn't film us in happier times but it was good in that it showed what the Army's all about, supporting our boys through thick and thin. No booing our team after 15 minutes here. It said it all when despite all the tormenting and banter we'd given them and they'd given us on the pitch over the years, McGrath, Warnie and Langer came over and applauded the Army and we saluted them. They recognised the support we'd all given and we appreciated their talent.'

Other highlights of Neil's supporting career include some dubious money exchanging. He once had a knockabout with umpire Steve Bucknor in a car park in Cape Town in 2005. He jokingly offered Steve a few rand to give the boys a break and that was the only Test England lost on that tour. During the World Cup game against Namibia in 2003 his group of mates were having a sweepstake and a Namibian fielder decided to join in, leading to deep suspicion of his fielding abilities.

Another very typical experience for a dedicated fan happened in New Zealand in 2002. 'We were legging it up the South Island in our Winnebago to catch the ferry in time to cross to Wellington for the 2nd ODI, only to find bad weather in the Cook Strait had cancelled all services.

We dumped the van, found a tiny regional airport and jumped in an eight-seater Turbo-prop to fly through the terrible weather, spilling our Guinness in the process, to get there. What happened next? England were 89 all out. Brilliant.'

Another of our brethren who is now as well known as Jimmy and Southgate is Deco. While he doesn't exactly shun the limelight, he doesn't embrace it quite as passionately. His notoriety comes from entertaining us with a song written when he was going about his business as a painter and decorator. It was shortly after the death of a friend of his who had *Lord of the Dance* played at her funeral and Deco came up with the following:

We sang in the morning at the start of the Test
We sang up to lunch then we went and had a rest
We came back from lunch then we sang till tea
It's fun being in the Barmy Army

(Chorus)
Sing sing wherever you may be
We are the famous Barmy Army
And we'll cheer England on wherever they may be
And we'll sing them on to another victory

Now an Ashes summer makes us all so proud
It's fun watching England hit the convicts round the ground
We'll sing for our batsmen and our bowlers too
'Cause they make all our dreams come true

Chorus

Now our ticket prices don't seem to be fair
But look at our faces do you think we even care
We've come in our numbers and we're gonna see
Another famous Ashes victory

The characters who form the backbone of the Army

Chorus

At the end of this song I hope the message is clear
We are the fans that will always come and cheer
So thanks everybody for singing with me
'Cause we're all part of the Barmy Army

Chorus

There have been many variations in the verses over the years as Deco tries to keep the song fresh and relevant to the country he is in, but the crux of it remains the same and his song is now as much a part of Barmy Army folklore as Jimmy's. Deco has a particularly strong bond of man-love with wicketkeeper Matt Prior which began in Sri Lanka when Prior promised to give him his shirt to lessen the hurt after he was robbed on tour. Because they didn't see each other for a while, Prior didn't come good on his offer until a couple of years later but having done so he now has Deco's unstinting devotion, which has manifested itself in four different songs and continual support from the stands.

Simon Humphrey, despite being a tremendously intelligent man, is as mad as a hatter and is usually to be found at a cricket ground wearing his blue and cream striped blazer, whatever the weather. (He's also been seen in full dinner suit, a snowman outfit and other wacky modes of dress). 'My first overseas tour to watch England was to Barbados for one-dayers in 1997, then I saw the light and concentrated on Test matches and my first "proper" tour was to South Africa in 1999–2000,' he explained when I asked him how he got involved. 'The blazer thing was just an impulse purchase from Kent and Curwen a few weeks before I moved out to work in Cape Town, a throwback to colonial times that sort of stuck when I wore it anytime I flew and anytime I watched cricket.'

Simon claims responsibility for Kevin Pietersen's bowling career in Tests. During the fairly lamentable display in Lahore in November 2005, as the hardy few watched Pakistan rack up 636-8 in the first innings, discussion revolved around what happened to KP's abilities as a spinner. Never shy, Simon stood up among a sparse and quiet crowd and told Michael Vaughan in no uncertain terms that he might as well give KP a bowl; KP reacted by warming up. Nothing happened that day, but at a home Test at Lord's in 2006, when Sri Lanka were proving obstinate, he repeated the trick. When KP finally did get to bowl for England he was a proud man.

None of this goes to show his more random side but during that same Lord's Test match he led a small group of us in a very long and detailed Christmas Carol singing session. In July. He once wrote a song about the Sydney Hotel in Galle that consisted merely of him singing the letters in the wrong order and then singing 'I can't spell the Sydney Hotel.' But his real signature is a version of Cliff Richard's *Living Doll* where he replaces the first few words with grunts and instead of singing 'Living doll' at the end of each line he puts in the name of an England player. It's not just that he does all this but that he will do it on his own in any crowd. I once saw him do it in front of a group of bemused Australians at the MCG.

That was during the 2006–07 Ashes when Roger 'Av It' first appeared on the scene. The Perth-based ex-pat is always to be seen with a cartoon cowboy hat and two pieces of cardboard, one of which says 'Av' and the other 'It'. On the reverse one says 'No' and the other 'Nonsense'. His schtick consists merely of standing up, emitting an amazing klaxon call from the back of his throat, and shouting 'Av it' before picking an opposition player and declaring that there should be 'No Nonsense'. This can clearly only be labelled under 'you have to be there' in terms of amusement but it makes everyone laugh no matter how many times they have heard it before.

Giles Wellington has been an Army stalwart for years and is one of the most respected people in it. He seems to know and remember everyone in the Army and while he was never as 'famous' as some of the others that all changed in the 2010–11 Ashes series with his remake of the *Sloop John B* song that Doug Mulholland made famous in New Zealand in 2008. If people didn't know him before then a thrice daily airing of that song in front of a few thousand England fans made the difference. But in truth most people knew him as the bloke who was always there and one who gets a real thrill out of selling merchandise. Indeed he's even got me doing it a few times. He does a lot of support work for the Army behind the scenes and is ridiculously passionate about it as a group of people.

There are many other characters that make up this crazy, weird, wonderful group of nutters, but the final word here will be reserved for another of our singing champions and perhaps the players' favourite, Big G. It's not hard to spot Graham Barber as he's a big lad, but if his figure is unmistakable then what does that say about his voice? A strange kind of high falsetto means he is irreplaceable for two of our songs. One is the classic *Rule Britannia*. G is one of the few people who actually knows the words and one of even fewer who can sing it properly.

When Britain first at Heav'n's command
Arose from out the azure main
Arose, arose from out the azure main
This was the charter, the charter of the land
And guardian angels sang this strain

Rule Britannia! Britannia, rule the waves
Britons never, never, never shall be slaves
Rule Britannia! Britannia, rule the waves
Britons never, never, never shall be slaves!

But his real party piece is *The Lion Sleeps Tonight,* a song translated for Barmy Army use like so many others, but one that requires someone of particular talents to sing the falsetto melody before the 'Eee-um-um-ah-weh'. Big G is that man and then we simply change the lyrics to fit the place we happen to be in:

In the jungle, the Mohali jungle
It's Kingfisher tonight
In the jungle, the Mohali jungle
It's Kingfisher tonight
We'll win away, we'll win away
We'll win away, we'll win away

The name of the town and the drink are interchangeable depending on where we are and what mood we're in, and the last line can also refer to how many away wins we have racked up by that stage. The reason the above version sticks in my memory the most was that the ground at Mohali was close to the airport and Kingfisher is also the name of a low-cost airline in India, not just a beer. Every time a Kingfisher plane flew over the ground we all looked expectantly at G and he didn't have much choice other than to get stuck in.

There are many others who bring colour, banter and enjoyment to the cricket-watching masses. They have become as much a part of the action as our heroes on the field and all are ingredients in the Barmy Army mix. The primary focus will always be watching the action on the field but there's always plenty going on in the stands as well and some of the characters are as well known to the players now as the players are to us. One thing's for sure, there's very rarely a dull moment with this lot around.

Six

Touring Pakistan

Let's twist again, like Shahid Afridi

Touring experiences in Pakistan
2005–06 3rd Test (Lahore)

IF AUSTRALIA IS THE 'Hollywood' or 'glory' tour, then Pakistan is definitely at the other end of the spectrum. It's the least glamorous country on the international cricketing scene, it is the least safe and the hardest to travel around. Oh and they don't approve of people drinking beer, which as you have found out is something we in the Army generally do quite often. Not that any of this is currently relevant as no one is likely to tour Pakistan for a long time to come.

Tours there were always tentatively embarked upon because of security reasons, but the terrorist attack on the Sri Lankan team and match officials in Lahore in 2009 changed everything and made what was always a tough tour into a completely impractical one. Terrorist attacks in this part of the world are nothing new but they became increasingly common. The attack on the Sri Lankan team was one of 50 terrorist incidents in 2009. In January 2010 there were 34 in the first three months of the year. And that 2009 attack came relatively hot on the heels of the Mumbai bombings that had such an effect on England's tour of India in 2008. But what made this particular incident stand out was that an attack on an international sports team and international match officials was unprecedented. And this didn't take place in one of the border areas, but in one of Pakistan's largest cities.

Understandably all cricket tours to Pakistan were called off and will be for the foreseeable future. Pakistan now play their 'home' games in neutral venues, such as England (v Australia in 2010) or the United Arab Emirates (v England in 2012). I doubt anyone gave a second thought to the safety of the fans when making this decision but in retrospect the British Foreign Office must be glad. Their advice as I write is 'we advise against all travel to specific regions of Pakistan and against all but essential travel to other specific regions of Pakistan.' That's understandable, but as we shall see terrorism doesn't stop the Barmy Army and there would undoubtedly be some of us who chose to travel anyway. But if teams can be targeted, who's to say terrorists wouldn't mind a crack at a group of international sports fans? When I made the decision to tour India in 2008 in spite of the terrorist attack on Mumbai I felt relatively confident that terrorist groups would not be overly interested in attacking cricket but I was obviously utterly mistaken.

I'm not really sure what the terrorist attacks against the Sri Lankan team were meant to achieve; in the same way it has always confused me as to what the terrorist attacks in Mumbai were meant to achieve. If you're reading this and you know who did it and why then you're better informed than me, but I guess the upshot is I should never try to second guess the motives and intentions of terrorists. And if they think they can achieve something by targeting a group of England cricket fans they might well get round to it one day.

This realisation was brought even closer to home by the fact that the Liberty Square roundabout where the Lahore attack took place was in a direct line between my hotel and the ground. I walked over it every morning and while the chance of me being anywhere near it at the same time as the team buses would have been slim, it's a slightly sobering thought to think that had they targeted England three years earlier I would have encountered the aftermath as I walked to a ground to watch a day's play.

All of this is a great shame because, despite the fact that Pakistan was hardly regarded as the safest country even in 2005, it remains one of my favourite tours and places to visit and I'm glad I took the opportunity to experience it when I did. You probably have to have a certain mentality to voluntarily visit a country such as Pakistan, but an adventurous spirit combined with a love of cricket made it a brilliant antithesis to lounging around Australia or South Africa. Both the travel and cricket bugs had bitten me badly by this stage and having had such a great time on the 2004–05 South Africa tour, having seen England win the Ashes in 2005 and having had my appetite for visiting far-flung corners of the world whetted, I didn't think twice about making the trip.

Strangely neither did Sam, my long-suffering girlfriend who had already joined the Barmy Army in South Africa and then taken umbrage at not being invited to the post-Ashes celebrations in 2005. I'm not even sure whether I even asked if she wanted to go to Pakistan – it would have been a strange request – but she decided to come anyway. I'm still not sure why. It's not like there was going to be anything else for her to do when the cricket was on and while we did some touristy things afterwards she still had to sit through five days of cricket. She didn't even know if there would be any booze to drink. I can only guess that in the absence of any other holiday plans she realised that if she wanted to go away with me that year it was Pakistan or bust. That's dedication, or desperation, I'm not sure which. I'm a pretty selfish person, and was certainly more so at that period, so the poor girl had to put up with me doing whatever I wanted to do most of the time. She knew how much this had started to mean to me so would never question my desire to go, but that she chose to come still amazes me.

Where Sam found my intention to go to Pakistan understandable, many of my friends could barely get their head round the fact. While some of them were worried for my safety, there was a more pressing matter on most people's minds. 'You do know they don't sell alcohol there, don't you?' was the recurring question thrown in my direction. Well, I have a vague knowledge of how the world works so I was well aware of that, but for all the Barmy Army's love of the occasional beverage it's cricket we love above all else. If there was no booze then there was no booze and we'd just enjoy the cricket. And if there was any booze then we would find it and have crazy adventures doing so.

In the end the week or so I spent in Lahore was not only safe, friendly and hospitable but booze-filled. There's only one real bar in Lahore, but it happens to be less than five minutes' walk from the cricket ground. Within half an hour of being at the game someone told me where it was and I simply followed him at lunch, a walk we were to make many times that week. You might think that the chances of having the only bar in a city that big near the cricket ground would be pretty remote, but the fact that it is an ex-pats' bar and that cricket is an ex-pats' game makes me feel there is nothing coincidental whatsoever about their relative proximity. We pretty much lived in that bar – Lahore is a wonderful old city, but doesn't offer much in the way of nocturnal activities. The roads are absolutely heaving 24/7 but where the locals go and what they do will forever remain a mystery to me. It wasn't just that the bar sold beer, but that it was a social epicentre for the hardy souls on that tour and it fostered a great community spirit. Without it the week would inevitably have been duller but as it was there we utilised it to the full.

But before we got to the bar we had to get to the ground. And this was more difficult than I had envisaged. Before leaving England I'd asked Leafy about how to get hold of tickets and he assured me that I would be fine. But when Sam and I turned up 15 minutes before the first day's play we got as far as a police cordon 100 metres away from the ground where a uniformed man demanded to see our tickets. When I explained patiently that I would like to get to the ground to buy some, he informed me that I needed to go to the bank. I have to admit this threw me a little bit. In England the idea of popping along to the local branch of Lloyds TSB and picking up a ticket for Lord's is hardly what you'd expect. I ascertained where the bank was and Sam and I trotted off to sort it out. I felt like a bit of an idiot walking up to the counter and asking for tickets for the cricket, but they didn't look at all surprised. They politely informed me that I needed to go to a different branch, one that was much further away. In a crazy world this made perfect sense – after all why would you sell tickets in the vicinity of the ground itself?

By this time I was getting twitchy. I hate missing the start of play on any day, never mind the first day of a Test. It's like a badge of honour, a weird thing that is strangely important to me and several other fellow Army people. On this occasion I would not see the opening exchanges, but thankfully I didn't miss much thanks to my first encounter with Pakistani hospitality. A group of guys had obviously sussed out the problem and they spilled out of a tuk-tuk near the bank to ask me if I was looking for tickets. They sold me two for the princely sum of £1 each and then intimated that we jump in their tuk-tuk for a ride to the ground. Sam looked somewhat suspicious of these activities but in my usual blasé 'everything will be all right even though they might be kidnappers' style I assured her all would be fine despite having no real evidence to back it up. The locals are experts at fitting a seemingly impossible number of people into a tuk-tuk, and while I wasn't sure beforehand how they'd managed to shoehorn themselves in they somehow found space for two more. They drove us round to the correct gate where two jumped out and insisted on escorting us to and through the gate, all for no favour or payment.

They had made an astronomical profit on the tickets though. They may only have charged us a quid for each, but they had a retail value of nought. While there is a love for cricket in Pakistan there is no money, so the majority of tickets for home fans are given away. Even then they struggle to attract crowds and for the most part the English support, small as it was compared to any other tour, equalled the number of locals. The English had in the main paid for tickets, but as that only amounted to the £1 a day we had been charged by our new friends it's a sum barely worth considering and I certainly didn't begrudge paying them that amount.

It wasn't long before we were making friends in the ground as well, with the locals very excited to meet these strange English people who had travelled all this way to watch cricket. It's easy to understand why. Lahore is hardly a tourist mecca, so the few hundred English held a huge novelty value and had celebrity status conferred by default. They were keen to speak to us, photograph us, stare at us and generally treat us as though we were exhibits in a zoo. This was particularly true of the female contingent but everyone got attention. On one occasion leaving the ground, Sam and I would end up doing our very best Pied Piper impression as hundreds of locals followed us as though we were Posh and Becks. Most asked for photographs but if we stopped for them to be taken the crowd would close in and it was slightly unnerving, especially for Sam. Eventually we insisted that if they wanted a photograph they would have to run ahead and take it as we walked past because we would not be stopping any more.

We weren't mobbed on that first morning but a group of young guys came over as soon as we were sitting and accosted us with questions about our lives, and life in

England generally. Before I'd managed to even ascertain what the score was I was being asked my name, where I was from and what London is like to live in. All of which were perfectly reasonable questions and I endeavoured to answer them while concentrating on what was happening on the pitch. Then the questioning took a random turn. When asked if Sam was my wife, I replied that she was my girlfriend. At which point my attention wavered from the cricket for a few seconds as my interrogator calmly asked me whether we had sex with each other. Before I could come up with a suitable answer my questioner's accomplice interrupted and pointed out that I had come to watch cricket and not to be quizzed about the details of my personal life. Thankfully his friend acquiesced and withdrew his query. The Q and A session ended there with the inevitable invitation to his family's house for dinner, the first of many such invitations. You can never accept them all and maybe I should have taken up at least one offer but I wasn't keen to face more questions about my sex life over the family dinner table.

We settled in to watch the game, in which the awkward questions were being asked by the Pakistani bowlers. England's Ashes-winning heroes were under pressure having lost the first Test after being in a winning position and then drawing the second. The third started well enough as England won the toss and batted, putting on an unbeaten century for the first wicket, but it unravelled somewhat after that as England closed on 229 for six. Before our evening visit to the bar that would become home I was keen to address the issue of tickets so that I wasn't faced with a trip to the bank the following morning. It transpired that our hotel was actually the pick-up point for those who had pre-ordered tickets and therefore I felt fairly certain that if we threw some money at the situation it would be resolved. I asked the receptionist at the hotel if he would be able to sort me tickets for the next four days. He pushed me on to the concierge who then got someone else on the case. The answers were negative but I couldn't believe it would be that tough to organise something. They told me they would call my room. Another negative. Half an hour later there was a knock on the door. With a flourish of his silver platter a man revealed two sets of tickets for the rest of the Test match, all for the sum of £1 a day.

That looked like particularly good value on day two. Although England had been bowled out for 288 Pakistan finished day two on 185-4 so the game was set up nicely. But for my £1 on day three I watched Pakistan bat all day for the loss of one wicket and take the game and the series away from England. Now any cricket fan can appreciate watching great batsmen playing great cricket even if they are from the opposition. But as a fan of your team there's nothing more demoralising than watching them field for an entire day for not much reward. And the only 'reward' that day was the wicket of nightwatchman Shoaib Akhtar; but as he had scored 38, including two sixes, even that was very much a pyrrhic victory.

It was demoralising so it came as something of a surprise that this was the only occasion I saw Sam watch an entire day's play. Usually she would retreat into her book for long periods or wonder aloud whether it was nearly beer o'clock but while Mohammad Yousuf and Kamran Akmal remorselessly racked up runs in a fairly unspectacular fashion she seemed transfixed and watched the whole lot of it. When I pointed out that even I was little bit bored she simply shrugged and said she was enjoying it. Strange creatures, women.

I would guess the highlights of that day were the lunchtime visit to the bar and the pizza delivery. It has to be said that the catering facilities in the ground were not up to much. Some might say that catering facilities in cricket grounds are never up to much but while that would be a tad harsh overall there was hardly anything on offer in the Gaddafi Stadium. It was like a concrete shell with seats in it and what passed as the occasional confectionery stall didn't exactly tempt the palate. But the manager of the local Pizza Hut knew a trick when he saw one, and every lunchtime a deliveryman would turn up with as many pizzas as his bike would carry and sell them at the back of the Barmy Army stand. Now that's good business practice.

Sadly Shahid Afridi wasn't playing thanks to the fact that he had been banned for his behaviour in the previous Test. A gas canister had exploded during the game and naturally everyone's attention turned away from the cricket; security concerns are real enough in this part of the world without unexpected explosions. But while everyone else was concentrating on the ramifications of the big bang, Afridi took the opportunity to rough up the pitch in order to aid his team's bowlers. As far as I know he's the only Pakistani player to have a song written about him, to the tune of *Let's Twist Again*:

Let's twist again
Like Shahid Afridi
Let's twist again
Like we did last Test
Do you remember when
You got caught for cheating
Let's twist again
Cheating time is here

Because of his ban, he didn't get to hear the song but I do have a vivid memory of making up for that at Headingley the following summer. Again Afridi wasn't playing but he was in the squad and at the end of the day's play I spotted him embarking on a lap round the ground. A few of us stayed back as the stand emptied and sang to him as he ran past. I don't think he knew exactly what we were singing but he knew it was about him. That summer series against Pakistan would also be marred by controversy when

Pakistan refused to finish the fourth Test after being fined five runs for ball tampering. And the next time Pakistan toured England it would be spot-fixing that would ruin the tour. The reason I mention this here is that after the spot-fixing scandal, the gallant knight on a white steed who rode to the rescue of the integrity of Pakistani cricket was... none other than pitch tamperer Shahid Afridi. As the always excellent Lawrence Booth pointed out in his *Daily Mail* column in 2010 there's something very wrong when Afridi becomes the good guy. 'No matter that Afridi has pirouetted on a good length in a Test match and bitten the ball in a one-day international. What counts is that he has not been implicated in spot-fixing, the crime of the day. It is moral relativism gone mad,' he succinctly summed up.

But that was all to come; for now he was out of the team and Pakistan didn't need to tamper with anything to complete a crushing victory. They declared on 636-8 and the only highlight for us was watching Inzamam-ul-Haq run himself out on 97. Inzy never liked running even when a century was there for the taking. England were two down as day five started and while the third wicket put on 175, the next seven totalled, erm, 43. It wasn't the first epic England collapse I saw, and it wasn't the last, but it remains one of the 'better' ones.

As the match came towards its conclusion, the ground filled up as it inevitably does in Asia when the home team is on the brink of a win. It seems to me that the majority of people couldn't be bothered seeing the team get to the win but they loved to be there at the end. And they had a double whammy because they not only got to watch Pakistan win, they also saw the Barmy Army in its element.

As the England collapse became more acute, the louder we got. This was the end of the tour and we were going to enjoy it, win, lose or draw. In doing so we became an even bigger novelty and the whole Pakistan crowd moved towards us, keen to see these crazy English fools closer at hand. Who were these strange people who travelled to Pakistan out of choice, watched their team lose, and sang and danced regardless? Welcome to the Barmy Army people. A fence separated us from the larger contingent of the home fans and the police heavy-handedly kept them away from us. Most of them would have seen nothing of the cricket because they were too busy looking at us to take any interest.

Despite the defeat, that night was a great one. At the end of a tour the players usually want and deserve a night out and when you're in a city with only one bar of note it's fairly obvious where they will end up. As that bar was our aforementioned Lahore HQ it was of little surprise when several of them arrived to share our end-of-tour party. This was the first time I would meet them in a social situation, and on top of my more incidental encounters with Hoggy and Flintoff in South Africa, it cemented the notion that cricketers are on the whole very nice people who are happy to share their time with the fans who support them. There's no hint of the standoffishness or arrogance that you often get with footballers. I remember spending half an hour talking to Marcus Trescothick, who was happily wearing a rather bizarre hat and chatting away as though we were old friends.

My other memory is a sporting one. Billy the Trumpet and I were playing another couple of lads at pool when Hoggy and Jimmy put their names on the board for the next frame. Bill and I were determined to win the current game and earn the right to take on our fast bowlers and despite our state of inebriation we managed it. In a blast of alcoholic overconfidence I insisted that we all put a tenner in for the game against the England boys. I don't know how pissed Jimmy and Hoggy were but it was either a) very or b) they aren't very good at pool, because somehow Bill and I won. I tried not to get too excited about it but someone came up to me afterwards and said,

'I bet that felt great didn't it?' and I couldn't argue. I would end up knowing both players well enough to talk to but neither of them remember, or choose to remember, their capitulation to my pool skills.

As I have already pointed out, my sporting prowess has never extended to cricket, but I did nearly end up playing a game the next day. The English press were playing their Pakistani counterparts in a social game and were a fielder short. They asked me if I would play and my initial reaction was to accede to their request but then I took one look at Sam, who had put up with five days of cricket without so much as a murmur of complaint, and figured that putting off our exploration of Lahore for another afternoon while I ran around after a red ball was pushing things a bit too far. While that was a disappointment, Lahore certainly wasn't.

It has a manic, vibrant atmosphere and it seems everyone is permanently on the move. Exploring the old town really is like stepping back in time with tiny, narrow streets inhabited by tradespeople whose ancestors were probably doing the same thing hundreds of years ago. The Badshahi Mosque is an epic construction and holds many more people than the cricket ground, 100,000 in total. Just sitting and riding through the city in a tuk-tuk is an experience in itself, albeit an occasionally dangerous one. Two of the England fans were in a tuk-tuk that overturned in a tunnel and when they were picked up by a friendly local in a car the guy who crashed still tried to get money out of them for the journey.

Our final experience of Pakistan was a visit to the Wagah border to see the daily closing ceremony. Every evening the border between Pakistan and India is closed with pomp and circumstance. There is a dramatic display where ceremonially dressed soldiers from each side posture and preen at each other. It draws a big crowd every night and is like a sports event in the way the locals cheer for their respective countrymen. As Rafia Sufi put it on the Asia Society website in 2010, 'it is a unique, masterly demonstration of how angry you can get without hitting anyone. The 45-minute parade manages to be by turns, ferocious, ridiculous, and touching, all in one.' Sadly he was writing about it because the authorities in India and Pakistan had decided to tone down the ceremony 'to help improve relations between the two countries'. I don't see the logic behind that as it brought the two countries together the way a friendly sports match would. The border between the two countries is still fiercely debated and occasionally fought over and other than the ceremony it often seems like cricket is the one thing that can bring them together. While Pakistani cricket is generally quite shambolic, it has played a small diplomatic part between the two countries.

I don't expect to be heading back to Pakistan to see their cricket team any time soon, which is a huge shame. For all its troubles, lack of infrastructure, chequered history and dubious sporting practices I enjoyed immensely my visit to the country. The people are generally friendly and welcoming and there is a vibrancy to the place that is unique to Asia. I can understand it is unlikely to be top of anyone's ideal destination list but I'm glad I had the chance to explore a tiny part of it when I did.

Seven

Getting paid to watch cricket

He'll tweet it on his blog

IS BEING PAID to sit in the crowd with your mates watching cricket and drinking beer the best job in the world? Maybe there are better ones but I can't think of any off the top of my head and certainly none that I might be capable of fulfilling. Somehow that's what I ended up doing for a while by virtue of a bit of luck and possibly a modicum of talent. If you can conduct coherent radio interviews at 11pm following an entire day on the ale after watching England win a Test match, or can write match reports while not always remembering the next morning what you had written, consider yourself qualified.

I'm not the only person who's ever been paid to watch cricket. The Sky commentators do it all the time and they don't even have to pick up a laptop. Being a Sky commentator is actually similar to being in the Barmy Army. They sit around all day, talk about cricket, watch cricket, tell stories about the old days and have a bit of banter. The only difference is they get paid lots of money for the privilege whereas we spend lots. Our advantage is that we get to enjoy a beer, sit in the sunshine and sing a lot. So when I got the chance to earn a few quid while not having to actually leave the sanctuary of the Army for the more staid press box I wasn't going to say no.

My first opportunity to make money out of being at the cricket came on the 2004–05 tour of South Africa and it came as a result of a drinking session with one of my best friends in publishing. He was editing mobile phone magazines at the time and wanted to find a way to spice them up with some interesting content rather than having page after page of dry reviews comparing screen sizes, battery life and features. This was back in the very early days of camera phones so we hit on the idea of me giving it a practical test. And where better to give it a proper trial than a live sporting event? As Vodafone was England's sponsor at the time we approached them and blagged the same model of phone as the players were using (the tight gits didn't include a SIM card or let me keep it) to see if it might replace my normal camera for holiday snaps. If that seems a tad strange in these modern technological times it's worth remembering that digital cameras back then were hardly amazing. To back up the images we also arranged for me to have a chat with Matthew Hoggard, deemed to be among the most tech-savvy of the England players. In retrospect that doesn't say much for the rest of them. Our chat about technology lasted only a few seconds and went roughly like this:

> Me: So, Matthew, do you use your camera phone much to take snaps on tour?
> Hoggy: No, not really.
> Me: Erm OK. Shall we just talk about other stuff instead then?
> Hoggy: Yes.

Ironically Hoggy would interview me several years later with a tiny video camera for his video blog on *The Times* website but for now we just nattered about cricket and life in general. There was enough to write about and added to the pics it made a nice fluffy feature for the magazine; so I met one of England's finest and got paid some money for taking a few holiday snaps. Not a bad way to swell the coffers when you're abroad. And that was just the start of it.

Before I'd left for South Africa I'd been chatting to the good people at *FourFourTwo* magazine who were planning to publish a cricket magazine for the 2005 home Ashes series and wanted to include a feature on the Barmy Army. Although at that stage my Barmy Army knowledge was hardly in-depth, the fact that I was due to go on tour again meant I was the perfect man for the job. Looking back now it was that feature that changed everything for me because in order to do the job properly I figured I should make an effort to go and talk to some of the main characters. When I approached Billy the Trumpet in Cape Town, a gruff character next to him offered me his card and said that if I wanted to write about the Army I should get in touch with him back in England. That gruff character was Barmy Army founder Paul 'Leafy' Burnham, who would end up employing me not long after.

I arranged to meet him when I returned from the tour and he was keen to tell me all about how the Barmy Army had been created and how it had developed. This information, coupled with my own experiences, meant that the feature pretty much wrote itself. It's the kind of overview feature I have seen written many times since, the irony being that it was often me in my future role as Barmy Army Media Bloke who would give the journo the story. Paul liked the feature and I was happy, so there was a basis for a relationship between us. (I was also happy because I was struggling to find tickets for that summer's Ashes and Paul mentioned during the interview that the Barmy Army had a section reserved for them. Thankfully he had some left over so I bought a few and witnessed some of that epic 2005 series.)

Coincidentally that summer was the first year the Barmy Army published anything resembling a proper magazine as opposed to the songsheets it had previously produced. I took one look at it and figured I could do a much better job, so in Pakistan later that year I cornered Leafy and said that if he was intent on publishing a magazine then

I was the man to do it for him. I am a magazine editor and journalist by trade, so why wouldn't he want me involved? Thankfully he agreed and I produced my first Barmy Army magazine the following summer. But before that there was the tour to India where I would develop my relationships within the Army only to have the whole thing jeopardised through no fault of my own.

I was sitting in the same pub with the same friend who had commissioned the South Africa mobile phone feature when he mentioned that he'd been talking to a guy from *Loaded* magazine and heard they were interested in doing a feature on the Army. By this stage I figured that if anyone wanted to write a feature on the Army then I was your man. I called *Loaded* to sound them out and they were interested. After a bit of discussion they teamed me up with a photographer and sent me to Mumbai for the third and final Test of the 2006 India series. Flights, accommodation and expenses were provided with payment on top; I could get used to this.

There was a slight issue in that while I had gained the trust of Paul Burnham and had met some of the gang in Pakistan, for many Barmy Army regulars I was still an interloper not to be trusted. I had become friendly with Billy the Trumpet in Pakistan but many people didn't know that, so when they saw us hanging around together they thought I was a dodgy journo trying to get him drunk to do a stitch-up on him. To my mind I was a cricket fan who happened to be writing a feature for *Loaded* but most people figured I was a staff member, especially as I was always with the photographer, who roped people in for the purposes of great pictures. 'That bloke from *Loaded*' was a tag that followed me for a while even after I started working for the Barmy Army, and it took me about five years to get rid of the moniker completely.

Had it been any other magazine it wouldn't have mattered so much, but *Loaded* was the original lads' mag and while that genre had begun as a combination of intelligent journalism mixed with some more puerile stuff they were at that stage erring towards the purely puerile (*Nuts* and *Zoo* were launched in 2004, lowering the bar considerably). Life in *Loaded* world was about drinking, drugs, shagging and being a lad. All of which wasn't quite what the Barmy Army was about. Sure there was lots of drinking and the fact that the name of the ground had a rude word in it would raise a smile (Wankhede Stadium, in case you're interested), but the rest of it was mainly about cricket and singing, which is not the same as drug-taking and shagging. I dumbed the copy down and bigged up the drinking side of it and they seemed content with my second draft.

Several weeks later a copy of the magazine came through the post and I proceeded to read a feature that was similar in content to the one I had written but with so many changes that it portrayed the Army as a bunch of drunken hooligan idiots. Rewrites are fine, but fabricating stuff to spice up a story and changing it so much that events described in the magazine bear only a vague relationship to what had actually happened is taking the piss. It won't surprise you to know I did not keep this shining example of my journalistic integrity and prowess so the precise details escape me now, but I do remember one story about Jimmy Savile vomiting down the back of the stands, an event that was entirely a figment of the sub-editor's imagination.

I was more than a tad concerned about what this might mean to my burgeoning relationship with the Barmy Army. Having gained access to the inner sanctum, with the friendship and benefits that this entailed, I was keen to start working for them and I could see all of the goodwill going right out of the window as soon as someone laid eyes on the *Loaded* masterpiece. I emailed everyone at Barmy Army HQ with a copy of my original feature that bore so little resemblance to the sensationalist waffle that had been published in the magazine. While no one was

The bouncebackability boys spell it out in style – Durban 2004

Amazing scenery and a brewery in front of it – what better place to watch cricket? – Cape Town 2005

Barmy Army co-founder Paul Burnham (Leafy) and his second-in-command Katy Cooke fill two of the empty seats – Lahore 2005

Hanging out with Marcus Trescothick and his fetching headgear in the expats bar – Lahore 2005

Bill Cooper plays the trumpet signed by the England players at the PCA awards 2006

The three amigos: Jock with the infamous drum, Billy the Trumpet and Jimmy Savile – Colombo 2007

Terrible food but a lovely bloke: Hotdog in action – Galle 2007

Morning imbibement on the fort wall with Simon Humphrey, Ed Salmon and Tim Haffenden – Galle 2007

Another trip to the dollar shop bears musical fruit – Hamilton 2008

Vic Flowers, aka Jimmy Savile, in familiar action – Hamilton 2008

"I saw the rage in his eyes…" Doug Mulholland – Wellington 2008

Matthew Hoggard gets a trumpet lesson from Bill Cooper at a Barmy Army cricket match – Napier 2008

"Dan Vettori, Dan Vettori, Harry Potter in disguise…" Serenading the spinner – Napier 2008

"We've got Tim Ambrose…" celebrating with the subject of my first song (right) in Napier 2008

A small but enthusiastic turn out for Dawn Patrol – Chennai 2008

Gilo, the author and Millers give it their best Liam Gallagher impression singing *"Swanny Super Over"* at Mohali 2008

Simon Humphrey prepares to entertain the crowds again – Chennai 2008

Swanning around: Hayley Wellington, Becky Fairlie-Clarke and Heather Storry in Mohali 2008

Christmas fun in India: Santa, Santa, Santa and Santa – Mohali 2008

The Barmy Army makes friends with the Mohali Army: Me, the unknown soldier, Big G, Heather Storry and Craig Millwood – Mohali 2008

Is that a scorecard or a phone number? A bad day at the office – Jamaica 2009

Hanging out with Courtney Walsh (far right) on a day trip to an idyllic island – Jamaica 2009

Hardly surprising the bowlers lost their run up when this guy can dig it up with his hands – Antigua 2009

A lovely grass bank, but no cricket to watch – Antigua 2009

The Oil Drum stand that somehow stayed in one piece – Antigua 2009

The Queen, aka Southgate, aka Neil Rowe, takes tea – Barbados 2009

"In a Swanny Super Over in Chennaiiii…" The author (middle) celebrating victory with Graeme Swann and Craig Millwood – Melbourne 2010

Just another Test match in Galle and we're not paying to go in the ground – Galle 2012

Enjoying beach cricket the day after the night before – Unawatuna beach 2012

particularly happy it was obvious to them that it wasn't my fault and so my reputation remained intact.

All of which left me free to concentrate on producing my first Barmy Army magazine in the summer of 2006. It was only a small magazine and hardly my greatest work – indeed in the scheme of things one of my worst – but for something done on a budget of £3.50 and a couple of packets of fags it was, in my humble opinion, a dramatic improvement on the previous year's efforts. In addition to the song lyrics that would always take their place in any publication there were features on the history of the Barmy Army, the Barmy Army Cricket Club and also a review of events in Pakistan and India during the touring season. It is not a magazine I would use in a portfolio, although I am still smugly proud of my 'Youth in Asia' coverline to describe using younger players on the tours of Pakistan and India.

But that publication was very much a case of dipping our collective toe in the water. I would soon have the opportunity to dive in and immerse myself in something more ambitious.

It's easy to forget just how hyped the build-up to the 2006–07 Ashes series was but England's victory in 2005 had served to build expectation levels that will perhaps never be exceeded. These were the days before the Global Financial Crisis so people had money to spend on touring and companies still had advertising budgets. The latter factor meant that we could fund the publishing of the 2006–07 Ashes magazine entirely with advertising revenue, although I still put it together on a creative budget three times smaller than I would usually require for such a publication.

For the first time, the song lyrics became an addendum to the magazine and not the *raison d'être*. We included an in-depth interview and bespoke photoshoot with Matthew Hoggard and something similar with Mike Gatting, at that time the last successful skipper of an England team in Australia. (I was actually editing Tottenham Hotspur's official magazine at the time and I had managed to get Spurs fan Gatting for that but it wasn't difficult to get him talking about the Ashes as well before using the leftover images that weren't in the football magazine.) We had round-table fan discussions and a variety of other features that basically allowed me to write any old crap about cricket. I adore magazine editing and to find myself with complete control of a cricket fans' magazine didn't really feel like work. With decent production and printing values established we published thousands of copies of a magazine that remains the favourite of however many it is now to which I have put my name.

I was firmly of the opinion that Paul should sell the magazine. To me it was an extension of his merchandising business pure and simple – a Barmy Army branded product which people would happily buy. But Paul had always been insistent that song lyrics should be freely available to anyone who wanted them, and seeing as the song lyrics were in the back of the magazine it would have to be given away. This made perfect sense in one way but as the magazine had become so much more than a songbook it also defied business logic. Once Leafy had actually seen the magazine he took my point, accepting that perhaps I was right. The dividing line between empowering the Barmy Army as a group of fans and giving the Barmy Army business a bit of cash was never more starkly apparent to me. Paul was having major issues at the time thanks to his travel partner not providing the services it was obliged to for his customers, costing him money and repute. Some extra cash from the magazine would have eased the situation, as Paul acknowledged when he realised the quality of the product.

By the following summer there was still enough money sloshing around the pre-recession coffers of our various sponsors to fund another magazine, although we still hadn't come to a realistic conclusion about whether to sell it or not. The issue in England was slightly different in that while in Australia we had specific merchandise stalls this was not the case at home. So even had we wanted to sell the magazine we wouldn't have had anywhere to do it, and selling on the streets is not strictly legal. I decided to stop worrying about it (ultimately it wasn't my call) and got on with producing another magazine on a shoestring. We featured Monty Panesar on the cover and if ever you wanted proof that journalism isn't always the glamorous profession it's cracked up to be that interview provided it.

Monty's star was very much in the ascendant but it was newly so and his representatives were not quite the media-savvy, hard-hitting, hard-dealing agencies that you would associate with someone like KP or Flintoff. That was a good thing on many levels. The great thing about cricket is the approachability of the players and the fact they are usually willing to help out. But once they're stuck behind a layer of public relations or agents the rules change and they become more inaccessible through no fault of their own. This had been proven during my interview and cover shoot with Hoggy for the 2006–07 Ashes magazine. As we were dealing with him directly without a PR bodyguard the five minutes we had for the photoshoot were more than enough because he was happy to pose and make a bit of an arse of himself. The interview itself took place in hospital as he was waiting for an MRI scan because he was apologetically short of time. It worked because two people can make things work but had there been a third party involved fretting about what was said and what was shot there would have been a lot of interfering and insistence that everything had to be done a certain way.

Back to Panesar, and after a bit of chasing his 'agent' informed me that the interview would take place at the Travelodge in Luton. If you can think of a less glamorous place to do an interview please tell me. The fact that it was handy for Monty and that he obviously didn't have an ego that would insist on a posher establishment was a good sign. But there was a real whiff of Alan Partridge about it and we were slightly concerned about how we would find a good backdrop for the pictures. As the interview was first thing in the morning I jumped in the car with the photographer, Giles Park, and headed up the preceding night. As any expenses had to come out of my payment for the magazine we shared a 'twin' room that effectively had Giles sleeping on a fold-out sofa. After getting there late we couldn't find anywhere to eat and ended up buying the last sandwiches of the day from a service station. Although their licensing hours had finished, the man behind the counter slipped me the wink and opened one of the fridges for me. My choices were cheap white or rosé wine; I grabbed a bottle of rosé, paid for everything and we headed back to the hotel. As I sat watching *Question Time* with a Travelodge cup (more of a thimble really) full of poor rosé wine in one hand and a slightly stale sandwich in the other I turned to Giles and observed that interviewing international sports stars was not always the rock 'n' roll lifestyle it was cracked up to be.

Monty was as good as gold though and we managed to get some great pics of him which disguised the fact we were in a Travelodge. Like so many cricketers he was open, honest, very down-to-earth and very generous with his time. In some ways he was probably less groomed for international stardom than many other England cricketers, who are usually earmarked years ahead of time, and he seemed amazed to be the focus of so much attention. His start to the summer did nothing to stymie his progress as he took 23 wickets at 18.69 in the series against the West Indies before coming unstuck against India when he took just eight at 50.37.

Although I was enjoying my involvement with the Barmy Army, it so far represented nothing more than a bonus client for whom I loved working and happily did so for less than I would charge anyone else. But as much as I was also enjoying my career as a freelance journalist I was getting itchy feet and considering moving abroad. I wasn't sure where I wanted to go but I knew I was bored with living in Blighty and needed a change of scenery. But my plans went right out of the window when Leafy collared me towards the end of that summer and made me the kind of offer I was never going to turn down.

He told me that he was going to instigate a membership scheme that would generate money to run the company in a more professional manner, that he had an investor lined up and a new guy to be the MD. More pertinently he wanted me to be a big part of it, taking over all their media activities from magazine publishing and website production through to media appearances and the like. This promised so much more than I had done hitherto and I was excited to meet the new MD and hear exactly what he had to say about his plans for the business.

I met Duncan Norris at Twickenham Cricket Club when the Barmy Army CC played there. He outlined his vision for the future, his plans for expansion, and I was impressed with his experience and ideas. I was even more impressed with his promise that 'no one works for mate's rates any more'. Oh how funny that sounds in retrospect. But back then the idea of having a more permanent, fulfilling and lucrative role excited me hugely. We didn't nail down exactly what that permanent, fulfilling and lucrative role might be but we agreed in principle that I would be involved and all thoughts of going overseas went out of the window.

Actually that's not strictly true; I had solid plans to go overseas, but only to Sri Lanka for the three-Test tour that winter. The lead-up to that tour saw me involved in planning meetings and working towards launching the membership scheme. Being involved in such a project was great fun and getting to do all of the collateral around it was great. I get a ridiculous buzz out of creating any combination of words and pictures and doing it for something I loved was extremely exciting. While that was all bigger picture stuff we also published a small magazine for the Sri Lanka tour and I wrote my first match reports for the Barmy Army website while I was there. With only a couple of months between the Sri Lanka and New Zealand tours we also started planning a small magazine for the latter tour.

Long-term planning about my particular role was still up in the air but I was busy and doing something I believed in so I just got on with it and trusted that everything else would sort itself out. Life got even better when Leafy decided not to travel to New Zealand, thereby missing his first tour for years, and asked me if I would travel in his place. My 'role' would be to support tour manager Katy Cooke, help the merchandise manager, put match reports on the website and be the point of contact for media and fans alike. This was a role I could fulfil and revel in.

While I was away cracks started to appear in the brave new Barmy Army world.

Firstly there were issues with the new website. In between the Sri Lanka and New Zealand tours I had planned and budgeted for a new website, working with a design agency to get the look and feel right. I had written all the content and briefed the techies and left them to do their jobs. I won't bore you with the hows, whys and wherefores, but suffice to say that while I was fairly sure I had led those horses to water they hadn't bothered to take much of a drink. The work I had assumed was being done building the site hadn't been. We were determined to launch by St George's Day and while we hit the deadline we did it without enough testing. A lot of work that should have been done had not been done. It took me a long time to get the site to where it should have been to start with and in the meantime I cobbled everything together so it looked as though it all worked properly.

We were also planning a Summer 2008 magazine and I wasn't short of ideas. But it seemed Duncan had ideas too, including giving someone else control of the magazine in order to get it onto the shelves of WHSmith. As you can imagine I was less than impressed at this as magazine publishing was my domain and I was supposed to be our media specialist. I also had my doubts over anyone's ability to get us into WHSmith because I knew just how difficult it was. I bit my tongue for a while and sure enough the other guy couldn't fulfil that promise. The day before I departed for New Zealand I was told that I had my baby back and I assured them that while in New Zealand I would get cracking on it.

I didn't agree a fee up front for the magazine as it was all organised at the last minute but trusted that we would come to the usual amicable agreement when I got back. I put together most of the content while we were away and then broached the subject of payment in a meeting with Duncan when I'd returned only to be told that there wasn't a budget. I called Leafy and told him politely that if there was no money to pay for the magazine content then there would be no content. I was a professional journalist and didn't go around publishing magazines for nothing, even for people I liked.

The basic problem seemed to be that the money invested had run out so by then anything to be spent had to be earned first. Which is a good way to run a business if you ask me, but not entirely in line with the new vision. The new membership scheme would have to start generating income pretty damn quickly to cover the cracks.

Looking back now I can't help but feel extremely sorry for Leafy. He'd had people telling him for ages that he needed to run his business more efficiently and had put his trust in experienced business people only to find himself right back to square one. He was used to scrabbling around for money on occasions but all that was supposed to have stopped and there he was having to deal with people wondering why he had no money. At least before he had always found a way to pay me for my work. Now he couldn't even do that.

We eventually agreed that a reduced fee would be paid when they could find the cash. So, despite my best efforts the website was not what I wanted, although it was better than people expected, and the magazine was pretty much the same. We seemed to have taken a few steps forward but several more back.

In the meantime I was homeless. Having vacated my rented flat before heading to New Zealand I was dossing on people's floors. Until I could get some sort of handle on what, if any, future role I would have in the Army I couldn't really make a decision about the rest of my life. The brand new website needed an editor but there was no budget to pay for one. There were other things I could help them with but again there was a limit to what I was willing to do for nothing. Eventually we agreed a relatively small monthly retainer for a variety of services rendered, including editing the website. I agreed to this deal on one condition. To make up for the lack of cash I insisted on going to every bit of cricket on the England calendar. I figured I could just about scrape enough other freelance cash together to live on and a summer of love doing not much other than watch cricket seemed like a fairly wonderful, if slightly irresponsible, idea.

As this meant I would spend much of my summer travelling I eschewed such basics as finding a place to live and bummed around on friends' couches, lodged with a family and then stayed with Paul Burnham during the cricket season. He had now taken over the reins of the business again and was trying to put right what had gone wrong. Leafy and I would discuss the future of the Army deep into the night, every night, at his flat, but I could tell that he was being pulled so many different ways that it was hard for him to make a firm decision on anything. After all, the last time he had done that he'd handed over the running of his company to people supposedly good at running these things and found himself very quickly back where he started. Although he ran it in his own inimitable, sometimes haphazard way, it seemed that others couldn't do any better.

Haphazard was also a word that described my nomadic lifestyle that year. I sold or gave away most of what I owned, paring my possessions to a small car load while doing some occasional 'proper' work along the way to pay for such basic things as food and beer.

All of which allowed me to watch phenomenal amounts of cricket, spend my time coming up with ideas about how the Barmy Army could evolve and progress, appear on TV and the radio a lot (I never have worked out whether it is possible to 'appear' on the radio) and introduce myself to the wider cricketing community. I made friends with the guys and girls from Cockspur Rum, one of our main sponsors (the amount of rum I bought at least covered the money they put into the business), got to know the people running *All Out Cricket* and also spent time with the people from npower. Unless you are a cricket commentator I can't think of any other way you could get to watch every single day of a Test summer but I managed it.

I was living the dream, and the staff of the sponsors would get used to seeing me slope into a ground every morning with shorts, flip-flops, a raincoat (it was a shit summer) and sunglasses hiding any evidence of last night's shenanigans. Not a bad work uniform really and while this wasn't the most lucrative work I'd ever done it was a loose definition of work so I revelled in it, enjoying my own personal odyssey of cricket. At a rough estimate I spent 50 days that year watching international cricket home and abroad. Away from the cricket I spent a lot of time in various meetings with people interested in hooking up with the Barmy Army in some way, working on the website and helping out with a wide variety of stuff that needed doing at BAHQ. No one would have suggested it was a sustainable way of life but it was bloody brilliant for a while despite the frustrations at having so many ideas for the Army that were not economically feasible.

That autumn I made my first appearance on *Cricinfo.* Type my name into the website's search box and you'll firstly come across the South African cricketer after whom I was named (when my Mum reads that sentence she's going to be rather angry with my father as she doesn't actually know that) and then you'll find the following from their Quote Unquote section:

> 'People would rather spend money [going to] a Test match than a Twenty20.'
> Paul Winslow, a Barmy Army spokesman, shows the organisation's purist tendencies
> (*Cricinfo.com,* Oct 16th, 2008)

I'd done an interview with the Press Association about the forthcoming Stanford Twenty20 for 20 palaver and *Cricinfo* had picked up on that quote in particular. Now as a journalist I'm quite used to seeing my name in print or online, but seeing a quote from me sandwiched between those from Ricky Ponting and Mark Waugh was a bit weird.

But *Cricinfo* life would get even weirder. Leafy and I had a meeting with them to discuss possible ways of working together. We agreed that I would write a blog for *Cricinfo* while I was in India for the December 2008 tour. I wouldn't get paid but we'd be able to advertise the Barmy Army website with the column so it had a benefit to the business, and writing for *Cricinfo* would be awesome anyway. I wasn't on official Barmy Army duty for that tour, but as I was going as a punter the Barmy Army website would have live daily match reports from a tour for the first time. But my Army audience was tiny compared to what I would get on *Cricinfo,* where one of my blogs got 100 comments. I even got a fan. I had been chatting amiably about all things cricket to an Indian guy during lunch in Chennai one day and in the afternoon he asked the person next to me if they knew who Paul Winslow was. When she pointed to me he was apologetic that he hadn't recognised me and excited enough to ask to have a photograph taken so he could show his friends. Inevitably everyone took the piss out of me mercilessly but it was a nice moment professionally.

That India tour saw my media profile rise quite dramatically because of all of the shenanigans surrounding the Mumbai bombings and how it would affect the fans. I'd be lying if I said I didn't enjoy being a media whore: I find it quite fun if a little strange that my opinion is worth putting on TV. But then in an age of 24-hour news channels nearly anyone's opinion is worth putting on TV – I certainly never got to the stage where I thought mine was worth any more than the next man. Strangely I have always got more nervous before playing football in a pub league on a Sunday morning than appearing on live television or radio, so I've always found it an enjoyable experience. And it always made me laugh when I turned on my phone after I'd been in the media to see how many texts I would get from people telling me to 'stop ruining my bloody breakfast and get off my telly'.

I did a radio phone interview with an Australian station during the 2009 Ashes and my Aussie mate Heath Ewinger, whom I once infiltrated into the Army during a home series, nearly crashed his car when he heard my voice on the other side of the world. The real highlight of all this media whoring would come on the next tour, an appearance on *TMS* during the West Indies series in 2009. And as part of that tour I got to meet yet another cricketing legend, both in deed and word, when I interviewed Courtney Walsh for the cover of our West Indies magazine.

I came up with a new idea for that West Indies tour – a tour video diary. With no budget I would have to somehow manage this myself but the video camera I bought for the project was, ahem, lost on a rather drunken night out so an idea I was finding quite hard to initiate with limited technical skills became downright impossible thanks to a complete lack of technical tools. I don't think the world of sports documentary lost anything though, if I am honest, although I'd rather have found that out without costing myself a video camera.

That was the first tour on which I got involved with selling Barmy Army merchandise and I found it strangely fulfilling. I'd never seen the attraction of standing around selling T-shirts before and while it's not something I'd want to do all the time the banter and chat you can have with people is great and you can almost feel the Del Boy in you coming out. 'Ah yes darling that's gorgeous on you – nah no need for a bigger size it's perfect.'

I would have liked to sell the magazine as well as T-shirts, caps and the like, but again it had been decided to give it away. We had managed to attract advertising and as it wasn't a huge magazine I wasn't too fussed although we did get proof that if you tried hard enough it could be sold. Some of the cheeky locals would come by and grab a large handful and we later discovered they would high-tail it to the other side of the ground and start selling them. I couldn't even get angry with them as I admired their enterprise. Maybe in retrospect we should have employed them to sell for us.

At the other end of the scale from merchandise seller I also added graphic designer to the list of roles I had played for the Barmy Army by designing the brochure for the forthcoming South Africa series. I'm no designer, but my background as a magazine editor meant I was better than anyone else. Professional pride wouldn't let me use the first incarnation that someone had rather horribly put together, so I spent much of my last two nights on tour designing it from scratch.

I left the design to the experts on our next publication – the Ashes magazine of 2009. With an ever-diminishing budget we managed something on tuppence ha'penny as usual and I was proud of what we achieved. With the Barmy Army in fairly dire financial straits at this point I was adamant the time for giving it away was over. I believed that if we had people dedicated to selling the magazine, people would buy it.

But with so few people to help out the Army and so much to do there wasn't much time to dedicate to selling the magazine so we ended up giving most of them away. On the few occasions some of us did put our backs into selling them we proved that people were prepared to pay money for it. I felt vindicated, but it needed a coherent strategy to really make it work and we didn't have one.

On any given tour a guy called Andy Clark produces a great fanzine called *Corridor of Uncertainty* on a budget far tinier than mine and always manages to sell a few. No one is suggesting he's making millions, but it pays for part of his tour. I never felt we made enough effort to sell ours at home or away, which probably pleased Clarky as we might have taken away some of his customers. But Clarky provides high-quality independent writing and the majority of people would have bought both, so it wouldn't have had a major effect on him.

Working for the Barmy Army for a few years was incredibly frustrating at times but also incredibly satisfying at others. I launched the website, edited a few magazines, designed some flyers, taught myself a bit of web design, came up with a communications plan, met some cool people, sold a load of T-shirts – hell I even wrote a song that was released, spectacularly unsuccessfully as it happens and more of which later. It was a crazy, mad rollercoaster few years as we/I dipped our fingers in more pies than I could ever imagine. I wrote for the *Mirror*, the *Metro* and *Cricinfo* as the Barmy Army's official blogger and appeared on *Sky Sports News*, *Sky Sports* and a host of radio and TV stations. (I got a call to do *Newsnight* once but they cancelled me at the last minute. Me and Paxman – what a battle that would have been. Not.) I managed to integrate myself into the world of cricket, the sport I loved. And I did it with a brief of having to sit in the stands, talk to other fans, sing some songs and drink some beer. At least that's generally the brief I gave myself. I could never be a cricket writer – I just don't have the implicit knowledge of the game others have. But given a brief of writing about being a cricket fan, well that's a role I can play.

All this 'work' had generally been a poorly paid way of financing my cricket habit in cash or in kind and it had worked out fairly successfully. In 2009 I eclipsed my previous year's cricket-watching total by attending 60 days of international cricket.

In 2010 I went travelling for the year and despite missing the UK summer managed more than 20 days of Test matches in South Africa and Australia. And somehow that year was relatively more profitable than any other. I got a job writing a column for the *Herald Sun* in Australia that paid me significantly more than anyone else had done previously. For the first time I didn't get paid mate's rates and it felt great. I still happily sold some merchandise anyway though. I'd got enthusiasm for that by then, and on an expensive tour like Australia it topped the coffers up a bit.

None of this really matches up to Leafy's own career running a business that allowed him to watch cricket all the time and make money out of it. But somehow I'd managed to enhance my CV, write about something I was passionate about and watch oodles of cricket at the same time. And while it wasn't always plain sailing and I am undoubtedly poorer now than I would have been had I just stuck to a more traditional way of running my business, I've had an amazing time and wouldn't change any of it.

And if you're reading this it means I managed to write a book on the back of all my experiences as well, which makes it all even more worthwhile.

Eight

You flew out to India, when your country needed ya

Touring India

Touring experiences in India:
2006 3rd Test (Mumbai)
2008 1st Test (Chennai)
2nd Test (Mohali)

INDIA GRABS YOU by the throat the second you walk out of the airport doors and never releases its hold. An immense country, filled with innumerable tuk-tuks, perennial noise, energy, madness and vibrancy, it seeps into your skin and never lets you forget where you are.

A traveller to India can escape the incessant clamour with trips to peaceful outposts but on a cricket tour you never avoid it, whether weaving through traffic to get to the ground, immersed in the cacophony of Indian crowds or being enveloped by the background noise in your hotel room.

Many travellers fall in love with the country and so it is hardly surprising that many cricket fans enjoy a tour there more than any other. As much as I like India and it ticks many of my travelling boxes (I much prefer developing countries generally), I've never fallen in love with it in the same way as many others. It does have a singular fascination and, while one can draw comparisons with

Sri Lanka and Pakistan, India is unique, in its approach to life and its approach to cricket.

My first visit was at the back end of a short series (there are far too many of these in India, which sums up much of what I believe to be wrong with the game over there) in the spring of 2006. The first Test had ended in a draw which England had the better of, and was memorable for the debut of Alastair Cook, who got straight off the plane from an A tour in the Caribbean to knock a century. It was a stunning start which inspired the song we still sing about him to the tune of *Give It Up* by KC and the Sunshine Band:

You flew out to India
When your country needed ya
Century on debut
What a find
Na na na na na na na na
Ally Ally Cook, Ally Cook, Ally Ally Cook

Although everyone knows the last bit, not many know the first few lines and even fewer know the actual tune. On the subsequent tour of India in 2008 several of us admitted to not really knowing it despite the fact we'd been singing it for two years. Thanks to technology (iTunes rocks) we downloaded it and now get it right every time. Not that it was required again on that tour as Cook totalled only 19 in the second Test, which England lost, and then became another victim of England's injury curse and missed the next game. Talk about a rollercoaster start to a career.

Another name to emerge was Monty Panesar, who claimed Sachin Tendulkar as his first Test wicket. With his Indian heritage the ridiculously over-animated celebration was perfectly understandable, although we would soon realise that it was actually standard behaviour and that he would probably do something similar if he bowled my Gran in her backyard. Tendulkar scored only 83 runs in the series and some people thought the end of his career was nigh. I wonder how that turned out. As for Panesar, he took only five wickets and would be remembered for an absolute shocker of a drop in Mumbai rather than his bowling; yet he still ended up as a cult hero among England fans.

He never really had what you would call a song of his own, but would always be serenaded with the classic *Papa's Got A Brand New Pigbag*:

De de de de
Monty Panesar
De de de de
Monty Panesar

This was the tour *Loaded* magazine was bankrolling but unfortunately that meant I didn't get to book my own hotel and was stationed near the airport. Anyone who has been to Mumbai will know how much hassle it is to get to the main part of the city from there. The photographer and I faced a two-hour cab ride every day and if you needed a wake-up call as to what Indian life was really like then two hours staring out at the slums every morning was more than enough. Kilometre after kilometre of shanty towns and hovels made for a fairly depressing sight and it was a daily reminder of how lucky we are to live the lives we do. A two-hour journey was no real hardship compared to daily living for most of the people we saw en route.

On arriving at the ground on day one there was a great example of Indian bureaucracy at work as the authorities don't like you to take anything into Indian cricket grounds. That includes newspapers (lest you set fire to them and throw them on the pitch), lighters (lest you set light to the newspapers you don't have any more), cigarettes (lest you somehow light them from the lighters you don't have any more), water (you can't start a fire so you won't need anything to put one out)... you name it, you're basically not allowed to take it in. I think they would confiscate your tickets if they could get away with it. While I was undergoing the statutory search on day one someone jumped over the fence behind my searcher and strolled into the ground without paying and with any contraband he fancied. That pretty much sums up the efficiency.

We quickly became experts at smuggling things into the ground, whether it was cigarettes under baseball caps or bottles of vodka down pants. Indeed we were so good at it that when the photographer decided he wanted a picture of the overzealous searchers at work we had to fake it. The idea was to get a snap of me having cigarettes confiscated, so we emptied nearly all the contents of a packet and went to have them 'discovered'. As we manoeuvred the searcher into the right position for the shot we wanted, I kept taking back the cigarettes and then giving them back to get the right shot. The guy was so confused that when we finished up he forgot to confiscate them.

More of this efficiency was on show at the Western Hotel, a local bar which became our de facto headquarters for the duration of the Test match. Anyone who has been to India knows that it generally takes about four people to get you a beer. One person takes the order, another writes it down, someone else reads it out and the last one hands it over. That's bad enough but the guy handing over the large bottles of Kingfisher we ordered incessantly would place the bottles on the bar and then walk away without removing the tops. It would take another five minutes to get his attention again whereupon he would inquire 'you want tops off, boss?' I think I managed to restrain myself from saying 'how the fuck do you think I'm going to drink them otherwise' but it was close on a few occasions.

The bar was full to bursting every lunch, tea and evening with England fans guzzling Kingfisher like there was no tomorrow. Everyone went through the same rigmarole. Every day. After five days you might have thought someone would have worked it out (well, after five minutes really), but, no, you still had to tell them specifically that you would like to have access to the nice amber liquid in the bottle you had just purchased. You could argue it was part and parcel of the charm of being in India. You could equally argue that it was just a silly waste of time for all involved.

Another frustrating part of the daily routine in Mumbai was getting a taxi at the end of the evening's festivities. We would show the taxi driver a business card with the address of our hotel and ask very politely if he knew where it was. He would equally politely say 'yes boss' while looking at the card with a confused expression that you just knew meant he had no idea where he was going but that he wasn't in the mood to turn down a fare. Within a couple of minutes he would stop the car next to other taxi drivers and hop out to confer with them about where he was supposed to be going. Obviously he didn't stop the meter while this was happening. This was bad enough for everyone else but as our hotel was so far away we often went through the hopping out and conferring thing several times before we got home. This got rather annoying. It didn't matter how insistent or animated we got, how much we told them we would be angry if they were lying to us about knowing where the hotel was, we just had to put up with it. Every night.

Someone who will forever remain nameless finally snapped and took matters into his own hands. Had the taxi drivers driven him to his hotel as efficiently as they had driven him to distraction there would have been no real issue. He'd had a few Kingfishers and the taxi bartering had begun. He aggressively told the taxi driver that if he was lying about knowing where his hotel was he would be most upset. Inevitably, said taxi stopped after five minutes for the obligatory discussion with his mates about where he was supposed to be heading.

At this point our hero was so pissed off that he jumped out of the back of the cab. And into the driver's seat.

I will never know what he had in mind and thankfully I would never find out because he immediately stalled the car, a not unexpected result of the fact that he didn't have a driving licence and had no idea how to drive even had he known where he was going. Another not unexpected result was that the driver appeared at the door going absolutely batshit mental. I know this because I was in the cab with him and while I was so stunned by the turn of events I hadn't even moved, I figured this was the time to get out of the cab, drag my mate from the front seat and disappear into the night. We've never really talked about the incident since so I'll never know what came over him and I don't really want to.

The next morning I was heading back in to the ground, sans the would-be cabbie, but with the photographer. He thought it would be good to get pictures of local kids playing cricket, so we stopped off at a large field where a few kids were having a knockabout. We took a few snaps and it wasn't long before they pressed the bat into my hands. The kids weren't to know that while I might be an English bloke wearing a cricket shirt I had no discernible talent for the game. It was all fairly friendly stuff at first as the photographer worked around us showing us having fun. But when one of the kids took a run-up that an international fast bowler would have found hard work I could tell the gloves were off and that he was intent on getting me out. Being rubbish at cricket I just figured putting bat on ball would be a good result and hopefully save any embarrassment. He delivered the ball pretty straight and I brought down my bat. It's fair to say I timed the shit out of it and it went absolutely miles. Although the park we were playing on was large, the ball went over the edge of it and was lost forever in dense undergrowth. Now these kids were only little, looked fairly poor and I'd just gone and smashed half of their precious sports equipment out of existence. Oops. We handed over more than enough money for them to get replacements and meekly sloped off to the ground. I've hit one glorious cricket shot in my entire life and it deprived some little Indian kids of their most precious possession. What a guy.

Another morning saw us playing a different kind of game as I was introduced to the concept of Dawn Patrol. This would become a regular feature of tours but this was its inauguration as an official Barmy Army event. The inspiration came on the 2004–05 tour of South Africa although I knew nothing of it then. The Barmy Army was proving to be its usual novelty attraction for the South Africans and also for a group of British ex-pats. Founder Dawn Patrol member Tim Haffenden takes up the story: 'We were invited to a pub for early morning hospitality by a load of ex-directors of major companies such as Boots, British Airways, British Steel and so on. These boys were all pushing 100 years old and had all retired to South Africa and had an exclusive little club which meant that they had to meet every Saturday morning, including Christmas Day if it fell on a Saturday, in the boozer at 8am for the first pint of the day. If one of them didn't show up then everyone else's beers would be put on his tab. They just invited us along because they were interested in meeting some of the Barmy Army that they had heard so much about on the telly and in the papers. So we all went along in fancy dress for a laugh and a tradition was born.'

The boys had so much fun they decided to create their own version, holding a Dawn Patrol in Mumbai and on every tour thereafter. Somehow I got roped in and after crashing on a mate's floor in the city to avoid a 6am taxi, joined a group of about 14 people around a table at one of Mumbai's more salubrious hotels at 8am. The only other punters were fairly well-off Indian families quietly having breakfast while a bunch of us noisily ordered gin and tonics and sambuca shots like they were going out of fashion. The fact that nearly all of us were in fancy dress made it even more incongruous. By 10am the bill was fairly monumental and Tim, without a trace of irony or humour, calmly turned to the manager and asked: 'Do you normally sell this amount of gin in the morning?' Before leaving Bill played a few tunes, we posed for photographs and off we went.

En route we stopped to buy a few bottles of choice spirits and smuggled them into the ground in the usual way. Already quite boisterous, we ordered a significant amount of lukewarm Pepsi and Orangeade and drank our way through the morning session. To this day it's the only time I've ever fallen asleep at the cricket having had too much to drink, although there has been the odd day when I've struggled to stay awake because of the night before. I am still blaming my state on the fact that I had climbed Mount Kilimanjaro the week before and been quite ill, so flying straight to India for extended drinking combined with Indian food was bound to have an effect on me sooner or later.

I still saw much more of the game than the average Indian in the crowd. Indian cricket fans are a strange old bunch. I've never been to an ODI there so I can't profess to know what that is like, but in terms of Test cricket they can be fickle in the extreme. Few Indian fans will sit engrossed throughout an entire Test match or even an entire day's play. To be fair to the Mumbai crowd the ground was always reasonably full but when an Indian says they like Test cricket there is a high likelihood that what they actually mean is that they primarily like watching Sachin Tendulkar bat, they like watching India win and they like watching the other Indian players bat as well. As for the rest of it, i.e. watching the opposition bat... well they can pretty much take it or leave it. When Sachin goes in to bat the crowd grows exponentially and when he's out the new additions seem to fade back where they came from unless he's taken them to the brink of victory, in which case they will stay on to watch India claim the spoils.

All of that would be startlingly obvious in Chennai two years down the line, but it meant the crowd had a particularly miserable time of it come the last afternoon of the game we were currently watching in Sachin's home city of Mumbai. England had opened with 400 all out before bowling India out for 279. At the second time of asking England scored 191, leaving India 313 to win in just over a day. Comparisons with that match in Chennai will be obvious as you read on but at 18 for 1 overnight it was a pretty even contest. India lost two more wickets before lunch for the addition of only 57 runs, with Rahul Dravid crawling along at a strike rate of 15. It was England's to win, with seven wickets required in two sessions to win the match and square the series.

Over our customary lunchtime beer we psyched ourselves up to get behind the boys while the boys were apparently preparing themselves by listening to Johnny Cash's classic *Ring of Fire,* soon to become a Barmy Army favourite. Now the lunchtime beer, like a great cricket shot, is all about timing. With 40 minutes minus walking time (minus waiting for the idiots to remember to take the top off your beer), there's always a question of whether to have one or two drinks. We decided to sneak in a very quick second before what we envisaged to be a long afternoon. It wasn't. Dravid was out while we were still in the pub, so we supped up quickly and hurried back. Before we could get there Tendulkar had gone as well and it was 76-5. But if we thought we had missed all the excitement we were wrong.

The next five wickets went down in quick succession and it had taken just 14.6 overs after lunch to get the seven wickets we needed. Shaun Udal managed 4-14, not a bad return for a man who took only eight wickets in the four Tests in which he played. And yet it was his spin partner Panesar who provided the most memorable moment, although not in a way he would have liked. With six wickets down, MS Dhoni played a pretty awful shot, clipping the ball off the outside edge down to long off straight to Monty for an absolute sitter. Well it might have been a sitter to anyone else but Monty didn't even get his hands on it. When I interviewed him a couple of years later he admitted that until he saw the replay on the big screen he didn't realise how far away from the ball he was. 'All you can do in that situation is hope you get another chance,' he told me.

Not only did he get another chance, he got it three balls later. See if you can spot the difference between *Cricinfo*'s online coverage of the two shots played by Dhoni:

> '44.1 Udal to Dhoni, 1 run, tossed up on the stumps, Dhoni comes down the track and swings hard, ball clips the edge and flies towards long-off, Panesar in the deep fails to spot it and the ball falls safely, Dhoni lives on.'
>
> '44.4 Udal to Dhoni, OUT, not this time! tossed up, Dhoni comes down the track and swings hard, ball clips the edge and flies down to long-off, this time Panesar judges it to perfection and nicely settles under it.'

The difference, evidently, was that Monty caught the ball but in the ground it felt like watching an action replay until the different outcome. Monty's fielding would always be the subject of ridicule (and occasional abuse from his team-mates) but he showed a bit of character that afternoon to make up for the earlier error and it was typical of India's tame resistance that Dhoni should play the same shot after nearly perishing the first time. Not that we cared. Not that Monty cared. Victory was imminent and the subsequent celebrations went long into the night before we all packed up to go home the next day.

Another character, who should remain nameless, was missing from those celebrations just as he had been missing from the afternoon session. He was feeling a bit shabby after four and a half days of hard touring and couldn't face the afternoon session despite England being on the verge of victory. He jumped in a cab to go and watch it from the safety of his air-conditioned hotel room but because he was staying a long way out of the city the journey took him about an hour and half. When he got there he was perplexed to find there was no cricket on TV. He was completely unaware that England had wrapped up the game while he was in the taxi and that he had missed one of the best overseas victories ever. All of which serves him right for being a wuss.

Our next tour to India was a completely different proposition from the relatively easy excursion to Mumbai. Several weeks before heading off on the 2008 tour that was supposed to take in Ahmedabad and Mumbai again, the latter city was rocked by a terrorist attack that involved the random killings of 164 people over four days. Whenever a terrorist attack or natural disaster takes place you can always identify with it more if you've been to the place, if you know someone there or you're about to go there. On this occasion I fulfilled all three criteria.

Cricket may well have actually saved my friend John's life that day. He and his wife had been living in Mumbai and had decided to go to the Leopold Cafe on the first day of the attacks. However, John was keen to stay and watch the end of a cricket match on the television and so they stayed where they were for long enough to keep them away from the terrorists who attacked the cafe and sprayed it indiscriminately with bullets.

My first reactions when I heard about the attacks were to think 'wow I've been there', 'oh shit John's there' and 'oh I'm supposed to be going there soon'. As the first was merely incidental and the second of less concern once I knew he was safe, it was the last that took up most of my subsequent thinking. While the city of Mumbai was recovering from the attack, those of us on the verge of heading off had our own, much less important, issues. Firstly we wondered whether the tour would go ahead at all. This was by no means certain and while it pales into insignificance in terms of the losses of the people in Mumbai, no one was particularly looking forward to losing the money they had shelled out. 'Cancelled cricket tour' is not on the list of things my travel insurance will pay out on.

Suddenly I was a wanted man by the media, not only as a representative of the Barmy Army but also as someone who was due to go out to India. There was no official Barmy Army tour; it wasn't going to be a hugely popular jaunt to start with because of the forthcoming tour to the Caribbean and it seemed obvious numbers would dwindle even further. My interviewers wanted to know whether I would still go, how I felt about going and how many others would go.

My answers became fairly rehearsed because my friends were asking me the same questions. Even before I knew whether the tour would go ahead I never wavered from the decision to go for several reasons. Firstly I was pretty sure that if the terrorists had wanted to target English tourists they would have waited a few weeks until we were in town. Had they done so the area they hit would have ensured that the Barmy Army would almost inevitably have suffered casualties. There is also an argument that there is never a safer time to travel than in the aftermath of such an attack as security is ramped up to the max. Also, as I tired of pointing out, Australia played an ODI against England at Lord's three days after London's 7/7 bombings and no one suggested that should be called off or that no one should go and watch it. I got on the tube the day after that attack – what else was there to do? Stay at home forever? Life goes on. It has to.

Not everyone was as blasé as I was about the situation and so the hardy souls who embarked on this tour numbered much fewer than usual on a visit to India.

It's partly for this reason it remains one of my favourite tours. There was an even bigger sense of solidarity and community than usual. A lot of that solidarity came from the difficulties we faced changing our entire itineraries to fit the new schedule.

While the England management were deciding whether to travel there were certain things they supposedly insisted upon before they would allow the tour to proceed and one of them was a change of venues. Mumbai had bigger and better things to worry about than holding a Test and no one was seriously going to suggest hosting one there anyway so it was understandable they would change that one. As far as we were given to understand, the request from the England hierarchy was to host the Test much further south. No one at this stage had really worked out the motivations and identities of the terrorists (indeed I still have no idea what they were trying to achieve) but the feeling was they were from the north/Pakistan so it made sense to move the cricket further away from that troubled area. When it was announced that the tour would go ahead with Chennai as an alternate venue those still intent on touring began to plan itineraries.

But then it was decided to change the other venue as well. Instead of Chennai replacing Mumbai for the second Test it would take the place of Ahmedabad for the first. Apparently Ahmedabad was also considered a security risk and in all honesty no one was too upset at the prospect of missing out on a place hardly alluring to overseas visitors. And the venue for the second Test? That was still undecided when the fans set off for India.

I landed in Mumbai early the day before the first Test thankful I hadn't bothered to book a flight to Ahmedabad in advance. I picked up my backpack intent on finding a seat on the next cheap flight to Chennai. That was simple, but getting from international arrivals to domestic ticketing was not as easy. Mumbai airport is crazy at the best of times but then it was crazier than ever thanks to the immense security. By the time I managed finally to battle my way through arrivals I was surprised to see that the thousands of people outside the airport were queueing in a relatively patient fashion to go through the extensive pre-security checks. I then realised the reason. Several men with machine guns behind sandbagged emplacements do make for decent crowd control, even in India. I found myself standing next to one of said machine gunners and asked politely where I might possibly find domestic ticketing. He pointed me in the general direction and when I asked if I would have to battle my way through all of the people he said I could cut across and through a gap in the fence. I know I got told that only because I was white and I knew they weren't going to shoot me but it did feel a little bit like being in a prisoner of war film, going through the wire with machine guns tracking me all the way. But I made it, bought my ticket and settled down for the trip to Chennai.

When several of us sat in a Chennai bar that evening our second topic of conversation, after recounting tales of the various routes and experiences we had undertaken to get there, was where we might have to go next. At that stage there had still been no decision on where the second Test would take place. We all hoped for Bangalore. It wasn't too far from Chennai (a mere 180 miles) and that made it an obvious choice for practicality reasons. It also fulfilled the ECB's desire to play in the south. From our point of view it would also make getting home a whole lot easier. Because the series would finish on December 23 most people had booked flights back to England from Mumbai on Christmas Eve to get home for the festive season. Flights from Bangalore to Mumbai were plentiful so it would make everything feasible.

Not that the fans would ever be taken into account, they rarely are, but our wishes were well and truly scotched by one of the more baffling decisions in a litany of baffling Indian bureaucratic cricketing decisions. When the reason for rearranging Test matches is one of security derived from a recent terrorist attack suspected to come from Pakistan do you:

A) choose the two Test venues furthest away from suspected danger?
B) choose the two Test venues that have the lowest security risk?
C) hold the second Test match as close to the Pakistan border as possible?

If you answered A or B congratulations, you are a normal, logical human being but I am sad to inform you that if you have any aspirations to be a cricket administrator you will have to come up with an alternative career plan. If you answered C then you are plainly bonkers, driven by internal politics and should apply to the BCCI for a job immediately.

It staggers me that the second Test was played in Mohali, as close to Pakistan as you can get without actually being there. Mohali is just 150 miles away from Lahore (as opposed to 1,300 miles from Chennai and 850 miles from Mumbai). If Flintoff could get hold of one properly in Mohali you'd need a passport to go and get the ball back. I still don't understand why the England management acceded to the suggestion given the obvious issues. I can only think that they figured it was safer because half of the Indian Army was already stationed up there to cater for the, erm, massive security risk. But not for the first time I am getting ahead of myself. Let us return to Chennai.

We rocked up to the MA Chidambaram stadium for day one of the series to discover one of those huge, shabby, half-completed concrete monstrosities in which Asia specialises. The walk from the entrance to the stands was akin to tramping through someone's allotment and then buying a ticket from their shed. Outside the ground we were surprised at the lack of obvious security. There were a few soldiers around but nothing noticeably out of the ordinary. Inside it was a different matter.

I knew there would be issues trying to get my camera into the ground but I decided to gamble on the possibility, safe in the knowledge that a bit of colonial bluster often goes a long way. Not surprisingly the soldier who searched me demanded I leave it with him. It's one of the quirks of developing countries like India that the authorities are so used to being obeyed that if a white guy questions their authority they usually look very confused. It is a sad fact, but as intimated it can work in your favour. I argued the toss with the soldier, especially when I found out that he would be 'looking after' my camera by putting it in a yellow plastic bag and placing it on an unguarded pile with lots of other yellow plastic bags.

I told him in no uncertain terms that there was no way I was leaving my camera with him and pointed out that it was very expensive. (£280 isn't that expensive for a camera in our terms, but it probably represented a sizeable chunk of his wages.) 'Indian lives are expensive as well,' he told me deadly seriously. I pointed out that while I appreciated this it would be rather difficult to kill anyone with a camera. The impasse was solved when his boss intervened to find out what was going on. I humoured him by taking a photo and showing it back to him to prove that what I was holding was not a lethal weapon aimed at razing the stadium. He smiled and told me to carry on, much to the hurt and chagrin of his subordinate.

Although the England fan numbers were depleted, we still matched the number of Indians in the ground for the first ball. I mentioned before that Indian fans are a funny lot and don't seem to have much patience for watching a game unfold, preferring instead to turn up just for the exciting stuff, although on this occasion perhaps I am being unfair because *Cricinfo* reported that morning that 'Cricket is under a cloud of fear and the MA Chidambaram stadium is now virtually a fortress, what with commandos and top-level security officials everywhere. Is that what's keeping the crowds out? There are hardly any spectators in.'

We quickly worked out that the reason there wasn't massive security outside was because the defensive measures were very much concentrated in the ground itself. The big group of soldiers 'guarding' the pitch in front of us changed with astonishing regularity as new deployments of men in different garish uniforms and with a variety of guns took their positions. We were certainly only the second biggest army in the ground that day as soldiers outnumbered both home and away fans.

These guys didn't worry us too much, but directly opposite there was a sniper on the roof and it seemed as though we were the ones in his sights. We would get used to having guns pointed at us on that tour but this was slightly surreal. I only realised just how much a few months later when I was ambling around a World Press Photo exhibition and realised that I was in one of the pictures. Admittedly I was a mere pixel or two but an enterprising snapper had got onto the roof and taken a sniper's eye view of the crowd and sure enough we were slap bang in the middle of his range of vision.

But we're nothing if not adaptable and so we soon settled in to watch cricket while keeping an eye on our protectors to see what they were up to. There wasn't too much to get excited about at first as England meandered to 63 for 0 at lunch and we meandered to the nearest watering hole to do battle with the Indian service industry. The score of 100 more for one by tea made us happy but by the time we bade farewell to the soldiers and motored in our tuk-tuks through Chennai to the hotel bar it was 244-6 after a dreadful last session. Nothing overly dramatic happened the next day until the over before tea. India had reached 30 for 1 in reply to England's 316 when debut boy Graeme Swann took his first steps towards Test stardom and Barmy Army hero status. As the song points out:

Hit for four with his first ball
Then took Gambhir and the Wall (Rahul Dravid)

Two wickets in his first over in Test cricket was definitely something to sing about and our homage to the event evolved over the duration of the Test match. Having read his columns in *All Out Cricket* magazine I knew he was a big Oasis fan and was determined that any song for him would be to an Oasis tune. Heather Storry started the ball rolling with the idea of 'a Champagne Super Over' in Chennai. Someone else changed it to 'Swanny Super Over in Chennai' and we tweaked the chorus a few times before adding in the rest of the song to come up with the following, to the tune of *Champagne Supernova*:

How many special people came
So many flights we had to change
Where were you when we were in Chennai?

Hit for four with his first ball
Then took Gambhir and the Wall
Where were you when we were in Chennai?

Some day you will find him
Taking loads of wickets
In a Swanny super over in Chennai

Some day you will find him
Taking loads of wickets
In a Swanny super over, a Swanny super over

Because people believe
That we should never have come here at all
But you and I will never die
And Graeme Swann is just one reason why, why, why, why...

Swann was interviewed on BBC Five Live after the series and was asked what was his favourite moment of the year. Instead of choosing the fact that he had taken a couple of big wickets in his first ever over in Test cricket, or that he had taken the wickets of Gambhir, Dravid, Sehwag and Laxman on debut, he said the best thing was that the Barmy Army had written a song about him.

That song will be the enduring memory of that Test match but it took a few days to fine-tune and according to my Barmy Army match report we had more fun with something else on day two. 'It was Yuvraj's birthday and so we thought about singing Happy Birthday to him but decided (in that stupidly optimistic way that we have) that we would sing it only after he got out. What we didn't realise when we made that decision was that he and Freddie (Flintoff) were about to embark on a war of words. We don't know what was said, but it was brilliant watching Fred give him the once over in all ways and then seeing Yuvraj edge straight into his huge hands. Oh happy days.'

Day three began with one of the more surreal Dawn Patrols. Dawn Patrol has always been an open invitation event but not many people are keen to start imbibing early in the morning. With so few people on tour and with a start time of 7.30am because play was due to start two hours later only a handful of people were ever going to attend this one. Arranging morning drinks in a city like Chennai at short notice was never going to be easy anyway, but when there is a Simon Humphrey, another founder member, there is a way and Simon decided that he would hold it in his hotel room. Not for the first time he would flummox hotel staff by asking for them to arrange a party for him in the early hours of the morning. He asked if they could deliver some ice, a couple of bottles of gin and some beer to his room at 7am. Now that's breakfast room service and a half.

Our numbers were bolstered when I received a text from Giles Wellington, who had just landed at Chennai airport and wanted to find out if there was a Dawn Patrol. When I replied positively he eschewed a visit to his own hotel to drop his luggage off and came straight to Simon's for post-flight, pre-match liquid refreshment, much to the 'delight' of his wife, Hayley.

The day continued in a positive vein as England finished off India's first innings and batted their way to a lead of over 200 with seven wickets left. According to *Cricinfo* 'The Barmy Army is chanting on their heroes.' Nice to know we could still make ourselves heard even in such small numbers. We'd come up with a very relevant version of *12 Days of Christmas* that went:

12 Warm Kingfishers
11 Returning players
10 Airport lounges
9 Immodium tablets
8 A dodgy curry
7 Potential venues
6 Cancelled flights
5 Days in Chennai
4 More runs
3 Proud lions
2 Cancelled Tests
And a win at the MCC

Every tour which takes place in the run-up to Christmas has its own version of that song. Our high spirits were dampened somewhat 24 hours later. Having declared and set India 387 we had been feeling quietly confident, but that was because we had no way of knowing there was a storm on its way in the shape of Virender Sehwag. In 102 minutes he scored 83 off 68 balls, smashing us to all parts of the ground and scoring so quickly that all of a sudden an Indian win became a possibility as we headed into the final day. And we all know that if there is a possibility that England can snatch defeat from the jaws of victory there is a fair chance they will grasp it with both hands. In a precursor of what was to come, the Indian fans were going absolutely berserk during Sehwag's innings, although they still had the good grace to shake our hands when Swanny finally got him out.

What happened in that last session and the next day was fairly depressing from a supporter's point of view. Having set India such an imposing target we genuinely thought we would see an England win. And we were even more excited about that possibility than usual because of the extenuating circumstances. To see us dismantled so easily was hardly enrapturing.

But looking back even soon afterwards we realised we had been fortunate. To see the most destructive batsman cricket may ever have seen (if you think that's being superlative check out Sehwag's strike rate in Test matches and compare it to anyone else's) turn a game in a heartbeat and then to see the second best batsman the world has ever seen take on the baton to carry his team to an unlikely victory, well it was just awesome cricket and a privilege to witness it. Once Sehwag had done the initial damage, Sachin scored a sedate century on day five to take India to victory. It almost seemed right that Mumbai's and India's favourite son was the man to bring some happiness to a city and a nation that had suffered such recent misery.

I pointed out earlier that there are three things Indian fans like to see at a cricket match, and this was all three rolled into one. Once victory became a possibility and once Sachin was at the helm the stadium just kept getting fuller. It was absolutely heaving throughout the afternoon and I've never heard noise like it. I would love to see the reaction of one of those cricket purists who believes the game should be played in funereal silence when 80,000 people spend hour after hour banging empty plastic bottles against chairs and walls. We tried our hardest to sing over it, but it was an impossible task. The great thing about the

Indian fans was the respect and appreciation they had for us. They were polite and friendly and in the wake of the recent terrorist attacks were genuinely appreciative of the fact that we had still visited their country. Several had written signs thanking us for visiting despite the attacks and there was a genuine bond between us. So a defeat, yes, but an honour to be there nonetheless.

While all that had been going on we had belatedly discovered that the trip to Mohali was in the offing for the second Test and so considerable time was spent working out the best way to get there. After exploring several options we decided to fly to Delhi and then get a five-hour taxi ride to the north. Delhi airport was being rebuilt for the Commonwealth Games at the time (and we know how well that went) so it was a fairly rubbish journey all round. The road from Delhi to Mohali is not one for the faint-hearted and the only highlight was when we stopped and found a choice of McDonald's or Domino's at the service station. Now most of the time I would find that choice fairly unappealing but on this occasion it was better than a gourmet meal.

Chennai did not make a positive impression on us and we weren't expecting much from Mohali either. Not that we actually stayed in Mohali, we were in the neighbouring town of Chandigarh. This has myriad charms compared to its neighbour although that's damning it with very faint praise. Chandigarh is a lot cleaner and more European in style than Chennai, but has very little going for it other than one posh hotel (where the players were ensconced) and the Blue Ice bar. The latter wouldn't look out of place in any English town but it stuck out like a sore thumb in this place and quickly became our favoured watering hole. But before that we had to run the gauntlet to get to the ground. And it was a gauntlet.

To get from Chandigarh to the ground in Mohali takes around 15 minutes in a tuk-tuk. But we couldn't get to the ground in a tuk-tuk because of the security cordon which stopped all traffic getting anywhere near it. And that was just the start of the security. It seemed like half of the Indian army was there (the other half we'd already seen in Chennai) and rather a lot of them insisted on pointing guns at us. As we walked down the empty street towards the ground we saw the first of many sandbag emplacements around the ground, each with a manned machine gun aiming directly at us. That was a fairly unnerving prospect. As we got to the checkpoint next to it a soldier asked us for our passports. We pointed out that unless we had taken a wrong turn we were actually trying to get to a cricket match, not across the border, and eventually he let us pass.

Obviously someone had realised that having a cricket match here was quite a high security risk (funny that) and the presence of the 'other' army made it feel like we were trying to gain access to a top secret military base rather than a shitty cricket ground in the middle of nowheresville. We passed through another checkpoint and got searched for the first time. Then we looked round for somewhere to buy tickets. If only they had remembered to employ ticket sellers, as well as soldiers, things might have been a bit easier at this point. It was Pakistan all over again as we were told that tickets were available from the bank, although no one seemed to know which bank or where that bank might be. More and more fans congregated outside the gate wondering how they might actually get into the ground.

Some chose to head off to try to find the bank while we chose to badger everyone in uniform or a suit to get them to sort it out. Everyone assured us there was something being done and we believed none of it because it was patently obvious nobody knew what to do. We sang *Jerusalem* outside the ground as we couldn't get in for the start of play and eventually an official appeared with a big wad of tickets and was instantly surrounded by people trying to buy them. The cynic in me would suggest that the money he took may never have made it into the official coffers but maybe I'm doing the guy a disservice. Anyway, we had tickets. Now we just had to get into the ground. History has told us that day one of a Test is always the one that throws up the strictest security and so it was. Cameras were examined, phones tutted at and the ladies had a separate tent to go through for their pre-entry search. We didn't want to know what was happening in there. Eventually we made it into the ground having missed 45 minutes of play to find a stadium even bleaker than the one in Chennai. Whoever runs cricket in Mohali must have some very compromising photographs of those who decide where India should play cricket, because there's no way you would award games there on merit.

But finally we were inside and as always we were determined to enjoy ourselves. And hey, there was cricket to watch as the sun beat mercilessly down.... oh no, my mistake, it was bloody freezing. We didn't miss as much play as we could have that morning by virtue of the fact that bad light prevented the match starting on time, as it would do pretty much every morning as a fog, eerily reminiscent of those I saw rolling in off the North Sea during my childhood, covered the ground. Not only had the game been moved to a ground close to the Pakistan border, it had been moved to a ground where early starts were scheduled because of bad light later in the day but were put back because of bad light early in the day. It was getting surreal and it didn't improve. My match report from that day sums up more random occurrences once we had finally got into the ground:

'So we were in, after missing the only wicket of the day, and then we watched our boys toil on a dead wicket. And then it was lunch. So we decided to go for a beer. Only they didn't have any passouts. Eventually they consented to let us out by having a security guard sign our tickets. So that was fine. The pub didn't have any beer so we went to the next one. They had some, but it wasn't cold. By this time it was time to head back to the ground.

'That's when it started raining. Not enough to send the players off the ground, but enough to make us cold. It's winter here up in the Punjab and we're not going to get a tan. After tea we decided there was only one thing for it and embarked on a 90-minute singathon going through the entire repertoire including a song for every player. They evidently appreciated it and it's been a while since we got applause from so many players as they left the field. There are so few of us here we enlisted some Indians who helped sing our songs.

'Just when we thought the day couldn't get any weirder as we left the road around the ground they closed the barriers for a minute or two because there was a stray cow on the road. Nothing surprised us any more so we shrugged our shoulders, waited for her to move on and went for a beer. God knows we deserved it.'

It was a fairly dull Test (only 28 wickets went down) and there was very little to warm us up so we just provided our own entertainment. Because of the low temperatures we were all wearing jackets of some description and upon starting another rendition of Graeme Swann's song three of us zipped up our jackets, donned sunglasses and bucket hats and did full-on Liam Gallagher impressions. What the locals thought of this I can only guess, but it remains one of my favourite images of touring. I can't remember which England player joined in, but there was definitely a collar up, hands behind the back, lean towards the microphone moment on the pitch.

We took the dressing up a step further the next day. The few locals who bothered to turn up had been wearing tank tops so we decided to instigate a tank top day of our own. Obviously not any old tank top would do, it had to be a garish number that your Auntie might think of buying you for Christmas. This led to a frenzied shopping spree in the morning as we all tried to find something suitably disagreeable. About 30 of us rocked up in uniform that day although I'm guessing the irony was completely lost on the Indians who probably just thought that we were wearing sensible clothing for a change. But we were quietly amused and warm as well.

There was an interesting sideshow to that shopping expedition. Our new bowling hero had inspired us to change the words of *The 12 Days of Christmas* to 'The 12 Days of Swanny' with one Graeme Swann, two Graeme Swanns etc etc and that song took on a life of its own on 'tank top day'. As a few of us mooched around the market to buy our attire we espied a man selling inflatables. This is not a rare thing in any part of Asia but this man was selling inflatable swans. That was his single product line. Where the demand for them had previously come from I don't know but it was an early Christmas for him as we bought 12. You can probably guess what happened next as a dozen of us were assigned a number and a swan and had to stand up throughout the song at the relevant time. I never did ask Swanny if he had worked out what we were doing but throughout India's second innings it did seem like the players were every bit as involved as us in the singalong. Matty Prior was definitely seen to be jigging behind the stumps although he may just have been practising his much-improved footwork or just trying to keep warm. We had a Christmas Carol service as well, although for some reason we decided to replace every single word of every song with the name Owais Shah and he wasn't even playing.

By day five there was a marked difference in the attitude of the soldiers who had made our entry to the ground on day one such a test of endurance. As we lifted our arms in expectation of the usual search, the soldiers instead grabbed our hands and shook them forcefully. It seemed they had worked out that we were not really prospective terrorists so much as English eccentrics who would follow their team anywhere in any circumstances. Everybody was all smiles as thank yous abounded and we thanked them back and had a laugh and a joke. This culminated in us getting a picture we had wanted on day one but were too scared to even take surreptitiously. Near our gate there was a truck with a machine gun on it. The guy manning it had a cloth wrapped round his head and looked like the archetypal terrorist – at least the western perception of one. Emboldened by our new found friendship with the military we asked if we could get a picture with him and the next thing a bunch of us were on the truck posing with a machine gun, bringing a whole new meaning to the phrase Barmy Army.

England will never have had fewer people watching them at the end of a series since the Barmy Army first began overseas touring than on the last day. That was December 23 and the majority of people were flying home the next day. The big issue with that was that people were flying home from Mumbai as the original itinerary had scheduled and Mohali was the best part of 1,000 miles away. There was no abundance of flights from Mohali to Mumbai so various differing routes were utilised. There wasn't a huge amount of drama on the pitch so no one was in danger of missing anything major and the ground started emptying from midday onwards as people went off to respective flights and lifts. I left halfway through the afternoon session for another five-hour journey on our favourite road back to Delhi. A couple more hours there were followed by a couple of hours on a plane to Mumbai. After a few hours I had a flight to Abu Dhabi and finally home to England where I landed at 6pm on Christmas Eve about 34 hours after leaving the ground. My trip didn't end there as I was going to Romania for Christmas and New Year so flew from London to Amsterdam to Bucharest where I landed in the early hours of Christmas morning after 48 hours on the go.

None of this prevented us from having an end-of-tour party; we just had it one night early. The Blue Ice bar was now used to our patronage and we had a favourite waiter whose name I have to admit has slipped from my memory. He was a legend though. When it turned out there was no Jägermeister in the place we quickly taught him how to make Monkbombs, which are the same as Jägerbombs but with Old Monk rum instead. Every night our man was ready with the shot glasses and the Old Monk and a smile. Our final night in Chandigarh was a Monday and, as you can imagine, Monday nights in Chandigarh are hardly rock and roll. But by now many of the few England fans in town had discovered the bar and a mini-party was in full swing.

Not surprisingly the licensing laws in this part of the world are not designed with the needs of a bunch of English nutters intent on having a large Monday night. The management seemed OK to bend the rules a bit until a few of the locals wanted in on the act and at this stage one of the managers pulled me aside and asked me very politely if it would be possible for my friends and me to leave the establishment. What followed was proof that befriending service staff and tipping them well is not only good behaviour, but can work heavily in your favour. I turned to our number one waiter and asked if we really had to leave and he said no sir it would be fine if I wanted to stay a bit longer and order just one more round. I immediately ordered 10 Monkbombs and my good friend and drinking partner Craig Millwood (Millers) chipped in with an order of 25 double vodkas. Our man didn't bat an eyelid and had the appropriate drinks whistled up. We saw him arguing with his colleague and I hope he was pointing out that while strictly speaking it was time to close, this would be the best chance they had to make this much money in one go for years so best to take it and run.

I'm not entirely sure of Millers' motives in ordering 25 double vodkas as it's not the most social of drinks but it proved to be an inspired move as we created the Kevin

Pietersen drinking game. This in itself was inspired by a bunch of lads who had come up with a song about KP to the tune of *Old MacDonald*:

Kevin Pietersen scored a run
Eey-aye-eey-aye-oh
And with that run he scored his ton
Eey-aye-eey-aye-oh
With a cut shot here and a cut shot there
Here a cut, there a cut
Everywhere a cut shot
Kevin Pietersen scored a run
Eey-aye-eey-aye-oh

The idea behind the song is that you sing as many verses as there are cricket shots you can think of – you simply insert a different shot instead of cut shot. They'd first tried it out in Sri Lanka, but as KP had been dismissed as soon as they started singing it they were given some almighty stick for jinxing him. But time had passed and this proved to not only be good fun (although only to be sung in a ground if the man in question had already got three figures) but a great drinking game. Everyone sings the chorus and when you come to the bit where you have to come up with a new shot you go round in turns thinking of a shot that no one has mentioned yet. If you can't think of a shot, you down a shot instead. A double vodka in this case. We sang it for about an hour before making our reluctant way out of the bar but the fun wasn't quite over yet.

The standard way to get to the hotel was bicycle rickshaw but we preferred to cycle them ourselves and give the drivers a rest. This inevitably turned into a race and on the last night I had the dubious honour of cycling Graham Barber home – and they don't call him Big G for nothing. Somehow I was way ahead of the pack but took a U-turn too tightly, tipping the whole thing over on its side. I was adamant we could still win so we got it back up, got Big G back inside and still made it over the finish line first. The only casualty was the driver's broken flip-flop so I gave him money for a new pair and we went into our hotel to order some more drinks. The hotel staff suggested that we go to our rooms to drink them but we insisted that we didn't want to disturb our fellow guests so it would be better for us to have them in the lobby. 'It's fine sir, your rooms are soundproofed,' is one of the biggest lies I have ever been told but they obviously wanted to get rid of us so we grabbed a few beers and carried on the party in our room.

Despite the trials and tribulations of that tour it was awesome and everyone had a fantastic experience despite the massive anti-climax on that final day when I'm guessing everyone was just glad to get home after a series that, like so many others in India, was simply too short anyway. We had been witness to one extraordinary Test match and one very dull one, but more importantly we had an adventure that would be hard to replicate.

Nine

Touring Sri Lanka

All in all it's just another Test match in Galle

Touring experiences in Sri Lanka
2007 1st Test (Kandy)
2nd Test (Colombo)
3rd Test (Galle)
2012 1st Test (Galle)
2nd Test (Colombo)

THE TEARDROP-SHAPED ISLAND 20 miles to the south-east of India shares many of its epic neighbour's characteristics and yet somewhere in those 20 miles the pace of life has slowed. Arriving in Colombo is still a fairly dramatic experience for those not used to Asia, but the welcome is not as chaotic as that faced in many other entrances to this grand continent. While there is an undoubted manic activity about the place, it's not as intense and once you've moved beyond the capital city, Sri Lanka is a country oozing beauty and tranquillity.

Admittedly tuk-tuks buzz about even the quietest backwaters like swarms of bees heading for the honey, but that's part of the charm and they remain my favourite form of transport – cheap, quick, easy, readily available. Many a tuk-tuk journey has turned into a race as several chariots full of Barmy Army numpties travel to the same place and implore their driver to get there as quickly as possible – not perhaps the most sensible thing to do in what can hardly be regarded as a particularly safe form of transport. We even have a song dedicated to the three-wheelers, to the tune of *Swing Low, Sweet Chariot*:

I looked over Kandy
And what did I see
Coming for to carry me home?
A thousand tuk-tuks
Chasing after me
Coming for to carry me home
Beep, beep
Cheap chariot
Coming for to carry me home
Beep, beep
Cheap chariot
Coming for to carry me home

There's always a tuk-tuk waiting to carry you home and there's always a driver willing to talk to you about cricket as you drive. Cricket is just as important to Sri Lankans as it is to Indians, indeed in some ways more so as it's a sport that managed to bring the country together even throughout its drawn-out civil war. As Kumar Sangakkara put it so eloquently in his Spirit of Cricket Lecture in 2011: 'The 1996 World Cup gave all Sri Lankans a commonality, one point of collective joy and ambition that gave a divided society true national identity and was to be the panacea that healed all social evils and would stand the country in good stead through terrible natural disasters and a tragic civil war.

'The 1996 World Cup win inspired people to look at their country differently. The sport overwhelmed terrorism and political strife; it provided something that everyone held dear to their hearts and helped normal people get through their lives.

'The team also became a microcosm of how Sri Lankan society should be with players from different backgrounds, ethnicities and religions sharing their common joy, their passion and love for each other and their motherland.

'Regardless of war, here we were playing together. The Sri Lanka team became a harmonising factor.'

The misfortune of civil war was exacerbated by the 2004 tsunami. Sri Lanka was the second hardest hit country, with more than 30,000 deaths and a million and a half people displaced from their homes. Again cricket helped the healing as the cricketing community got behind the relief efforts, donating money and playing games to raise funds, while the Sri Lankan players were among the leaders of the aid effort. To return to Sangakkara's lecture:

'Refusing to delegate the responsibility of distribution to the concerned authorities, he [Muttiah Muralidaran] took it upon himself to accompany the convoys. It was my good fortune to be invited to join him. My wife and I along with Mahela [Jayawardene], Ruchira Perera, our physio CJ Clark and many other volunteers drove alongside the aid convoys towards an experience that changed me as a person.

'We based ourselves in Polonnaruwa, just north of Dambulla, driving daily to visit tsunami-ravaged coastal towns like Trincomalee and Batticaloa, as well as southern towns like Galle and Hambantota on later visits.

'We visited shelter camps run by the Army and the LTTE [Tamil Tigers] and even some administered in partnership between them. Two bitter warring factions brought together to help people in a time of need.

'In each camp we saw the effects of the tragedy written upon the faces of the young and old. Vacant and empty eyes filled with a sorrow and longing for homes and loved ones and livelihoods lost to the terrible waves.

Yet for us, their cricketers, they managed a smile.'

The southern town of Galle mentioned by Sangakkara is a Test match venue but the ground was destroyed in the tsunami. It hosted its first match since then on England's

2007 tour and was very much a symbol of the country's recovery from the disaster. Originally designated as the first Test venue, it eventually held the third Test in order for more time to be given over to repairs. This meant that we began our Sri Lankan adventure in Kandy, a wonderful town in the hills that occupy the centre of the country. That trip to Murali's home town was followed with a Test in Colombo before moving on to Galle.

Because of its recent history Sri Lanka has struggled to attract tourism. That is a shame for them and a joy for those of us who have enjoyed its delights (I've been lucky enough to visit four times now) as it retains much of its charm and innocence. It's true that the fewer tourists a country has the warmer the welcome often is. You are not perceived as 'just another tourist' but as someone who has found their way slightly off the beaten track and people are genuinely thankful you have visited their part of the world.

Lack of tourism also meant that Sri Lanka was a very cheap place to visit in 2007 (prices have gone up since, although it is hardly wallet-busting even now). It was pretty much the only place in the world where you could buy a dozen beers for five quid – at a cricket match. It wasn't the best beer and it rapidly became a lot worse than 'not the best' if you didn't drink it within ten minutes, allowing it to warm up, but at that price who cared? Every time you walked past the bar, even if a visit there wasn't your primary focus, you bought a dozen because it was rude not to. This ensured a steady supply of beer and probably led to this being among the booziest of tours. Not that you could get your hands on a beer at the start of play for that first Test in Kandy. The gas supply was broken, but then that wasn't an issue for most people as they were still stuck outside queuing to get in. It wasn't like there were 50,000 people trying to attend and it wasn't like they had never hosted a Test before but as in so many countries we turned up on day one to wonder whether anyone had bothered to tell the people who were hosting that we were coming. Once we did get in, Kandy turned out to be a wonderful little ground.

There were hints of division in the Barmy Army at this time. The membership scheme had been announced and there was a fair amount of negativity from many people about how it was going to work. And there was also a group of relative newcomers, who would go on to become regulars, who had yet to mix with the old hands. Another thing adding grist to the traditionalists' mill was that the Barmy Army had its own stand. And, in truth, it did look faintly ridiculous with its bunting and comfortable chairs looking as if they had just been dragged from a wedding reception. But if your hosts are willing to provide such advantages, who's going to complain? Not the majority and while you could just as easily get in with the locals for 20p a day, those who had purchased their tickets from the Barmy Army in advance were enjoying the comfort. It didn't stop many of those 20p-a-day people gate-crashing it later anyway, although that was mainly to bring the singing masses together.

If you did buy a 20p ticket to sit on the grass bank you could be fairly safe in the belief that you were sitting on a pretty stable structure, which is more than you could say about the rickety stands that had been hastily erected for us and others. They were not so much stands as shelters, consisting of uprights with sheets of corrugated iron forming the roofs. Kandy is much cooler than the coastal resorts and can get a little breezy, and when the wind got up the flimsy nature of the stands was very quickly highlighted. The corrugated iron was not well attached to the rest of the structure and on one particularly blowy day we saw one sheet whipped from the framework of the stands, followed by another and another. As you can imagine this didn't impress the people in the stands although they needn't have worried. It was the people stood nearby who had to watch out as they dodged the flying sheets of iron.

In England this would obviously never have been allowed to happen in the first place but had it happened the game would no doubt have been called off while Health and Safety people came in and enforced structural repairs. In Sri Lanka all it took was a few of the local kids to shin up the vertical struts, have the roofs handed back up to them before weighing them down with some car tyres to ensure it wouldn't happen again. A minimum of fuss, a quick fix and all was well again. Who needs Health and Safety?

The crowd weren't the only ones ducking for cover as once we saw the teams and umpires suddenly dive to the ground. It transpired there was a swarm of bees flying over but as we couldn't really see them it looked strange. What also seemed odd was the first morning of the match when Hoggy took four quick wickets, Sri Lanka were 42-5 and England made the whole thing look easy.

It wasn't supposed to happen like that and as it transpired it didn't continue. That was as good as the whole tour got for us on a sporting level. It was the cricketing equivalent of a spectacular premature ejaculation followed by repeated failures to get it up again. And that, in a sense, was inevitable. Because the cricket gods had decreed this would be Murali's Test. He needed five wickets to overhaul Shane Warne's total of 708 and become the highest wicket taker in Test history. Now Murali could usually be banked on to take five wickets in most matches against England, especially at home, but the fact he was born in Kandy meant it was a dead cert that he wouldn't miss out this time round. He duly obliged and while we respectfully applauded his efforts the Sri Lankans went mental and fireworks were set off around the ground. Considering their efforts at building stands I'm not sure they should have been allowed to be in control of fireworks but I don't think anyone died.

The Barmy Army has never been quite sure what to make of Murali. He is hated by the Aussies because they think he's a chucker, and because he took more wickets than Warne, but the English are ambivalent. We know he's been cleared by the ICC and that the reason his action looks wrong is because of a birth defect in his elbow. We also know he's one of the nicest men in cricket and that his philanthropic work is mightily impressive. And if the Aussies don't like someone that's usually good enough reason for us to think the opposite. So there is commensurate respect from England fans but at the same time the furore over his action is such a glaring target for a song that it was inevitable someone would write one, which is why he was occasionally serenaded to the tune of *Row Row Row Your Boat*:

Throw, throw, throw the ball
Gently down the seam
Murali, Murali, Murali, Murali
Chucks it like a dream

But as I said, generally we're more interested in singing about our own players and that occasion saw us composing for the man playing in his first overseas Test, Ryan Sidebottom, who was to become the undisputed star of the winter. He was quickly adorned with a song to the tune of *Robin Hood*:

Sidebottom, Sidebottom
Swings it through the air
Sidebottom, Sidebottom
With his curly hair
He bats at number eight
He likes to masturbate
Sidebottom, Sidebottom, Sidebottom

It's amazing the amount of discussion you can have over the inclusion of the word 'masturbate' in a song and this time it provoked plenty, including some from the man himself who later said 'I suppose I like the rude version best. I think my mum likes it, you know. It gets everyone laughing, and I don't mind.' We came up with alternatives, but we never loved any of them as much as the original. It was much easier after the first Test in New Zealand on our next tour because he took a hat-trick and was batting one lower in the order so it became

He bats at number nine
His hat-trick was sublime

Everyone was happier about that on a decency level, but we still used to sing the original a lot for old times' sake. Apart from that the Sri Lanka tour was heavily reliant on old classics rather than new songs. We sang Jimmy's *Everywhere We Go* to absolute breaking point and there was a lack of real creativity. Someone did come up with a song for Ravi Bopara, who made his debut in that first Test, to the tune of Queen's *Radio Ga Ga*:

All we need is, Ravi Bopara
He's better than Lara
And Sangakkara

A quick look at Bopara's stats for that tour proves that it wasn't ever going to be used much. He scored 42 runs at 8.4 and all of those runs came in the first Test with three ducks in his last three innings, including being run out from slip in the third Test. Lara and Sangakkara eat your hearts out.

We were one shocking decision away from drawing the first Test and eventually the series but Murali's record breaking wasn't going to be sullied with something as inconsequential as a draw. He had taken the record-breaking wicket (bowling Paul Collingwood) in England's first innings on his way to 6-55, but England still had a first innings lead of nearly 100. That evaporated quite quickly as Murali wasn't required to bat again. Sri Lanka scored 442-8 in their second innings and Murali contributed three more wickets when England batted again and we were out for 261. The only surprising thing is that he didn't get a ten-wicket haul in front of his home fans. After all, this is a man who took his 800th and final wicket with his 44,039th and final ball in Test matches. He had, as Graham Gooch might have said, a good scriptwriter.

My other overriding memory of that Test is that it was the first time I have ever unwillingly missed a day's play while on tour. I have no idea what bug hit me but I was unable to move from my bed on day four and whether the beers were £5 for 12 or not I wasn't indulging in many of them when I made it back on day five, preferring instead a steady diet of antibiotics. Another great thing about Sri Lanka is the ready availability of antibiotics without the need for something as bureaucratic as a prescription.

My health was not helped by the fact that Sri Lanka is without a shadow of a doubt the worst tour when it comes to food inside the ground. It's generally bloody awful and yet strangely the number one food-seller quickly became a Barmy Army mascot. Hotdog, as we so originally titled him, was at all three Tests selling spring rolls and hot dogs from a little plastic box. I'm not sure how he managed to blag the same job at all three matches as this was hardly specialist work but he was ever-present. He was a lovely bloke who revelled in his Barmy Army hero status while serving largely unpalatable food. Well, it was unpalatable to me; Billy the Trumpet ate it religiously. But then Bill always complains of indigestion. Maybe Hotdog secretly worked for the indigestion tablet company as Bill went through more of them that tour than I went through beers.

Either way, Bill, Hotdog and I were fighting fit again for the second Test which, as is always the way nowadays, was played hot on the heels of the first so there wasn't much time for exploring the delights of Sri Lanka. Thankfully I had visited Sigiriya before but if you ever find yourself in that part of the world do visit that mountain fortress because it's spectacular. I opted instead to recover properly from my illness with a half-day Ayurvedic treatment session before heading to Colombo.

The capital is a fairly typical big, dirty Asian city although there's enough of an old colonialism whiff to raise it above the norm. And it does have the advantage of being by the sea and there's nothing like going back to the Galle Face Hotel and having gin and tonic by the waves to wash the dirt of the city out of your mouth. There are two standards of rooms at the hotel and the cheap seats were well within our budget so we moved in and enjoyed many breakfasts and dinners on the lawn terrace as the sea crashed incessantly against the wall. It was something of a throwback to the old days and we consumed a lot of tea and a lot of gin in true English style.

We also consumed gin and tea at another of Colombo's finest hotels, the Taj Samudra. Simon Humphrey and Tim Haffenden, those purveyors of Dawn Patrol excitement, were in Sri Lanka and Simon excelled himself with his hosting on this occasion. He organised a breakfast buffet with a gin bar on one of the fabulous lawns within the hotel. This was perhaps the largest Dawn Patrol gathering and with the majority of people making an attempt to dress up (contrary to popular belief the Barmy Army doesn't usually do fancy dress but makes concessions for Dawn Patrol) we made quite a sight for everyone waking up and pulling back the curtains to see our little gathering. Simon himself was dressed as a snowman.

The thing about Dawn Patrol is that once you've had a drink or two in the morning, and if you're mainly topping up from a couple of big nights beforehand, you don't really want to stop drinking when you get to the cricket, so we didn't. Alcohol-fuelled or not, I don't think the Barmy Army has ever sung so much in one day. It was one of those days when England toiled and toiled in the field, taking only two wickets, and seeing as we knew this was when they needed us most we tried to get behind them as much as possible.

Harmison, in particular, was struggling and if we sang his song once we must have sung it a thousand times. The song goes to a tune no one seems to know the origins of:

My name is Super Steve Harmy
They all think I'm barmy
I bowl right arm fast for England
England!
When I walk down the street
All the people I meet
They say Hey! Big man!
What's your name?
My name is Super Steve Harmy

Repeat

It was one of the few times I have seen an England team applaud the supporters when walking off the pitch during a Test match as opposed to at the end. I'm not sure everyone appreciated our efforts but the players did and as usual they were our foremost concern. By the time I got to bed that night I needed eight solid hours' sleep – after all we were only halfway through a Test match. Unfortunately I got about an hour because every time I tried to get to sleep I had the Super Steve Harmy song going through my head and it sent me absolutely mental. As this was Stuart Broad's Test debut I'm sure I must have had his song doing the rounds as well:

He's big, he's bad
He's better than his Dad

The madness of the day was summed up by the playing of inflatable Twister at lunch. I believe it was Nicky Bowes, another great Barmy Army personality who had toiled far more hours than anyone should ever have to during her time working at the business end, who had the inclination to bring this to the cricket. It was an inflatable pool with the Twister board printed on the bottom. The only issue we had was how we were going to fill it. The nearest tap was more than one hundred yards away and clearly doing it jug by jug would take all five days, never mind one, so we gripped the bull by the horns, or the pool by the walls, and carried it to the tap and waited for it to fill up, before carrying it back full of water. I've never seen eight grown men carrying a paddling pool full of water around a cricket ground before, nor since, and perhaps I never will again, although one should never say never. The locals, not for the first time, must have thought we had taken leave of our senses. It only remains for me to include the detail that I am the unbeaten, reigning Barmy Army Paddling Pool Twister champion. Ahem. I thank you.

If all that was memorable the Test match wasn't. Only 22 wickets fell in a dull draw. I remember a Jayawardene double ton (actually 195 now I check my facts) and I remember a lot of rain and now I come to think of it I remember another of the rather stupid events that seemed to characterise this tour. On a particularly dull day, that man Simon Humphrey decided to organise a version of *It's a Knockout* which involved two teams carrying people and chairs from one place to another. One of my friends said he had seen me on television carrying some bloke on a chair and asked me what I was doing. I really couldn't answer his question in any sensible way but it seemed like fun at the time.

As well as being the tour of the cheap beer and dreadful food, Sri Lanka is also the tour of the drum. For some reason someone decided to take a good old-fashioned marching bass drum on the 2001 tour and it was rescued from its storage and reinstated for the second Test in Colombo. Our resident Scotsman, Allan Fairlie-Clarke, originally referred to as Jock, although that did evolve to Bale of Hay when his wicket-keeping in a Barmy Army game was likened to that inert object, was the drummer. He occasionally shared duties with Ed Salmon, who pulled rank as he previously played one in an Army marching band. I think everyone, including Jock and Ed, is glad that the drum is not a permanent fixture, but it has a certain novelty effect and would prove invaluable when we came to include some Pink Floyd in our repertoire later in the tour.

We moved on to Galle, but there was still concern about whether the ground would be ready in time. As this was to be the first Test at the ground since the tsunami had swept over it nearly three years previously it had a huge significance. The effects of the tsunami are startlingly evident in this part of Sri Lanka. There are myriad signs to 'new' villages built by aid agencies and outside agents to house people made homeless. We visited the opening of one of them – it was nearly three years after the event, remember – where the medical facility is named after the Barmy Army in thanks for our support. There are tsunami memorials down the west coast and in our base of Unawatuna you could walk down the beach and feel the foundations of the washed-away buildings beneath your feet. Everyone had a story to tell. I visited the Lighthouse Hotel just outside Galle and the manager explained to me how his guests had watched people washed from the rocks below.

Another man told me how he climbed a palm tree to escape the wave. The tsunami can only really be a concept until you can get this close to the people and places it affected. We soon realised how much this match would mean to the country as a symbolic gesture.

The problem was that the rebuilding of the Galle International Stadium wasn't complete. The SSC in Colombo was hardly Lord's, but the Galle ground barely looked ready for club cricket. We figured that if they were struggling then maybe the Barmy Army could help. A big group of people went out and bought cleaning implements, rocked up at the ground the day before play was due to start and offered their services to those in charge. I'm not sure how seriously they took us but our offer was refused, which seemed a bit churlish at the time. While we were hanging around at the ground the sum total output of about 200 staff seemed to be the cube root of not very much. Indeed about 30 people were employed to do nothing but sit on the outfield.

As is always the way in Asia they bodged and fixed enough so that the game did get under way on time although it was a good job they changed the itinerary and put this one at the back end of the tour instead of the front. Seeing as we weren't overly confident about their ability to have the ground ready (and we were a tad disgruntled about some of the umpiring during that series), we put our songwriting skills to good use the night before and introduced a bit of *Another Brick in the Wall*:

We don't need no seats to sit on
We don't need no stands at all
No dodgy catches in the outfield
Umpires give us one good call
Hey, umpires, give us one good call
All in all it's just another Test match in Galle

It's very hard to get the timing right on that song, so the drum came in handy for us. iPods and the internet revolutionised Barmy Army songwriting because all of a sudden you could nail songs you couldn't quite remember but I do seem to remember calling my Mum to find out the lyrics of a Barry Manilow number during that Test. Not sure why but whatever I was writing obviously didn't get past the cutting room floor.

As it happened we did end up with seats to sit on and a stand, although it wasn't until after lunch that I availed myself of those facilities. Indeed for the majority of the early sessions I sat with others on the famous fort wall. The fort overlooks the ground and while you are a fair way from the action you can see what's going on. Not only that but there is a great atmosphere as many locals congregate to watch the cricket from a bird's-eye view without having to pay for the privilege. They were always quick to approach us and talk about all things cricket and enquire whether we were enjoying their country. That's something that doesn't often happen when you are with your mates in a cricket ground.

Not only did Galle offer a unique way of watching the game, it also offered possibly the best place in the world to go after a day's play. We based ourselves in the beach town of Unawatuna, a short tuk-tuk ride away. It remains one of my favourite places in the world, an idyllic slice of relaxing beach life, the perfect spot to chill out after watching cricket. There wasn't much to keep us in Galle anyway (the nearest pub, the Sydney Hotel, is probably the worst cricket pub in the world) so we just headed to the beach for sundowners and evening festivities. Indeed if you mix all that up with a couple of great lunchtime drinking hotels in Galle old town and a couple of upmarket hotels if you fancy splashing out (splashing out still being relatively cheap in Sri Lanka), you'd be hard pressed to find anywhere better to watch Test cricket.

We were challenged again with cricket that wasn't hugely fulfilling (rain provided continual disruption and Sri Lanka's first innings took two and a bit days despite filling only 150 overs), and in order to amuse ourselves we decided to have an inflatable day on day three. There was nothing particularly complicated or sophisticated about this, it was simply a response to the availability of inflatables of various kinds all across Sri Lanka. As we shopped for ours I have an overriding memory of Billy the Trumpet lying over his Father Christmas inflatable struggling to deflate it before paying for it. It wasn't a good look.

The night before we'd met a couple of female English backpackers and coerced them into joining us at the cricket the next day. They turned up to my room in the morning when I was still very much bleary-eyed. I had promised to wear a Sri Lankan sarong that day so joined them in a tuk-tuk wearing it while carrying an inflatable parrot and looking dreadful. Later that night I would have a romantic assignation with one of them although I could never really suss out how I had managed to attract her. It's not like England's cricketers looked any better, getting bowled out for 81 that day as we had our inflatable party before heading back to Unawatuna for a tour party to raise funds for the tsunami victims.

On day five I went straight into the ground, avoiding the fort, which meant I could see the banner hanging down which stated '15 days of misery: Thanks for nothing'. There are many retorts to that. My favourite line remains that a bad day at the cricket is still better than a good day at the office, so it's still not miserable. While the cricket wasn't great and England hadn't performed particularly well, I certainly hadn't been miserable at any point other than during my illness in Kandy and that was hardly the players' fault.

It was an honour to be present when Murali broke the record for Test wickets and while we hadn't played particularly well I'd certainly seen worse. Admittedly I never saw much worse than getting bowled out for 81 on a pitch on which Sri Lanka had just scored 499 for 8, but hey ho. Life's too short to be miserable because your cricket team is rubbish.

The banner upset quite a lot of people who, like me, believe in supporting your players through thick and thin. Several people wanted to go up there and rip it down. I couldn't really see the point in giving it that much credence and after all we live in a free world where we're allowed and encouraged to vent our frustrations. But what I had always loved about cricket supporting as opposed to football supporting was that it almost always meant just that: supporting. Let's face it, slagging your own players off is counterproductive. You want them to do well, so support them. It also struck me that it was a hell of a lot of effort to go to in order to vent your fury. Most people can be content to just whinge and complain to their mates over a pint or two.

If I may digress a moment and switch to football, I have long been of the opinion that the common habit of shouting abuse at your own players is a strange thing to do if you want the players to improve. This is especially true of international football, where transfers can't be made and you have a finite number of players from which to choose. It was something that never seemed more apt than when I was at Wembley to watch England's Euro 2008 qualifier against Croatia and Scott Carson made a huge blunder to give them the lead. Thereafter he was continuously booed by his own fans. Which if you give it any thought is a pretty silly response. The player himself is going to be feeling fairly dreadful and with most of the match still to play the last thing he needs is fans knocking his confidence still further. Imagine if everyone at Wembley had started singing his name in support. The player would know the crowd were still behind him, which would help him shrug off his mistake and regain confidence for the rest of the game. As everyone wants England to win, building up your player's belief in himself would seem a more sensible ploy than eroding it even further. As Gary Neville summed up in his recent autobiography, *Red*: 'The whole lot of us got it in the neck at other times. Sometimes we deserved it, but playing for England was one long roller-coaster: some ups and downs, but also quite a few moments when you're not really sure if you're enjoying the ride. It should be fantastic, the best moments of your life. But there is no doubt that too many players spend too much time fearing the consequence of failure when they pull on an England shirt.'

The ironic thing about the banner on the wall is that while it wasn't usual Barmy Army style some of my mates had been busy with a sign of their own. The grapevine had been working overtime and we'd heard that Vaughan was thinking of retiring as England skipper. In our little group we wanted to show our support for him (funny how the 's' word keeps popping up) and so we did a banner of our own saying 'Michael Vaughan – Our Most Successful Captain – We Still Support You'.

Now I wasn't hugely involved in its creation and you could argue that if we have the right to show a banner saying we support him then matey boy on the top of the wall had just as much right to do one that slated the England team. You'd be right as well. But I wonder which would be more likely to inspire Vaughan to greater deeds.

Vaughan never had a particularly witty song written about him, but what he did have was simple, direct and to the point. To the tune of *Kum Ba Yah* we sang:

Michael Vaughan my lord, Michael Vaughan
Michael Vaughan my lord, Michael Vaughan
Michael Vaughan my lord, Michael Vaughan
Oh lord, Michael Vaughan

On occasions we would sing this for ages and change the lyrics to things that we supposedly associated with him, although it did get a bit surreal at times. We sang:

English born my lord, English born
Mows his lawn my lord, mows his lawn
Earns his corn my lord, earns his corn

And almost inevitably:

He likes porn my lord, he likes porn

Not that we had chance to sing about him or inspire him to perform great deeds that day as he had already lost his wicket by the time it began, but perhaps the banner would inspire some of the others. Erm, not so much. In the time it took us to carry it halfway round the ground to put it up we lost three wickets in four balls and Ravi Bopara contrived to suffer that run out from second slip. Maybe we should have put it up at the start of play to counteract the other one rather than wait until the wickets were tumbling.

I remember standing by the fence after helping erect the banner and not wanting to move during the over. There were some locals watching from the other side of the fence and they got quite upset with us. When I pointed out that I had paid money for my ticket and so was entitled to stand where I wanted unless I was interrupting the view of someone else who had also paid, he didn't quite get where I was coming from.

England managed to save the Test and despite '15 days of misery' we lost the series only 1-0. To qualify that statement it is probably worth pointing out that rain was probably our best player on that tour and certainly in Galle, where only 275 overs were bowled. As England had only four wickets left and were still 160-odd behind it's clear that England's Man of the Match was the water cascading from the heavens every afternoon and we acknowledged that by singing the rain dance song a lot. No one wants to see rain instead of cricket (unless it's 2005 at the Oval and England need a draw to win the Ashes) but if you're only going to watch another hour or two as your team loses then why not? We asked for and got rain on that final afternoon. And it wasn't just rain, but that torrential stuff that has a beauty all of its own. Confident that this meant the end of the Test and the end of the series we embarked on our end of Test party. We danced in the rain, sang *Singing in the Rain, Raindrops Keep Falling On My Head* and anything else water-related we could think of. We behaved like people who fully expected to get in a tuk-tuk and go and get a dry change of clothes presently. Deco was even spotted lying lengthways in a big puddle attempting the front crawl.

Half an hour later the sun was out again, the ground dried and we all sat there soaked to the skin regretting our earlier exuberance. It was only a temporary hiatus as play soon ended again with rain even more violent than the earlier stuff. And this did not stop for the rest of the night. We managed to get back to Unawatuna and then our end of series party just went on and on because we couldn't be tempted to go home in that weather. My last memory of that tour is finally giving into tiredness and walking home at about 6am with water up to my waist and the rain still lashing down. England had struggled to keep their head above water for the entire series but this was, quite frankly, as ridiculous as that analogy.

In terms of England's performance and the excitement of the cricket as a whole that Sri Lanka tour was probably the dullest I've been on, yet still I cite it as one of my favourites. The beauty of touring is that you can get fulfilment in so many different ways. In enjoyment of the country, the people, your fellow cricket fans, the experiences you share and the friends you make. I like my team to do well as much as the next man, but there's so much more to a cricket tour, which is one of the reasons I find it so appealing. Sri Lanka offers enough to have tempted me back since and I was excited about renewing acquaintances with the country and its people in 2012.

Ten

Press and players' view of the Army

Drink with the Army, sing with the Army

IT'S FAIR TO SAY that over the years the Barmy Army has had something of a love–hate relationship with the press. Actually that should perhaps be clarified. Generally the press in the country we are visiting is positive. I have rarely seen any negative publicity overseas and generally the press are keen to write about us in an enthusiastic way as we give them something else to write about – a phenomenon they seemingly can't get enough of. Indeed it was the Australians' respect for us that coined the name Barmy Army and the Australian Press Corps even bought us a load of beer after the Ashes win in Australia in 2010–11. We are respected for the devoted support we offer and the atmosphere we bring to cricket grounds around the world.

Back in the UK though it's been a different story. In truth the behaviour of the Barmy Army was always going to come as something of a shock to cricketing traditionalists. Cricket has evolved in other countries and the atmosphere at matches is a million miles from the village green, smattering of applause and jolly good old boy environment of Britain. West Indies supporters always made a right old racket during their glory years, Asian crowds are hardly renowned for their placidity and the Aussies wouldn't even know what funereal silence was. But you always get the feeling that the old boys' network thinks that England should rise above such nonsense and sit there cocking a snook at bothersome oiks while drinking one's Pimm's and discussing the latest goings on at Eton.

But a new generation of England cricket fans wanted more than that, especially when they are overseas. It's where the Barmy Army came from and perhaps why it is still predominantly an overseas entity but there was always going to be a clash between old-school cricket fans and this new breed who wanted to bring an element of football-style support to the game. As Simon Briggs pointed out in the *Daily Telegraph* in 2010: 'They do tend to polarise opinion. While some credit them with keeping Test cricket alive, others claim that they are an eyesore and an earache – a gang of beet-red Englishmen who ruin everyone's fun by droning away as monotonously as a trapped bluebottle.'

Those who disapprove are the staunch traditionalists, and because cricket writers are often of that ilk it is not surprising that the gentlemen of the press have often been at pains to point out what a terrible bunch of people we are. The late Ian Wooldridge was the first to raise his head above the parapet and fire opening salvoes at the Barmy Army when it was conceived during the 1994–95 tour.

His disapproval was again highlighted in a *Daily Mail* editorial in 1997 when the Army had moved to New Zealand. He wrote of 'an appalling cacophony of discordant noise [has been] inflicted on those wishing to watch a Test match in the traditional manner. The Barmy Army are not cricket hooligans. They are not destructive. What they lack is a single line of the incisive, original wit that used to come off the Sydney Hill and could convulse an entire Test match crowd.'

It's tough to work out what offended him. First, it seems to be the noise but then he backtracks somewhat to admit we are not destructive. By the end our main crime seems to be that of not being particularly funny. Wooldridge was a bit like a dog with a bone in that he never gave up an opportunity to have a go at us.

In 2002 he wrote: 'It has been reported that several thousand of England's Barmy Army cricket followers are about to depart for Australia to support England in the imminent Ashes Test series. Pray God this isn't true. Ten would be too many. They are not bad people. They don't set fire to pavilions or cars, they don't wreck bars or violate the local womenfolk. They don't indulge in racist chants. What they are is excruciatingly boring...

'They are hugely mistaken if they believe they have added any joie de vivre to a Test match. They are courteously tolerated by Australians who regard them as a bunch of self-promoting berks.'

All I can say is he must have been talking to different Australians than those I meet, who banter with us, and enjoy our songs and style of support.

Another who has not been shy of voicing his disapproval of the Barmy Army is perhaps the very epitome of cricket traditionalists, Christopher Martin-Jenkins, a past president of the MCC no less. At the end of England's successful 2004–05 series in South Africa he wrote: 'Why the countries they [the Barmy Army] invade are too polite to tell them the truth, heaven knows. Worthy souls dwell among them, no doubt. As a group, they too often demean English cricket. As Betjemen prayed of Slough: come friendly bombs and fall on them.'

The mischief-maker in me is tempted to leave the quote there, but to be fair to CMJ he did finish it off 'Water bombs will do'. CMJ can often be heard on *Test Match Special* bemoaning us with comments such as this in January 2010: 'I'm sorry about this Barmy Army lot, interfering with your listening back home.'

The issue for Wooldridge and CMJ seems mainly to be with the noise we make, and ultimately they are both intelligent enough to appreciate that we may not be bad people just because we make a bit of a racket. If it's just a question of noise then we have to agree to disagree and move on. Everyone is entitled to their opinions but it does help if those are based on fact, which is why we really do get annoyed when attacks on the Barmy Army are factually incorrect, unnecessarily abusive and scathing. And for examples of those we should look to two of the Barmy Army's best friends, Matthew Norman and Dominic Lawson – neither of whom, it should be noted, is a cricket writer.

Let's begin with Norman. During the 2010–11 Ashes series he penned an attack on us in the *Daily Telegraph* (ironically when we were being praised by nearly everyone else for our awesome support) in which he said:

'I refer to the self-styled Barmy Army, that coalition of desperate saddoes who are the sons not only of Thatcher, but of Dave Lee Travis as well. What an overpoweringly rich gene pool that one is. All it's about with these self-styled warriors is them. They are the only faction of any sporting audience in history whose primary motivation for attending games is not to watch but to be watched.'

If you think that's bad I'm saving the best bit until last but for now let's just have a look at this. So we're all saddoes are we? And desperate? Sweeping generalisations from a man who has not to my knowledge spoken to any of us. But while that was simply generic typecasting, I just can't get my head around the Dave Lee Travis and Thatcher references. Apart from the obvious fact (obvious to anyone who bothered to do any research anyway) that the wide age range of the Barmy Army should really preclude lazy generational stereotypes I honestly don't really see what DLT and Thatcher have to do with a bunch of people singing songs at cricket. I mean there are some strange characters in the Army, but the love-child of Thatcher and DLT? The mind boggles.

I assume he's got an issue with the 'self-styled' nature seeing as he used it twice in two sentences but short of using the name the Barmy Army – which we did not originate – I'm not sure we're any more or less self-styled than a certain self-styled restaurant critic, sports critic and political commentator.

If people wanted to pay thousands of pounds to travel round the world to 'be watched' then they have that right. However, you'll probably find that they do so to watch cricket and support their cricket team. I didn't do a poll of the thousands who invested so much in travelling to Australia for that series on their motivations but I suspect that 'to be watched' wouldn't come too high on the list.

But look at me biting. I promised myself I wouldn't. He's not worth the effort. But wait a minute – what was that other thing he said, hang on I have it here somewhere. Oh yes:

'Whatever their other failings, football thugs had integrity.'

In case you think this is a misprint I'll put it in again.

'Whatever their other failings, football thugs had integrity.'

Now it's really quite hard to know where to start with that as a comment. Integrity is defined as having moral and ethical principles. I'm not sure where fighting people because they come from another country or support a different football team fits into that definition. Or where turning up to cricket and singing a few songs shows a lack of integrity. So basically the people who would beat the crap out of each other because they supported a different bunch of 11 people on a football field had more integrity than a bunch of people who turn up to a cricket match, support their side and sing a few songs? Riiiiggght.

I know I've taken the bait but he does anger me a tad. I'm not sure it's his opinion that riles me so much or the fact that he gets paid so much money for it.

Perhaps I should have left the right of reply to those who commented on the piece online, all of them scathing in their opinion of it, such as 'angeldust' who described it as: 'Truly, one of the most unjustifiably bile-ridden and venomous articles that I have ever had the misfortune to read in the Telegraph.'

But Matthew, if there was an award for best piece of vitriolic crap written about the Barmy Army you come a distant second compared to the Barmy Army's true hero, Dominic Lawson. He showed his hand in the run-up to the 2006–07 Ashes in the *Independent*. It was a general diatribe against us and as usual all too easy to pick apart. And I'm never one to turn down an easy opportunity. He insisted that the Barmy Army was 'the self-appointed official England Cricket Team supporters' club'. Erm, sorry Dominic but we're not the official England Cricket Team supporters' club at all, self-appointed or not. Not a good start really if you can't even get that right.

Apparently we have 'a sort of uniform: shiny black soccer shorts, white ankle socks, a T-Shirt (two sizes too small) displaying the flag of St George, a royal blue cap, and sunglasses.' I don't know anyone who wears 'soccer' shorts and even if we did we wouldn't call them that because only Aussies refer to it as soccer; we would call it football.

Generally we wear cargo shorts. Our T-shirts are generally the right size and at this point the Barmy Army logo incorporated the Union Flag as opposed to the St George Cross and even then it was only tiny, but apart from that he was spot on. And anyway what the hell are people expected to wear when the sun is shining? What, pray tell, Dominic, do you wear on holiday to foreign climes? Shorts perhaps? A T-shirt? A cap? Maybe a pair of sunglasses to protect your eyes from the sun? You strike me as the kind of guy who might wear white ankle socks with sandals. Although I would also guess that for England matches you wear beige slacks, navy jacket, MCC tie and brown brogues. But let us continue.

'Vast amounts of lager go in, and an equally copious supply of chants emerges from the same orifice. Actually, it's chant, singular.'

Can't argue with the first point, can't argue with the second. As for the qualification of the second you should have stopped while you were ahead. I dunno how many songs are in this book but it's more than one. And while we do have a few chants there are more songs. But anyway, I really should leave him there and not waste too much energy as it's all too easy to pick him apart.

And I would leave him there but he likes to waste energy on us so I may as well return the favour. He was at it again in the *Independent* three years later during the 2009 Ashes in the aftermath of Ricky Ponting getting booed at Edgbaston and his missive was even more scathing. I'm surprised he calmed down enough to put fingers to keyboard and splutter: 'Instead, we got a cacophony of churlishness from people who had not the faintest conception of how privileged they were to be present.'

Sorry old boy – most people had paid 80 quid for a ticket. And none of us get paid truckloads for spewing ill-informed rubbish in newspapers. Or have a Daddy who was chancellor of the exchequer or mother who was heir to the Lyons Corner House empire. We didn't get educated at Westminster School or Christ Church college, Oxford. And that means that 80 quid is a lot of money, so we have every concept of how privileged you are to be there when you decide to spend it on a day at the cricket.

He went on to say: 'I don't know if the boos for Ponting emanated from the ranks of the so-called Barmy Army, the self-appointed "Official England Cricket Team Supporters' Club", but I wouldn't be entirely surprised.'

So you don't know whether it was us but you're using it as a stick to beat us with anyway. Great journalism that. More extensive research caused him to say that 'one former international, when I wrote an article critical of the Barmy Army, emailed me to say that he had found them nothing but a tedious nuisance when he was on tour.' That's fair enough. But did you bother to ask any other players? Perhaps those I'm going to quote soon who love us to bits and appreciate the support we give them? No, thought not.

He also went on to say that the behaviour of the Australians in the crowd was uniformly exemplary and there were more women in their section. I must at that point take my hat off to him. He is obviously some kind of omnipresent cricket fan who can be everywhere at once and also carry out a demographic check on cricket crowds with just a quick glance of his all-knowing eye. Although equally it would not surprise me to find out he wasn't even there.

The rest of the piece was a simple rehash of what he had written in 2006, with little original thought. But he did stop short of including his last sentence from that 2006 piece again. 'Can we have our game back, please?' Our game? Since when was it your game? Which is this group to which you belong that owns cricket? No one owns the game, least of all you.

But enough. I'm getting drawn in. Although there remains one thing for Messrs Norman and Lawson to note. If you are going to abuse us... if you are going to accuse us of only having one song... if you are going to print the lyrics of that song to back up your argument... it really does help if you actually print the correct lyrics. There were enough inaccuracies in their pieces anyway but they could at the very least have got that right. We even have it on our website for them to cut and paste. Kind of sums it all up really.

Incidentally, can anyone spot the irony in Norman and Lawson being on the same side of the fence on this issue? If one of the sticks Norman likes to beat us with is that we are 'children of Thatcher,' what then does he think of Dominic Lawson, the child of Thatcher's chancellor of the exchequer for six years, one Nigel Lawson?

The Dominic Lawson tirade in 2009 caused a huge amount of media interest and the topic du jour became whether the Barmy Army was good for cricket. Unfortunately for Dominic most of the coverage was positive. England cricketers past and present came out behind us as did Australia's, including Matthew Hayden and Ricky Ponting (the booing of whom had kicked off his rage).

In my then role as Barmy Army media type I ended up doing lots of interviews but the most intriguing promised to be on BBC Five Live with none other than Dominic Lawson himself. I had all the above reactions ready to go. But I was sidelined, firstly by the fact that the Five Live presenter introduced the segment using Lawson's comment as fact not opinion and then by finding that such a self-important man was just going to talk over everybody. I was far too polite, not shouty enough for that interview. Which is ironic as you'd probably think it should have been the other way round. After all I was one of the 'boorish and chauvinistic' Army he hates so much.

I remember him insisting that England's success at Lord's was probably down to the fact that there was no Barmy Army presence there, thus showing his complete ignorance of the fact that it was the first victory over Australia at Lord's for 75 years and that might suggest that it's libraryesque atmosphere was not particularly helpful. He didn't, as a matter of interest, mention anything about the fact that the MCC members had, erm, booed Ricky Ponting at Lord's. Strange that.

James Lawton was quick to back up his fellow *Independent* writer Lawson, emphasising in 2009: 'The Army believe that the old role of the spectator to watch and appreciate skills of a very high order, to express emotions that flow naturally from the action, long ago became redundant in face of a more pressing need to participate.'

To be fair Lawton has a point. Some people do enjoy the participation element of the Barmy Army. And why not? But that's not exclusive to enjoying the game as well.

It doesn't help that these opinions of the Barmy Army are formed from very small encounters, and as we have already discussed, the Barmy Army can be a very different entity from one day to the next. But all we ask for is some research and thought before writing about us.

The *Telegraph*'s Simon Briggs has, as we have already seen, a more measured view of the Army and when I was working with the business side I appreciated his impartiality and that he would occasionally ring me up for quotes on things that affected England cricket fans or to give us the right of reply when we were under the hammer.

As he pointed out shortly after Matthew Norman's piece: 'Whatever they wear, and however loud they sing, isn't the most important thing that the Barmies show up at all? In an age of declining Test attendances, can we really afford to reject a group of at least 5,000 hardy fans – and often two or three times that – who travel on just about every England tour? There are those who claim that the rise of the Barmies has encouraged a boorish, beery atmosphere that drives away families. And yet, despite the decline in Test attendances around the world, English crowd figures have held up better than anyone's, both home and away.'

Other journalists have been disapproving without being overly and overtly critical, but even some of the more traditional cricket writers have belatedly begun to appreciate what we can bring to the game. Scyld Berry, the outgoing editor of *Wisden*, wrote of us in 2011: 'My opinion of the Barmy Army was not favourable when it began, because the songs contained foul language which should not have been imposed on children watching. But last winter their songs were no worse than bawdy, ridiculed senior Australian players rather than the juniors and were surprisingly tuneful, and the focus was on the cricket rather than on themselves.'

It was an interesting and welcome observation from Berry but our behaviour had not really changed on that tour, so perhaps the difference was not in behaviour but in perception. Certainly it seems to reflect a fairly seismic shift in opinion of late from dislike to appreciation.

George Dobell, senior correspondent of *Cricinfo*, is more forthright in his positive views of the Army. 'The Barmy Army are bloody fantastic, very knowledgeable, very enthusiastic and you never have any trouble from them... what would the grounds look like today if it wasn't for them?' he told the Spin Podcast in January 2011.

Penny Wark, of *The Times*, is also a fan, intimating in the summer of 2009 that, 'As a cricket widow who has been persuaded to go on tours abroad, I have come to regard their exuberant singing in the face of unmitigated sporting disaster as a triumph of the human spirit, and I like their wit.' We like Penny too, not just because she wrote nice things about us but because she made the effort to come to the office and to events to actually find out what the Barmy Army was all about before writing about us. Revolutionary idea that one. She also described me as 'strikingly good looking' so maybe we shouldn't really rely on her opinions as having any real weight. You can imagine the ribbing I got when I turned up at the cricket and everyone else had read her piece before me.

That apart, getting to know us before putting pen to paper is surely worthwhile. It's why I particularly like the view that manifested itself in the form of a comment from 'pazaz_pool' following a Jim White article in the *Daily Telegraph* during the 2010–11 Ashes series: 'You see, I haven't lived the life of a Barmy and I have not been there on countless overseas tours, supporting and supporting and supporting. I imagine my (like many others) view is distorted by the relative nature of my own brand of support and how it contrasts to the Barmy image. The things I witnessed at Trent Bridge were, to many Barmies, themselves examples of bandwagon jumping. So I think, in spite of myself, that I will happily commend the Barmy Army for their support and sod how they do it. The MCG would have been a quieter place without them. After all, it's possibly not our cup of Tea... but don't say it's not Cricket.'

It's about the most measured comment I've read and all the more so because it comes from someone who does not necessarily like our brand of behaviour but who at least took the time to consider it from all perspectives. I leave the last word of the outsiders to one of my heroes and another epitome of the English gentleman at cricket, the great Stephen Fry, who tweeted after the 2010–11 Ashes: 'Congrats to the much maligned #barmyarmy their commitment, loyalty, good humour and wit an inspiration to sports fans everywhere'.

We can undoubtedly be a bit precious about what people say about us. Indeed I've proved that in my reactions to articles that still get my back up. But while the negative opinions of the likes of Norman, Lawson and Wooldridge annoy us and while we equally relish the nice things said about us by disabusers such as Berry and Fry, there's only one group of people whose opinions really matter to us and that is the players we pay thousands of pounds to support round the world.

We weren't necessarily welcome immediately. Michael Atherton, the captain who was named on the first ever Barmy Army T-shirt, has always seemed a bit ambivalent and told the *Telegraph* in 2005: 'I found them neither an inspiration nor an irritant because I don't notice the crowd when I'm playing. If they want to believe that [they have an effect on the performance of the team], fine. No one wants to dampen their spirits.'

But I've heard enough tales from the early adopters to know that a lot of the players do like the Army. Angus Fraser, part of the team on that inaugural Barmy Army tour, is more forthcoming in his praise. In the *Independent* in 2010 he wrote: 'Travelling abroad to watch cricket is a major commitment and the players really appreciate the support they are given. Ian Bell and Kevin Pietersen did not go drinking with the Barmy Army because they felt they had to. They want to. The players enjoy the fun, songs, revelry – and free booze. They want to celebrate special moments with people who it means just as much to. The ritual has always begun with several beers at the ground, then the hotel. A quick shower and change would be followed by an enquiring visit to the hotel bar, which would usually be where the party started. Then off to the Barmy Army's favoured watering hole. What time you got to bed depended on your stamina.'

The relationship between the players and the fans seems to have grown closer as the Army has become an established part of the cricketing fabric. If you ever wanted real proof a look at the podium after England's 2005 Ashes win should suffice as Jimmy Savile and Billy the Trumpet were invited onto the stage to share in and lead the England players' celebrations. This is now translating to the media, as the ex-players now being used as commentators have a closer bond with the established Army than their predecessors. It is particularly true of Michael Vaughan, a champion of ours during his Test captaincy, who has now transposed that to his work on *TMS* and other media outlets, much to the annoyance of CMJ, with whom he has clashed on many occasions as to the relative merits of the Army. His appreciation was evident when he stood down from the England captaincy and sent a personal letter to Barmy Army HQ thanking us for the continued support and referring to the Army as England's 12th man – a tag he adopted as much from Liverpool's famous Kop stand as a cricketing term.

I didn't attend much cricket before Vaughan was captain but it always seemed like he got us and he realised how important we could be. I never spoke to him much either other than during an epic night out at the Thirsty Whale pub in Napier following the third Test victory over New Zealand – more about that later – but the fact that he was the first to demand more singing that night and was, if a little reluctantly, willing to lead it proved how much he liked it. I bet he would have liked to have been around when we sang about Mitchell Johnson in 2010–11. He was heard laughing on air and tweeted that it was his favourite song.

There was one guy who didn't make it to that New Zealand party and I couldn't work out why until I read his autobiography. Matthew Hoggard, 'Hoggy', was the first Barmy Army patron, one of our biggest fans and always an amiable bloke. His autobiography tells you that his history with the Barmy Army went back a long way to a rather big piss-up on the eve of a Sri Lankan Test. After learning he had been dropped he hung around with the Barmy Army, got smashed and had to rely on Leafy to look after him – even Leafy would tell you that is a fairly desperate state of affairs. Somehow Hoggy managed to blag the resultant hangover by sleeping at the back of the changing room and letting other guys do the twelfth man duties. If Fletcher had found out about that night it's just possible that the Barmy Army could have ended the career of one of our favourites before it had properly begun.

Anyway our relationship with him was good. Indeed it was better than that as he was our champion on the field. I interviewed him several times, with the most bizarre taking place prior to the Ashes of 2006–07. I travelled to Leeds to meet him at Headingley. I hooked up with a photographer we had for the day and waited for him to show up. And waited. And waited. When he eventually showed up he was hugely apologetic, but explained that he had been in physio because of an injury scare. Not only that but he had to go for an MRI scan in about ten minutes so was there any way we could do the pictures quickly and then do the interview at the hospital? Note that at no time did he actually say he was too busy – he always had time for the Army.

Fortunately Hoggy is a born buffoon, which may well be an act, but that's what you need when you're doing a photoshoot so ten minutes was more than enough. Bidding the photographer goodbye we then jumped into Hoggy's car, rocked up to the hospital and had a chat while he was wearing nothing but a green gown. Before we'd actually discussed anything he pointed out that it was a waste of time me coming all the way to Leeds as he didn't care whether I just made up the interview. He was deadly serious as well but seeing as I was there I figured I might as well get it from the horse's mouth.

He really does love the Army and pointed out that we were at our best when the team were struggling on some hot, dusty pitch on the subcontinent and he was knackered. Apparently we could give them that extra lift. I always use this example as proof that, whatever you think of us, the players think we can help them, so who gives a toss what anyone else thinks? We all want a winning team. If the players say we can play a part then we'll carry on playing that part.

Anyway, by the time I bumped into Hoggy again he was our official patron and I spent a particularly dull afternoon with him as I unwrapped a few thousand books, he signed them and I put them back in boxes. Yawn. We chatted again about our role and he asked whether he could be the official team link so when they needed a boost he could give us the nod and we could kick in. That was a bit of a no-brainer as far as we were concerned. Unfortunately he wouldn't have the opportunity to do it very often as we were about to witness the end of his Test career. Dropped for the second Test against New Zealand, he would never play for England again.

At the end of that Napier Test he was still the guy who led the players over to the supporters at the end of the game and instigated the singing, getting Big G to belt out a rendition of *Rule Britannia*. So it seemed strange that he didn't turn up at the party. I can imagine he was upset at being dropped but he was a team guy, a good guy; read his autobiography and it's obvious his problems went much deeper than cricket so I can now fully understand why he didn't want to be around us lot. The fact that he had turned up and had such a good time with us a few days before was testament to him being one of the good 'uns. Just as Hoggy was one of our big fans then his replacement in the team, Jimmy Anderson, is also hugely appreciative of our efforts. In the backlash that followed Dominic Lawson's column after the Ricky Ponting booing incident he told the *Independent*: 'We get booed when we go to Australia so I'm fully behind it. I haven't found the crowds irritating at all. I've enjoyed it. The atmosphere at every ground has been fantastic. When the crowd are singing along it makes you want to win that little bit more – and play harder.'

But then it seems that every member of the current team appreciates what we do for them. Matt Prior is a huge fan and the new unofficial conduit between us and them. He is always the first in the field to start dancing when we start singing, especially when we burst into this to the tune of *Ring of Fire*:

He always takes the top edge skier
He bats at Hove where his average gets higher
Four, six, four
He's Matty Prior, he's Matty Prior

He fell foul of the jellybean enquire
He has no need for a Brylcreem supplier
Four, six, four
He's Matty Prior, he's Matty Prior

Prior is the leader of the England fielding unit and he regularly turns to us when he wants the volume turning up. If he wants us to be part of it we're all too keen to get involved. The opinions of the rest of the team are so well known now because they're all kind enough to tell the world on Twitter and in their newspaper columns.

Alastair Cook said in *Metro* after the 2010–11 Ashes series: 'I'm not saying we couldn't have done it without the fans but they have been a real help. Their songs have been brilliant and very, very catchy. When we went into the Aussie dressing room for a drink on Friday afternoon after our victory even their players were singing Barmy Army songs. They get in your head and that's how catchy they are.'

Tim Bresnan tweeted after the win in Melbourne: 'How to make 75 thousand empty seats vibrate. Let the Barmy army sing. Unbelievable support from the best supporters in the world.'

KP was another to utilise Twitter to acknowledge the support, saying 'Our Barmy Army are absolutely amazing!! All of you that are on twitter – thank you so much for your support!! You are unreal!!!'

Twitter king Graeme Swann was not slow to join in after the Sydney celebrations, declaring a 'brilliant night with the best travelling support in the world. Barmy army, I salute you.'

Andrew Strauss, whose Australian wife Ruth loves the Barmy Army, was also quick to acknowledge that 'The support from the Barmy Army was outstanding', while Jonathan Trott was quoted in the *Telegraph* in 2010 as saying that: 'the Barmy Army gives us real support and I enjoy every minute when they are singing. I know the team enjoy it and it lifts us.'

Now when the players are coming out with those sorts of endorsements then the rantings of a few self-important columnists pale into insignificance. But I leave the last words here to a man whose opinion probably has more weight than most. A man who gets the opposite of the adulation we pour on our heroes, the Barmy Army pantomime villain Ricky Ponting.

'I have said for a long time that the Barmy Army are the best sporting crowd in the world. I don't care what sport you are talking about, or what country – they are unbelievably good supporters. There is never anything untoward, it is always good light-hearted stuff, and when England have a sniff of winning the volume goes up tenfold. They add a lot to the whole experience of the Ashes.'

Eleven

Touring New Zealand

Around Wellington town we did roam

Touring experiences in New Zealand
2008 1st Test (Hamilton)
2nd Test (Wellington)
3rd Test (Napier)

WITH FEWER THAN FOUR and a half million inhabitants, New Zealand is sparsely populated and its cricket grounds reflect that. While statistics suggest that cricket is played by more people than rugby, it is undoubtedly rugby that is king here for spectators, and domestic rugby matches can attract higher attendances than international cricket. That, and the laid-back nature of the country in general, make this the most relaxing tour on the calendar. There's none of the craziness you get in Asia, none of the noise and vitality that pervades the Caribbean, no big city venues like those visited in Australia and South Africa. Here it's small grounds with small crowds in small towns separated by small distances and the cricket is punctuated with the opportunity to explore this beautiful, accessible country with friendly locals.

While I don't quite agree with New Zealanders' assertions that they live in God's Own Country it is undoubtedly a stunning place and overland travel here is a delight whether you are in a car or on foot. It's easy to see why it was chosen as the Middle Earth of Tolkien's *Lord of the Rings* trilogy, such is the unspoilt, timeless nature of many of the rolling landscapes. And unless you're talking about rugby or sailing, the locals are generally an unassuming and laid-back mob, fiercely passionate about their homeland without being overbearing.

There is the fact that it's even further away than Australia to contend with but once you've put those miles under your belt a visit is a hugely rewarding endeavour. At first I was somewhat disappointed and surprised to find that the 2008 tour would not be a step-by-step itinerary of New Zealand's bigger cities (Auckland is home to one third of the national population and after that even the cities are only big towns), but much smaller, lesser-known venues. We ended up in Hamilton, Wellington and Napier. I'd never heard of two of them until the schedule was announced and I'd spent a fair amount of time travelling in New Zealand.

When you consider the huge population centres we often end up in, these were tiny. You might assume Wellington is a fairly big city but it is home to fewer than 400,000 residents. Hamilton has around half that and Napier about a quarter of Hamilton. Even in big cities it can often seem as though the Barmy Army has taken over a place; in Napier we represented a significant percentage of the population that week.

Hamilton is a pleasant, if completely unremarkable, town with one main street that encompasses all the shops, bars and restaurants and there's really nothing else to get excited about, yet it hosts a wide variety of top sporting events. As well as international cricket it provides Super 14 rugby (it is the home ground of the Chiefs) and V8 motor racing, which is a big deal in these parts. We attended a Chiefs' match and the town was preparing the track for a forthcoming V8 round when we were there. Cricket came a distant third in terms of excitement factor for the locals.

The ground was nigh on empty most days, which we didn't mind because we could make it our own. It's a good enough venue with temporary seating and random four-tier Portakabin edifice that Sir Ian Botham famously refused to climb in order to commentate on the game. But the grass banks were awesome, the queues for beer and food were mercifully short and we generally had the place pretty much to ourselves. And to be fair to the locals who eschewed the chance to watch international cricket on their doorstep, they weren't missing a great deal on the pitch for the first three days.

That grass bank would have been ideal for sleeping and it's a miracle we didn't as England scored at a rip-roaring two runs per over throughout the whole Test. Snooze. We crept to 348 in response to New Zealand's 470 and the only real opportunity we had to get excited was towards the end of day four. New Zealand were 101 for 2 and a fairly dull match was meandering towards a draw when a Ryan Sidebottom hat-trick with a Monty Panesar wicket in between meant four wickets fell in nine deliveries. That gave us the faintest sniff of victory. But as Gilo said at the time, 'that hat-trick might just have bowled us to defeat'. It hastened New Zealand's declaration and they set a target of 300. England were bowled out for 110, with only one score above 13. Of all the post-match nights out this was almost certainly the most anti-climactic. Usually we can get over a miserable defeat with a big night out, but with us not really in the mood, the rest of the town safely tucked up in bed and the players stewing in their hotel, there was absolutely nothing doing.

Ryan's hat-trick did inspire Gilo to write another song, although not one that would get much use (to the tune of *Molly Malone*):

In Hamilton city
Where the batting was gritty
I first saw our Ryan get three in a row
He bowled left arm over
Got em caught by our opener

That's when our Ryan got three in a row
Three in a row
Three in a row
With Fleming, Sinclair and Jacob Oram

It speaks volumes that we will remember the Test as much for the 'gritty' batting as the hat-trick, but those of us who remember the song (about five people I think) would at least be able to reel off the victims of England's second last Test match hat-trick in a pub quiz.

Another song that we used to amuse ourselves during a dull few days was one that Gilo had assured me would never take off. I actually agreed with him, but perhaps the circumstances and desire for new songs helped. Either way we began singing, to the tune of *When The Saints Go Marching In*:

Our racing driver
Is called Hamilton too
Our racing driver's called Hamilton too
He's called Lewis and drives real fast
Our racing driver's called Hamilton too

It's easy in retrospect to see why Gilo thought this wasn't much of a goer. But with Barmy Army songwriting you never really know what will and won't work. And for some reason this did. Other verses included:

Our Scottish Test player
Was called Hamilton too
Our Scottish Test player was called Hamilton too
He was rubbish and played one Test match
Our Scottish Test player was called Hamilton too

A Scottish football team
Is called Hamilton too
A Scottish football team is called Hamilton too

They're Academical and they're rubbish
A Scottish football team is called Hamilton too

Sarah Connor
Was called Hamilton too
Sarah Connor was called Hamilton too
Linda was in the Terminator movies
Sarah Connor was called Hamilton too

It's fair to say that as we sang this throughout the Test there was a lot of Googling going to see what other people could come up with. But Hamilton was fairly simple. When we got to Wellington we figured the same trick would work and there were some obvious ones:

Our favourite boot
Is called Wellington too
Our favourite boot is called Wellington too
They keep our feet dry when it's wet
Our favourite boot is called Wellington too

Our favourite Duke
Was called Wellington too
Our favourite Duke was called Wellington too
He was the one that beat Napoleon
Our favourite Duke was called Wellington too

Our favourite food
Is called Wellington too
Our favourite food is called Wellington too
It's got beef and lots of pastry
Our favourite food is called Wellington too

And then we got to Napier, which was always going to prove very tricky. We managed:

Our Essex player
Is called Napier too
Our Essex player is called Napier too
He's called Graham and he scores sixes
Our Essex player is called Napier too

Our Edinburgh University
Is called Napier too
Our Edinburgh University is called Napier too
It's where Jock did his degree
Our Edinburgh University is called Napier too

That was all to come though. In Hamilton we not only amused ourselves with one of the more obscure songs we'd ever sung but also by daily trips to the dollar shop where we challenged each other to buy the most random stuff we could find – most of which was supposed to make some sort of noise. There were toy drums, tambourines and clappers, whatever took our fancy. I've said it before and I will say it again – sometimes you just have to make your own fun.

On the fifth day of the Test we made our final visit to the shop and the guy behind the counter who had been serving us all week asked us what we were in town for. We were not really expecting that question and we certainly weren't expecting his next one. When we replied that we were there to watch cricket he asked 'Who's playing?' There were hundreds of English guys in Barmy Army shirts wandering round his little town and he hadn't cottoned on to the fact that there was an international cricket match taking place round the corner from his shop. No wonder we had the ground to ourselves.

Despite the terrible result and fairly mundane cricket, this Test represented a watershed in my Barmy Army career. While the 'Our racing driver is called Hamilton too' song had been my idea it was never destined to have much longevity and each verse was sung by individuals as we challenged each other to come up with new variations. But I also managed to write my first ever hugely popular song, one picked up quickly, which would be sung by all the fans, the players and get distributed on the internet as well.

We were having dinner on a boat cruise early during that first Test when Gilo and I started discussing the fact that we needed a song for our new wicketkeeper Tim Ambrose. We struggled at first. Ambrose doesn't rhyme with much after all. I just couldn't get the fact that it sounded like Ambrosia out of my head. And Ambrosia was the favoured tinned dessert manufacturer of my youth. But this seemed like a stupid road to go down so I tried desperately not to. I explored some other avenues but nothing seemed to be right so I went back to where I started and came up with this, to the tune of *You Are My Sunshine*:

We've got Tim Ambrose
Sounds like Ambrosia
They make good custard
Comes in a tin
They make creamed rice too
That's not important
Just as long as England win

Ahem. Gilbert and Sullivan, Rodgers and Hammerstein, Webber and Rice, eat your hearts out. In all honesty I can't say I was overly convinced with my creation that evening, but by the end of the tour I was bloody delighted with it. It became bigger than I could ever have dreamed of and hearing an entire England crowd singing a song you put together gives you a special kind of buzz. When random strangers come up and ask if you wrote the song and then pat you on the back, telling you it's brilliant, you get a weird kind of sense of pride.

There are no hard and fast rules about what makes a successful Barmy Army song but it does help when the man in question gives you a good excuse to sing it. Ambrose did just that during the second Test, scoring a century, and from that point on the song was a winner. By the end of the tour everyone was singing it, including the players. I had a drink with Tim on the end of tour night out and he was so happy he had a song and very thankful. I remember him saying to me at some stupid hour of the morning that 'he hoped we were going to be friends for a long time'. I wasn't naive enough to think that he liked me that much, but that he hoped he was going to be England's wicketkeeper for a long time. Sadly, his Test career would only last 11 games, but he always had Ambrosia.

I read something on the Barmy Army forum about that song, saying it was juvenile and stupid. I think it was meant as criticism, but I couldn't agree more. Most of the good songs are exactly that. Coming up with a song that becomes successful is a curious mix of timing, size of crowd and easily memorable lyrics. This was catchy, each line linked into the next and it was completely and utterly ridiculous.

It was to start my songwriting addiction that would see me picking up bits of paper at any stage of a Test match to jot down some new lyrics. I'm not sure now whether any of them have ever attained the level of popularity that one did so maybe I should have done a Stone Roses and stopped before I had even begun. But where would the fun in that be?

Even then my songwriting was well and truly eclipsed on that tour by Doug Mulholland, a man with no fear of standing in front of a crowd, with a voice that could carry over it and a songwriting ability that made him famous in the Barmy Army within a week of turning up as a complete stranger. Type in 'Barmy Army Jesse Ryder Song' to YouTube and you can see for yourself. The lyrics to his two opera magna, based mainly on the drunken misdemeanours of New Zealand batsman Jesse Ryder in the run-up to that tour, go as follows, firstly to the tune of *Sloop John B*:

We came over from old Blighty
The Barmy Army and me
Around New Zealand's towns we did roam (we did roam)
Drinking all night (drinking all night)
A grand for the flight
Well I feel so pissed up
I should have gone home

So hoist up the John B sail
See how the mainsail sails
Call for the captain ashore
Let me go home (let me go home)
I wanna go home, I should have gone home
Well I feel so pissed up
I should have gone home

Jesse Ryder's an evil man
He gets drunk whenever he can
He doesn't give a toss
About Vettori and the boys (Vettori and the boys)
Jesse Ryder's a sod (Jesse Ryder's a sod)
He thinks he's a God
When he felt so pissed up
He should have gone home

Chorus

Now Jesse Ryder he got drunk
He smashed a window to have a dump
The constable had to come and take him away (take him away)
Sheriff John Stone (Sheriff John Stone)
Why don't you leave Jesse alone

When he felt so drunk then
He should have gone home

Chorus

And secondly he penned this to the tune of *Delilah*:

I saw the rage in his eye as he looked for a toilet
I saw the glass on his hand as he smashed down the door
I stood there laughing
He saw the blood on his sleeve and we laughed no more

Why, why, why, Jesse Ryder?
Why, why, why, Jesse Ryder?
Long before the selectors say no more
Forgive me Vettori I won't be a twat anymore

As Jesse woke up paralytic in Christchurch Hospital
The Doctor came in to offer Jesse a hand
But Jesse was still mortalled he said
(Spoken) Well I've had just about enough you, so you can go and shove it down your...

Why, why, why, Jesse Ryder?
Why, why, why, Jesse Ryder?
Long before the selectors say no more
Forgive me Vettori I won't be a twat anymore

The choruses were easy for everyone and as Doug was more than happy to stand with a pint in hand and belt out the rest of it the songs were instant hits. That tour was a hugely successful one for new songwriting after the relative paucity of Sri Lanka, and Adrian Raffill also came up with a cracker for Kiwi opening bowler Chris Martin, also to the tune of *You Are My Sunshine*:

You've got Chris Martin
He's not in Coldplay
He's not had Gwyneth
He cannot sing
He's got no albums
Or record contracts
But he's just as boring

It's not often we pay so much attention to opposition players but sometimes the events and personalities just lend themselves to songwriting so obviously then it is hard not to. All of these came on top of an old classic that we used to serenade Dan Vettori, to the tune of *Oh My Darling, Clementine:*

Dan Vettori
Dan Vettori
Harry Potter in disguise
We are going to
Steal your glasses
And poke you in the eyes

Rumour has it that Vettori is not a big fan of the song, so he was probably less than impressed when Gilo turned up with a bag full of joke thick-rimmed glasses from the shop in Napier and we put them on before singing. You're never sure what effect these songs are having on opposition players and the rule is pretty much in place that banter is good while abuse is not. But they evidently get heard. When skipper Stephen Fleming made his speech at the end of the series and the end of his international career he acknowledged the Barmy Army and said he was just thankful that we hadn't come up with a song about him. This was also the Test series that saw Deco come to prominence with his Barmy Army classic *We Are The Famous Barmy Army.* All of a sudden from having all the pressure on Jimmy Savile to sing his one song we had numerous people willing to stand in front of the crowd with a load of new songs and a bunch of new crowd favourites that everyone would sing as well. It was like new life had been breathed into the Army choir and everyone revelled in it.

But again I am getting ahead of myself. We were on our way to Wellington for the second Test, still somewhat shell-shocked by the insipid performance in Hamilton. What we didn't know at the time was that it was the last time we would see Barmy Army patron and the seventh most successful England bowler of all time, Matthew Hoggard, play Test cricket. What a horrible way to go out.

The great benefit of the choice of host venues was that they were all on the North Island and thus travelling from one venue to the next didn't take too much time. That meant there was the opportunity for sightseeing – something all too rare in the modern game now back-to-back Test matches are the norm. In the West Indies you have to fly between islands, in Australia between states, in South Africa it's also internal flights (the only two Test matches in the close vicinity of each other are, of course, at opposite ends of the schedule) and in India, well just read the chapter and you'll kind of get the gist. In New Zealand there was time for visiting geothermal sites, bungee jumping, and even a bit of relaxing. That meant we were primed and ready for the Wellington Test.

Of all the pubs to have hosted the Barmy Army during my years of touring, none went out of their way so much to make us welcome as The Feathers in Wellington. Being a Barmy Army venue is a bit of a no-brainer as pubs rake in so much money in a short period of time they can afford to go on holiday for the rest of the year. But the ones that really win are those that truly embrace us and Geordie, our host for the week, not only embraced us, he liked us so much he would be seen at the next Test in Napier and also on the upcoming Ashes tour. In truth we should have hated him as he used us as an excuse to dispose of umpteen bottles of foul gin. Admittedly he didn't charge us for it but we should really have been charging him.

By this point in the evolution of Dawn Patrol it wasn't so much a case of whether we would have one but when and where it would be. The notoriety of the event was growing from that first small gathering and now everyone wanted a bit of the action. In the absence of founders, Tim Haffenden and Simon Humphrey, I became organiser but that was a fairly simple exercise. We told Geordie about our tradition and he readily agreed to open up early. As usual we only had one instruction. We need lots of gin. As you already know he had plenty of that although we did insist on the good stuff for Dawn Patrol. So, not many hours after we'd left The Feathers at the end of the night we were back in there warming up for a new day. By now the ramifications were almost set in stone. Dawn Patrol would be the loudest day of the tour and the day after would be the quietest as everyone recovered from a 16-hour drinking session. We consider we have stamina, but even we have a limit. The highlight of that day in Wellington was the lunchtime game of cricket featuring the celebrity slip cordon. At one point our game of cricket involved Paul McCartney (in his Sergeant Pepper days) bowling to Ginger Spice, a monk keeping wicket, with Batman, Robin and some transvestites in the slips. It was quite a sight.

We liked the ground nearly as much as the pub (and the fact that the gap between them was easily walkable). The Wellington Basin is a proper cricket ground and yet still one at which most county teams in the UK would turn up their noses. That's because half of it is actually a cricket stadium and the other half is grass banks. And, as I might have mentioned, the Barmy Army loves a grass bank. The only issue with the one at Wellington is that it is quite steep and the busier it got the more inevitable it would be that gravity would take its effect and by the end of the day we would end up compacting down towards the bottom of the hill.

With a bunch of new songs to bed in, a great pub to host us and a new-look bowling attack we settled in for round two and it proved to be spectacularly successful. Day one ended with Tim Ambrose on 97 not out so we had plenty of opportunity to sing his song. By the end of day two the decision to drop Hoggy and Steve Harmison looked vindicated by Jimmy Anderson's five-fer. Sadly we've never really cracked Jimmy's song despite several discussions with him about what he wants. When everyone else has proper songs and all he gets is 'Ohhhh Jimmy, Jimmy. Jimmy Jimmy Jimmy Jimmy Anderson' it's understandable he'd want something better. The nearest we've got to anything taking off was to *Viva Ronaldo* during the South Africa tour of 2009–10:

Jimmy Anderson, Jimmy Anderson
When he makes it swing
The Barmy Army sing
For Jimmy Anderson

He'd prefer something Stone Roses inspired but Stone Roses songs are not very easily singalongable so we never cracked it. We will get there though. After all he has already eclipsed the man he replaced in terms of England wickets so he deserves more. At that time Ryan Sidebottom was foremost among our bowling heroes after his efforts in Sri Lanka and the first Test here. He was revelling in his role as Barmy Army hero and with his five-fer in the second innings we had reason to roar him on. I will always remember him for taking the winning catch in front of us and turning to celebrate before running to join his team-mates. An iconic image for those of us who were there.

If you ever needed an example of how the Barmy Army can polarise opinion then I have never seen a better example than that Test. The security guards loved us. The head of security actually thanked me on behalf of his staff for making the five days an enjoyable experience for them and for being polite and courteous. The security guards actually made an effort to come over at the end of the Test and applaud us, which was a first. They followed it up with a letter to BAHQ from all the security guards over the three Tests thanking us for being such a good crowd.

But as usual with the Army you have to take the rough with the smooth. And the rough in this instance was a very, very angry old cricket fan who we noticed berating Jimmy Savile for something. Gilo and I took it upon ourselves to go and see what was going on with the result that he left Jimmy and turned his ire on us. He ranted on about how cricket should be played in absolute silence at all times and how the racket being made was tantamount to heresy. We tried to reason with him and point out that while we appreciated his views there should surely be a place for those who wanted to sit in silence and those who wanted to sing – especially in a game like cricket where the grounds were so big (he was, after all, sat on the opposite side of the ground to the boisterous masses). But he wasn't to be mollified.

Then he became personal. 'I bet you guys have been to university, haven't you?' he asked. We agreed that we had and he went on to say that he was only a lowly railway worker but that 'intelligent guys like you' should know what the Barmy Army does and stands for is a terrible blight on the game. I'm not entirely sure how we kept a straight face at this time. I still wonder what he would have said if we'd pointed out that Gilo had been on more tours than anyone else there, that I actually worked for the Barmy Army, and that between us we were responsible for half the new songs that had been written on that tour and were the first to pipe up singing them. We decided that he could live without that knowledge and, finally agreeing to disagree, we went our separate ways.

After a victory celebration we departed Wellington and headed off via the beautiful Lake Taupo to the small town of Napier, which had almost certainly never seen anything like the invasion of English fans that hit it. If the population is only 60,000 then the arrival of 1,500 England fans is going to boost it by two per cent. I'm not sure if that is an accurate reflection of the numbers we boasted but you get the point. And never has a town as a whole embraced us so much. We were made welcome everywhere from the local cricket club that hosted the Barmy Army cricket game in which Matthew Hoggard would get a golden duck, to the social clubs that got us on stage to sing songs, to the other club that made us feel as if we'd all been members for years and the waterfront pubs that would send their red double-decker bus to take us over. (No, I haven't got a clue what a red double-decker bus was doing there either.) If the Barmy Army ever had a twin town I reckon this would probably be it and I think if England ever play there again most people could probably find accommodation with the locals, such was their hospitality.

That hospitality was equally evident when we were welcomed by the Hawke's Bay Cricket Club to play a match against them the day before the Test started. This was a landmark occasion as it proved to be the last overseas match Matthew Hoggard played for a representative England side. Hoggy was still out of the Test team and he turned up to this game, although not with the intention of playing. It wasn't purely out of love as he was contractually obliged to the Barmy Army to be there but when he asked what he was supposed to do someone came up with the idea of him fielding. I pointed out that if he was going to field he may as well bowl and when he replied that he was only wearing flip-flops I pointed out that as he was an international bowler a handicap might not be a bad thing. Besides it meant he could get his own back on one of the local lads who had been bowling to him in the nets. He had bounced Hoggy, little knowing that he would be facing him a couple of hours later. Hoggy's performance was more memorable for his batting, or lack of it. I suggested he open and when he magnanimously pointed out that he didn't want to deprive our guys of a bat I suggested he smash a few and then retire hurt after an over. Neither of us needed to worry. He holed out first ball, doing so to a local journo who wrote about the whole thing in next day's paper.

As much as we liked the town the same could not really be said of the cricket venue, which was actually a rugby ground. It doesn't take a genius to work out that cricket grounds and rugby grounds are different shapes and it did feel as though they were trying to shove a circle into a square. Or vice versa. That apart we still had a grass bank on which to sit so we were still happy. Not for long though as after half a dozen overs we'd lost three wickets for bugger all. KP got us out of the shit with a hundred and we managed to bat through the first day but for a fairly soporific 240. I took to taking pictures of the scoreboard when it declared a 'Maiden Over' as a weird aside, but there were far too many to catch – 88 in total throughout the match. That mean we effectively watched an entire day of maidens. Awesome.

New Zealand were rolled over within a day and it was our new hero Sidebottom doing the damage again with seven wickets. His song got a hell of a lot of airing on that tour. Then began an innings that would have a fairly dramatic effect on English cricket. We're not so overloaded with great openers that Andrew Strauss would not have made his way back eventually but it certainly looked like his career was about to have a forced hiatus. He'd scored less than one hundred runs in five innings in New Zealand thus far after being 'rested' for the Sri Lanka tour and was horribly out of form. But he made his position safe by collecting 177 runs and a year later he would be England captain. Three years later he'd be the England captain who won the Ashes in Australia. If everyone else was writing him off one of our number didn't. In one of the more famous Barmy Army spread bets he bought Strauss's runs at five quid a run over 40 something. Easy money.

England declared, setting New Zealand 553 to win. Six years previously, on the 2001–02 tour, England had set New Zealand 550 to win in the first Test and New Zealand had scared the bejeesus out of them by scoring the second highest second innings total of all time, 451, which included Nathan Astle's 222 off just 168 balls. This time round they would hit the fifth highest fourth innings score ever, with a late 77 from 40 balls from debutant Tim Southee just giving us a small scare. But England worked their way through, we had the rather bizarre vision of watching Monty Panesar fielding at sixth slip and we had our first overseas series victory since South Africa three years previously.

We found time during that Test to rectify a glaring omission from the Barmy Army songbook. Kevin Pietersen had smashed onto the scene in the 2005 Ashes, but despite featuring in nearly five overseas series since then we'd never put anything in words for him. It's true that there were certain people who thought his ego was large enough that it didn't need the extra massage of a song. Personally I found this a bit silly and churlish (although I had to laugh when were sat in a pub one day and started singing 'You're KP, You probably think this song is about you' to the tune of *You're So Vain* while discussing the issue).

Anyway, we decided it was time to sort this out and to get some inspiration we even had a word with Hoggy when he played for us. By this time there were enough budding songsters around that given a challenge there would be more than one result. Adrian Raffill came up trumps again, even though none of us had any idea of the song he was referring to and when we downloaded it on iTunes it sounded nothing like the tune he gave us. Heard of Gogol Bordello? No, neither had we. So the song *Start*

Wearing Purple meant nothing to us. When we finally heard it, it meant nothing to us either but by then we'd bodged a tune to the following:

He's got an average over 50
He likes to score a massive ton
His ego's bigger than his batty
He's Kevin Pietersen

Batty was originally batting, but upon consultation with KP's wife we found out that KP thought we were singing batty, which means backside in South Africa. So we changed it. Gilo also came up with a winner to the tune of *Hi Ho Silver Lining*:

You're our spinner and fourth in KP
That's where you bat
Showing your bling at fourth slip
With your big bold tats

Blinding us with your earrings,
From where we're sat,
You cut and drive the new ball
With your Woodworm bat

And its Hi Ho Super KP
Everywhere we go now Peter
You'll score a double century
Or maybe just a ton
You're Kevin Pietersen

But while those were both good, one of the most creative and apt efforts turned up out of the blue from a Barmy Army veteran and general legend, JV. Bearing in mind that KP's missus used to be in Liberty X, what better way to show our appreciation than by using a Liberty X song? So he used the tune of *Just A Little Bit* to come up with:

KP
When you walk out to the crease
You're sexy
You are England's number four
You've got a ton to score

Hook! Just a little bit
Pull! Just a little bit
Drive! Just a little bit
Score just a little bit more
KP score a little bit more

Just a little bit more, just a little bit!
Hook! Just a little bit
Pull! Just a little bit
Drive! Just a little bit
Score just a little bit more
KP score a little bit more

He came up with it on the last couple of days of the tour and bizarrely he got the opportunity to sing it to KP's wife Jessica down the phone. A group of friendly locals had invited us up to their box for a beer or two so we'd taken to paying them a daily visit to share an ale with them. We took Bill and Jimmy up there to sing and play from the box which entertained both the Barmy Army on the bank and the more sedate fans in the stand below us. After England's victory we popped up to say goodbye and thank them for their hospitality and as we were hanging out looking at the post-match interviews we noticed the WAGs sat around below us having a drink. We dispatched Gilo's wife Hayley down there to see if Jessica liked KP's new song.

The next thing we knew the girls were beckoning us down so Gilo, Doug, Raffill and I descended and joined their party. They asked us to go through the repertoire, paying particular attention to the song we had for their other half. We had to ring JV and get him to sing the song to Jessica. It was yet another surreal moment in our Barmy Army 'careers' and we enjoyed it thoroughly. When we thought we might be overstaying our welcome they were quick to keep us around and plied us with some wine. There was an awkward moment when Ian Bell's lovely girlfriend, now wife, Chantal, asked us what song we had for him. We knew there was one but we'd never sung it much and stumbled a bit.

I met her again in South Africa a couple of years later and triumphantly told her that I had come up with a new song for him. I couldn't quite remember it at the time (something to do with Stroh Rum), but she asked me to email it to her. It's never made it to the stands, but I sent her the following in honour of his 199 against South Africa, to the tune of *(I Would Walk) 500 miles*:

When we were at Lord's
And Belly came up to the crease
He said today I'm going to score a double ton

And when he went out
He smacked the Saffas round the ground
He was scoring boundaries for fun

And he would have scored 200 runs
If he'd have scored just one run more
If he'd have run three instead of two
Or just hit one more ball for four

Ian Bell, Ian Bell...

That encounter with the lovely wives and girlfriends in Napier was the preamble to an epic night. Everyone had been asking me where the end of tour party would be and I quickly realised that in my role as Barmy Army liaison I'd better sort something out. We settled on the Thirsty

Whale and arranged for their double-decker bus to pick us up. There was method in the madness in that we knew this was in the vicinity of the team hotel, although we had no solid plans to interact with them. Big G then said that if 'a few' of us wanted to go over there we would be made welcome. But we'd always preached inclusivity so it was decided that rather than a few people leaving our party the players would have to come to us if we were going to mix. We didn't tell them that but we just figured it wouldn't be fair if some of us got to enjoy their company but not others. We needn't have worried.

The bar was already full and good times were being had when the doors opened and pretty much the entire squad descended on us. This kicked up the atmosphere and the singing started in earnest. We went through much of the repertoire while the players mixed in or stood on the stairway looking over the crowd.

I was happy enough that they were there and that everyone was having a good time although I had little idea what to say to any of them. Mind you I had little idea of what one reserve wicketkeeper was saying to me which may just have been his broad Durham accent or maybe one too many vodka and red bulls. What I did get out of Phil Mustard was that he had asked Peter Moores if he could sit with us on that final day but was rejected.

The singing had ceased as everyone continued to have a good time when Big G came up to me and said that Vaughany wanted us to start singing again. I'm not really sure what inspired me to do this but I went up to the skipper, whom I had never met before, and told him that we would be quite happy to start singing again but if he was so keen then maybe he might like to kick it off. For a man who has faced up to the world's fastest bowlers he looked scared shitless and insisted he didn't know the songs. I told him I would feed him the words and we headed to the staircase running alongside one wall of the bar. It wasn't hard to get the whole army singing

'Vaughany, give us a song, Vaughany Vaughany give us a song', at which point he looked to me. I have no idea which songs we started with but he came out with the first line and we took care of the rest.

What I really wasn't expecting was him asking me to get other members of the team to sing. None of the players escaped as the Army asked them one by one to 'give us a song' and they all had to remember a tune to sing. Monty Panesar in particular looked petrified before coming out with *God Save The Queen*. The real hero of the night though was Paul Collingwood. Big G's version of *The Lion Sleeps Tonight* was famous but having tried the falsetto bit myself once when he wasn't around I discovered it's very hard to do. Not that that stopped Colly, who stood on the bar and gave it a bloody good go.

A couple of the players who did make that night told us a couple of years later that it was the best night of their lives – Alastair Cook still talks about it. That might suggest that cricketers don't get out as often as some people think they do – or that we're even better company than we thought. My memories of the tour drawing to a very late close were having a cheeky fag and beer with Tim Ambrose, clearly revelling in his introduction to Test cricket, and then not being able to sleep because Jägerbombs in the Thirsty Whale had a whole can of Red Bull in each one.

For new songs, new people, friendly locals, lack of hassle, an overseas tour victory and a beautiful country to enjoy that New Zealand tour was one of my favourites, although it's fair to say my liver does not agree.

Twelve

There's much more to the Barmy Army than watching cricket

It's fun being in the Barmy Army

MANY PEOPLE ARE amazed when they find out that the Barmy Army is a business as opposed to an ad hoc collection of cricket fanatics, so they'd be even more surprised if they knew just how many different activities it gets involved in. As I've pointed out the business has never made a huge amount of money and it's usually a case of finding ways to keep the business going rather than a desire to make millions that inspire some of the more random commercial partnerships, and it's taken us down some very strange roads.

If the Barmy Army is not particularly good at making money for itself, it has proved spectacularly successful at raising money for charity. This has long been a strong part of the Barmy Army ethos and as far back as 1996–97 the Army raised £900 for the Soweto Cricket Club by playing them in a charity game.

Durban orphanages have also benefited from Barmy Army fundraising and when the tsunami hit during the 2004–05 tour of South Africa money was raised to help the relief effort. The Barmy Army will be forever immortalised in Hampton village in Sri Lanka where its name has been emblazoned on the local medical facility as thanks for its help.

Other beneficiaries of the Barmy Army's generosity have been the Pakistan Earthquake appeal during the 2006 tour and Help for Heroes, for whom we sold wristbands and raised money during the 2009 Ashes. There has also been a lot of support for established charities such as The Ben Hollioake Fund, the Chris Cairns Cancer Appeal and close links with Chance to Shine. In Bangladesh in 2010 people even went to the extreme of wearing Australia shirts to support the Shirt of Hurt campaign for Sport Relief. Those charities benefited to the tune of more than £100,000 between them over the years but if that was proof of the Army's fundraising efforts then the work during the 2010–11 Ashes series in getting behind the McGrath Foundation put all that in the shade. Throughout that series the Barmy Army sold the McGrath Foundation pink T-shirts and stubby holders, held McGrath Foundation events in its headquarters and dedicated its Fans Ashes events to the cause, raising £25,000.

Ever since that first match in Soweto and up to the Fans Ashes the Barmy Army has often managed to combine playing cricket with raising money. The Barmy Army Cricket Club has played hundreds of matches, sometimes for charity and sometimes just for the joy of the game. The match against Soweto may have been successful at raising money but BACC's performance left something to be desired. After running round the park for 40 overs they found themselves chasing a target of more than 300. Without Darren Stevens, who was to become a Kent regular, BACC would have been completely humiliated as opposed to completely embarrassed because he scored 50-odd of the sub-100 total. As the tenth wicket fell the Soweto fielders started to leave the field to celebrate their victory but they had reckoned without BACC's cunning plan. Oblivious to the laws of the game, they sent in batsman after batsman although it was no use. Despite using 25 batsmen they still didn't get anywhere near the target, or even close to batting out their overs!

There's never any lack of sides willing to take on the Barmy Army and there have been a few famous faces taking part along the way. Mark Butcher opened the batting for the Army when they took on Bunburys in 2005. Matthew Hoggard also opened the batting as we've chronicled elsewhere when in New Zealand. Jimmy Adams donned the Barmy Army colours against his old friend Courtney Walsh in the Caribbean while Nick Knight and Graeme Hick were just two of the stars turning out during the inaugural Fans Ashes.

The Barmy Army had always played games against its Australian counterparts, The Fanatics, but this became more serious in 2009 with the creation of the official Fans Ashes tournament. It attracted media coverage, had its own sponsor, npower, and great cricketers turning out on either side with Ian Harvey and Jason Gillespie turning out for the Fanatics. The rivalry was rekindled in Australia, where England took back the trophy Australia had won in England.

Another regular feature on the BACC calendar is an annual game between the Rest of England BACC and Stafford CC Barmy Army. The event has raised more than £16,000 for the Leukaemia Research Fund over the years.

If the adults games are semi-serious, the Barmy Army Colts definitely represents a step up in competitiveness. Mark Stear took the idea of the Barmy Army CC one step further by creating a Barmy Army youth side and this quickly developed into an entity with numerous representative teams from different age groups. The Colts come from all over the country and as there is no real England Colts team it is perhaps the closest thing to an international colts set-up there is. They tour all over the world and provide great experience to young cricketers. The recent Ashes series saw the kids win 10 games out of 11 against various Aussie sides. With many different age groups and a huge variety of games it's a great way to get the kids involved in the Barmy Army at the same time as improving their cricketing experience.

The Fans Ashes in 2009 was also a handy platform to launch our attempt at having a hit record. It was an attempt doomed to a fairly dramatic failure, but one that still amuses me as an experience to this day. We had had some preliminary internal discussions about releasing a song for that summer anyway and we'd had initial chats with the PR company of a foodstuff I won't mention about getting involved in their single. But they were only interested in a PR stunt and any budget they had was going to be spent on having an ex-England cricket player singing, which meant they would be just using the Barmy Army for their own commercial ends. We'd been down that road before and didn't fancy it again so we reckoned there was nothing in it for us.

As we contemplated what, if anything, to do next we were approached by Matt Jagger, a man with a history in the music business, who already had an idea for a song. It was originally a one-minute wonder proposed for use as a promo for a gaming company but they didn't understand the concept so he approached the Barmy Army with the proposal to turn it into a hit record. This sounded more up our alley so we collaborated with him on making it into a complete song. In this case collaborating meant me rewriting existing verses and adding new ones to make it worthy of the Barmy Army. All of which meant I ended up on the credits and had my own record deal. The final version went as follows:

(Chorus)
Hey Hey Ricky, what you gonna do?
Hey Hey Ricky, get on your kangaroo
We're taking back the Ashes, they don't belong to you
Cos we're the Barmy Army, we're England through and through

You tried to find a bowler but it ended up in tears
You once had Warne and McGrath now it's just that
Brett Lee 'Spears'
You'll try to get a century, but we know how you bat
So go on back down under or we'll bring out Gary Pratt
Repeat chorus

Symonds has gone fishing, Gilchrist is long gone
You have got no spinners, we've got Panesar and Swann
You'll always be a whinger, when will you ever learn
You'll never get your hands on our little Ashes urn
Repeat chorus

You cook shrimps on the barbie, drink beer that's really
weak
Your country isn't quite as old as some of our antiques
You didn't like our Bodyline, wish Beefy had been yours
Now we've got Freddie and KP to hit sixes and fours
Repeat chorus

Not content with recording the song, we also needed a video and after finding a very nice and friendly gambling company to put up the money in return for a bit of branding we did exactly that. A bunch of Barmy Army stalwarts turned up to a ground in North London not knowing what to expect apart from a fun day. But for the film crew this wasn't about fun, it was a serious business. The director was an absolute luvvy who thought he was dealing with pros, not amateurs who were more interested in a beer than having someone shout at them with a megaphone.

Beer was actually banned so we could concentrate on our jobs and as you can imagine that not only went against the ethos of the Barmy Army but meant we couldn't get the Dutch courage many of us needed to appear before the cameras. We had the singer playing himself and another guy playing Ricky Ponting. The setting was a traditional

England cricket afternoon and we put Ricky in a series of situations where he was getting hounded by the Barmy Army.

If you watch the video (it's still available on YouTube) you will notice a tall guy with stubble, wearing a blonde wig and a couple of cricket balls instead of breasts when it gets to the line about 'Brett Lee Spears'. If you hark back to my first Australia tour you will remember that I had been likened to Brett Lee then and so when it came to finding someone to play that particular role I was always going to be favourite, only this time with more embarrassing consequences. I'm still not sure what was worse, the wig and boobs or the Cricket Australia T-shirt they made me wear. Yuk.

There were lots of extras in Barmy Army shirts, but the concept also required some great historical English figures to appear. When the call came for someone to play Robin Hood I somehow got railroaded into that as well. After Brett Lee Spears I figured things couldn't get much worse anyway. You'll see him running through forests and near the front when we do the Ricky Roo – a dance created specifically for the single. I've never been much of a dancer anyway (not unless smashed at any rate) as you can probably tell if you make it to the end of the video. The real glamour was provided by the Marston's Maidens and some other lovely ladies who took attention away from the less aesthetically pleasing Barmy Army types.

The video culminates in a chase scene where we all hassle Ricky across the cricket pitch until he makes his escape in a hot air balloon, the one with our sponsor's name on it. Now our actor was no hot air balloonist so he got clear instructions on how to operate it. The real balloonist crouched down in the basket so he would be out of shot, but on hand if anything went wrong. Unfortunately he was in no position to affect what did go wrong. As Ricky jumped into the basket and hit the hot air burner a sudden gust of wind resulted in him setting the balloon on fire instead of filling it with air. They had to bring a new balloon down on a different day to finish the shot.

The record was backed by *The Sun* and it was on this we pinned our hopes of success. With the support of a big paper like that we thought we might have a chance of selling a few. Unfortunately on the day the record came out Michael Jackson died. His death took over the entire paper, meaning our little song was starved of any publicity and there was no chance of it regaining lost ground. It did get played on a few radio stations and I had an on air record-off with Phil Tufnell (the ex-cricketer who released the song with food company links) but it was all destined to be a fun and interesting exercise rather than a money spinner. I'll stick to Tim Ambrose ditties in future.

We should have known better. It wasn't the Barmy Army's first assault on the pop charts, that was *We Are England* for the 1997 Ashes series. Unfortunately the record was released two months too late, just after England had been defeated. In 1999 they had another go, with *Come On England* for the World Cup. Despite appearances by many sports personalities and celebrities in the video it was also doomed to failure, as were other sporadic attempts.

As well as the magazine publishing arm you have already read so much about there has been book publishing. *Barmy Cricket* was released in 2006 and the official history of the *Barmy Army, Everywhere We Went,* came out in 2011. And occasional stabs at video documentaries of the tours have been made. These were completed in Mumbai 2006 and Pakistan 2005 but without great success. The best televisual record of the Barmy Army exploits came during the 2006–07 Ashes series in Australia when Fox commissioned a show called *An Aussie Goes Barmy* where Gus Worland spent his waking moments with the Barmy Army throughout the whole tour. The show was narrated by his best mate, film actor Hugh Jackman, and was a big hit.

The Barmy Army's real success has always been merchandising. It is what the business and indeed the entire entity was built on and on which it continues to thrive. Barmy Army travel has evolved over the years and takes many people overseas to watch the cricket. The Army has bought and resold thousands upon thousands of match tickets at home and abroad and even has a financial services arm but it's merchandise that is the stable business.

While the Barmy Army logo has been applied to more things than you can imagine and the BA office is like an Aladdin's Cave of odds and sods the staples remain the same. How many Barmy Army T-shirts have been sold over the years? No one can really hazard a guess but one thing's for sure. Thousands more will be sold on every tour so while they may not ever be top of the pops, the best-seller lists or the DVD charts, you'll always see evidence of the Army around.

Thirteen

Touring the Caribbean

There were no more balls in the second Test

Touring experiences in the Caribbean
2009 1st Test (Kingston, Jamaica)
2nd Test (St John's, Antigua)
3rd Test (Bridgetown, Barbados)
4th Test (Port of Spain, Trinidad)

IF AUSTRALIA IS THE glory tour, then a trip to the Caribbean is not far behind. The word Caribbean has a magic all of its own and conjures up images of sun-kissed beaches, preternaturally blue seas and ice-cold beverages consumed in beautiful heat under the shade of palm trees. And for cricket fans there is an even bigger attraction. The Caribbean is Sir Viv Richards, it's tall, scary fast bowlers, it's the three Ws, Sir Garfield Sobers, Brian Lara and many more.

The West Indies is unique in that the team does not represent one nation but several and as such is the only one not to use a national flag. The flag they have chosen sums up everything about this part of the world: cricket stumps and a palm tree on an island with blue sea in the background. Although there is national identity within the team and supporters there is also a great collective pride in the area.

I was once asked why the Caribbean tour is so popular and my answer explained all of the above and more.

Because this is the tour where you can bring your non-cricket loving partner and they will probably be happiest. I somehow managed to persuade Sam, my then girlfriend, to go to Pakistan but there's little doubt she would have been happier had we been heading off to Antigua. And on my visit to the Caribbean in 2009 I had little difficulty persuading my new girlfriend, Klara, that ten days in Barbados was a good idea. When I answered that question I actually said that it's easy for men to 'bring wives and girlfriends' on tour to the Caribbean. Unfortunately for me I was asked it on live radio (more of that later) and one of the girls in the Barmy Army took umbrage. She never said anything to me directly but insisted to one of my friends that I was a horrible sexist man who didn't take into account that some girls like cricket and bring their boyfriends and husbands, not the other way round. Perhaps I should have said people can bring their partners, but the truth is you only had to look around you to prove my point. For whatever reason cricket remains a predominantly male arena and there were more wives and girlfriends on that tour than any other.

I was on duty again in the West Indies as a Barmy Army staff member. In truth I couldn't have picked a better tour to work on as it's the most expensive tour to complete. Instead of flying to one country and travelling around internally this tour entails visiting several different countries with lots of international flights and they don't come cheap. Neither does accommodation as there isn't a great deal of budget offerings. The Caribbean lends itself to holiday-making, not backpacking.

But before we could worry about accommodation and getting around, we had to get to Jamaica for the first Test and that was a real issue for a lot of people. The day before the majority of fans were due to fly out snow fell heavily on the UK and as anyone who has lived there during a blizzard of the white stuff will testify we are singularly dreadful at coping with such weather. The country generally grinds to a halt in a way that must bemuse the likes of Russia and Canada. Airports struggle to function and getting to an airport becomes a lottery as transport services implode. If it hadn't been for fortuitous circumstances I, like many others, would have missed the first three days of the tour because of the snow. I had Klara to thank for it.

We had met in late November and had been on just a handful of dates before I had trotted off to India for the two-Test 2008 series. I went straight from there to Romania to spend Christmas and New Year with friends and she joined me, partly because she knew I would be back in the country for only four weeks before disappearing off to the Caribbean for six. Upon arriving back from Romania she booked a trip to Barbados as well but because we'd been apart for much of the few weeks we'd known each other we decided to go away for my final weekend in the country. Of all of the places I could have chosen for a romantic, or should I say dirty, weekend, a hotel between Croydon and Gatwick Airport was hardly ideal, but it was practical. We were at the stage in a relationship where being together was more important than where we were and as I was due to fly out from Gatwick on the Monday morning it meant we could stay an extra night and she could head straight into London to get to work.

We had been for a walk in the snow on the Sunday as it gradually covered the country in a blanket of virginal whiteness and I shivered because I didn't have much in the way of winter clothing with me; big coats are hardly de rigeur in the Caribbean. Come Monday morning we hopped on the airport shuttle bus and were at Gatwick in a few minutes. I said goodbye to Klara and turned my attention to the numerous text messages and phone calls I had been receiving. Most of them were asking the same things. Where was I? Had I got to the airport? How delayed was the plane? The answers were: Gatwick. Yes (evidently). Not at all. Gatwick was so quiet that morning because most of the people who should have been there were stuck on the motorways and byways of Britain, including the guy who would have given me a lift had I not been away for the weekend.

I was forced to be the bearer of bad news, explaining to those struggling to get to the airport that the only plane not delayed that morning was the Virgin flight to Jamaica. In the end the plane was half empty and just to rub it in for those who arrived a little late they spent two hours de-icing it while refusing to allow anyone else to board. I had four seats to myself, chatted to some new and old faces and had a generally pleasant flight. And if I thought my friends stuck at the airport were having a bad time then the person I should really have worried about was Klara. With no trains, no taxis, no coaches and pretty much nothing moving she was stuck in Gatwick airport, making it back home only shortly before I landed in Kingston. It's one thing being stuck in an airport waiting to go on holiday but when you haven't even been on holiday that must have sucked. She cursed me a lot, apparently.

But enough of the vagaries of the English weather and our inability to deal with it. The lucky ones who had made the flight were in high spirits and after landing in Kingston we checked into our hotel and headed to our HQ for the next week. We have had many Barmy Army HQs over the years. We have had fantastic hosts, average hosts, brilliant bars and shabby pubs. In truth we're not overly fussy as we can turn any venue into a party venue but there was something rather special about this one. Our host was none other than Courtney Walsh. That is the legend that is Courtney Walsh, he of 519 Test wickets at an average of 24.44 (and a Test record 43 ducks – sorry Cuddy). He had done some work with our PR girl Becky Addley on another project when I first met him to interview him for our tour magazine. He was effusive in his praise of the Barmy Army and what they brought to cricket but also generous in his offers of hospitality and organisation, offers he more than lived up to.

We were warmly welcomed to Cuddy'z, his bar in Kingston, and Courtney was geniality personified as we downed the first of many Red Stripes and eased our way into another epic adventure. I missed most of the pre-Test Barmy Army CC game he had arranged the next day by virtue of attending a press conference to pick up my press credentials, much to Cuddy's chagrin.

'Hey Winslow, I thought I was going to be playing cricket against you today,' he chastised when I finally turned up. I don't think he believed me when I told him I couldn't play. When it comes to Barmy Army CC tour games I usually don't get involved, partly because of the lack of any obvious cricketing talent but also because I know there are a lot of people who want desperately to play in the games. On this occasion I would have been happy to get involved and I was needed because we couldn't get a full team out. My replacement, as it happens, was a friend of Courtney who said he would make up our numbers. As ringers go Jimmy Adams is not the worst you could pick, although even he couldn't even out the teams in spite of his batting and bowling heroics.

Despite the amazing welcome and hospitality of Courtney and his gang there is a downside to touring Jamaica. Because while it may have magical connotations, Kingston is not the world's safest city. I'm sure if you go on holiday to Montego Bay you would rave about Jamaica as a tourist destination, but spend a week in Kingston and you won't have the same feeling. The advice was to not go anywhere on our own and try not to walk anywhere. As usual the reality was not quite as bad as the warnings, but we still had a couple of muggings and occasions when our brethren were told in no uncertain terms to get themselves out of a particular part of town.

The real mugging was on the pitch though. England were in a right old muddle as in the six or so weeks since they had left the field in Mohali they had somehow contrived to lose both captain and coach as KP's attempted coup, if that's what it was, backfired spectacularly and both he and Peter Moores left their jobs. It's hard to believe now England are the world's number one Test playing nation (as I write in June 2012) that the Flower–Strauss axis started off so uncertainly, ignominiously and with neither really sure if their roles were temporary or full-time.

Not that we were really giving this too much thought as we headed down to Sabina Park for the first day of the tour. Sabina Park is one of those great cricket venues which conjures up visions of sporting glory. This was the ground where Sir Garfield Sobers hit 365 not out, a Test record score that would stand for decades and is still the fourth highest in history. Less gloriously it was also the venue for one of the shortest Tests ever on England's 1998 tour when the game was abandoned because the pitch was deemed unfit. With the Blue Mountains in the background and a quintessential Caribbean feel it was a great cricket ground. Unfortunately the use of 'was' in that sentence is perhaps the most important word in it. Now it's a ground with two concrete monstrosities facing each other, not much in between and it has about as much character as a cricket ball. You can't walk around the entire ground, which is a basic amenity any decent cricket ground should offer, and it's soulless.

But if we were unimpressed with the development we were too excited to worry much at first. The ground was almost empty on that first day and we wondered where the famed West Indian support was. We knew they had fallen out of love with cricket a bit, but this was ridiculous and made the hideous stands seem all the more ugly and needless. But if you want to fill a cricket ground with otherwise apathetic townspeople the way to do it is to win matches so it would help if the England cricket team had one of its calamities. By day four the place was heaving and partying thanks to a performance of such woefulness as to make all of the other performances of woefulness seem not that woeful. You expect the odd disaster against ridiculously good Australian sides, or on the subcontinent, but in the West Indies against a pretty poor side we were expecting to improve our win ratios, not to be subject to something that came straight out of our worst nightmares.

The Test had been meandering along in a non-exciting fashion. England scored a fairly undramatic 318 in the first innings, with ex-captain KP lambasted by everyone for playing a shot too many and getting out for 97. This castigation conveniently ignored the fact he was the highest scorer in the team by some distance. Besides, it wasn't really KP's fault. He was on 97 when Hereford Rich, who had been with us on that epic last night in the Blue Ice bar in Chandigarh, started singing:

Kevin Pietersen scored a run
Eey-aye-eey-aye-oh
And with that run he scored his ton
Eey-aye-eey-aye-oh

By the time I had turned round to tell him to shut up unless he jinxed it KP was out, and I have neither forgiven Hereford nor let him forget that moment.

In reply the West Indies racked up 220 for 1 and were well on top, but England pulled it back to 392 all out, which didn't seem too disastrous in the circumstances. Both teams were trundling along at about two and half runs an over (when Chris Gayle's strike rate is just over 50 you know there's not a lot in the way of fireworks and Ryan Sidebottom's 24 overs had gone for just 35 runs); it seemed like a pretty sedate Test match.

And so we turned up to day four expecting nothing dramatic. The West Indies were still in, but with three wickets left it was merely a case of finishing their innings, putting on a decent total with a draw the obvious if uninspiring start to the series. Hmmm. Reading the scorecard of what actually happened is still painful, so much so that I won't include it here. Suffice to say England were all out for 51. Nearly half of those runs were scored by Andrew Flintoff as no one else made it to double figures. Alastair Cook, Matt Prior, Stuart Broad and Stephen Harmison got ducks. Kevin Pietersen and Paul Collingwood only went one better. Jerome Taylor conceded only 11 runs off the nine overs it took him to take five wickets, and two of those were no-balls. If we thought the strike rates had been low before then the 1.53 runs per over England scored made this torture even worse. If you are wondering why I am reeling off all these statistics when I said I wouldn't reproduce the scorecard you would have a fair question. I'm finding it therapeutic to be honest and at the same time hard to believe. This is probably the first time I have actually brought myself to analyse what happened that day. You can actually have quite a lot of fun with it. The six extras, for example, represented nearly 12 per cent of the team total. How cool are cricket stats?

Anyway, enough of that. As usual cricket giveth and cricket taketh away. Even in the worst of times there is usually something good to find and this was no different. My press accreditation included photography credentials which meant I could go where I wanted when I wanted. Now these were genuine as I was writing daily match reports for barmyarmy.com but in truth they were most useful because they saved me the cost of entry into the ground, which was where I needed to be because the whole point of my match reports was that they came from within the crowd and not from the press box. But as the presentations were about to start a mate suggested this might be the time to make use of them. He had a point.

I struggled through the crowds of West Indian fans, waved my pass at the security guy and found myself on the pitch in the midst of a celebrating West Indian team. My Canon Powershot G9 is a great little camera but it doesn't exactly make me look like a pro (at least I had a camera, otherwise I would have looked very stupid). But who cared? I did my best to look like a pro as I walked backwards around the ground in front of the lap of honour, snapping away as if I had a deadline to keep. As the lap came to an end in front of the Barmy Army section I heard our band of brothers shouting 'Winslow, Winslow, Winslow'.

Someone pointed out that my ego was big enough without any of that nonsense thank you very much and he may have had a point but what the hell, I drank it all in. If I thought that was the surreal end to another surreal moment I then realised that I was walking next to the fastest man on earth, Usain Bolt. And people were chanting my name!

The lad who suggested I go on to the pitch, and the same one who then admonished everyone for chanting my name, was one Ben Osbourne who, coincidentally, was the guy who would have given me a lift to Gatwick but missed the flight. My match report that day largely involved him and here it is:

'Any England tour is always hugely anticipated by those who are fortunate enough to be going on it. A trip to the West Indies has something magical about it. Not just the romantic notions of islands with brilliant beaches and azure waters, but the people, the enthusiasm for the game and the recent happy memories for England fans.

'So imagine it's Monday February 2 and you're due to fly out to Jamaica. You get in the car, pick up some friends and make your way to Gatwick. Only there's a problem because traffic on the M25 is moving about as fast as an asthmatic snail. You get stuck in traffic for hours and when you finally get moving you call your friend at the airport (that's your humble writer) who is the bearer of bad tidings as he is about to board the plane.

'The next flight out is not for three days, which means you have to spend your time in a country that seems incapable of coping with any weather condition other than mild. You watch England struggle along with a cup of tea in one hand and the heating on full. But that's OK as you'll still be there before long. You arrive in the country at the end of day two and although things aren't looking great, at least you've made it. Day three is not the worst for England and things are looking up.

'As you arrive at the ground on day four you realise you've left your ticket at the hotel. A ticket is about the same price as a two-way taxi so you utilise the ridiculously inefficient queuing system to buy a new ticket. Admittedly you have to scrounge $20 from someone when you realise that you've also left your money at home, so maybe that Red Stripe at 9am wasn't such a good idea. Then you have to sit through one of the most embarrassing capitulations in English history (and god knows there have been a few) and get on the bus back to your hotel in the knowledge you have paid for six days of Test cricket, seen one and a half and most of that was dreadful.

'That is the story of Ben Osbourne, bless him. He could be forgiven for being depressed, but an hour after play had finished he was in his pool with another Red Stripe in his hand which wasn't the worst place in the world to be. In between the morbid jokes there were moments of complete and utter despair. No-one could remember anything worse – and with the collective experiences of people there, that was truly saying something.

'As we lost the last Ashes series 5-0 there was a devil-may-care sing-song, but here there was just a collective disbelief. Yes the sun was still shining, yes we were a lucky group of people to even be here, but really did we deserve that? For the first time we actually don't want to see any of the players when we head out tonight. We wouldn't know what to say to them anyway. And even the idea of heading down to Courtney Walsh's bar is tempered by the fact that the chances are most of the West Indian team will be in there celebrating... probably singing *London*

Bridge is falling down which seems to be a favourite round here when beating the English.

'By then we will hopefully have had enough beer and rum to join them and congratulate them – there was the usual appreciation of the winning team as they did a lap of honour but this was as bitter a pill as we have had to swallow for a long time. At least Ben has got five more weeks in the sun, but any more of this and he may be wishing Gatwick never opened again.'

We did head down to Courtney's bar, of course, and met defeat in the way we do victory. We certainly looked to be having more fun than the West Indies players, who stood around moodily as the band played and Courtney got a few of us up on the mike to sing Barmy Army songs. One of the girls was awestruck by the sight of Chris Gayle but too scared to approach him, so I went up and asked him if he would mind having a picture taken with her. He grunted, which I took as assent, and when I congratulated him and asked him if he would be so kind as to not beat us like that again he looked at me as if I was a piece of cricket dirt on his spikes. I'd hate to meet him if he'd lost although I get the feeling he meets those two diametrically opposite spectres with equal reactions. I used to think he was the epitome of cool but not so much now.

We introduced Courtney to the joy of Jägerbombs that night. Lots of them. On the next day he had arranged a trip to a small island where we could finally buy into the Caribbean hype with great weather, a barbecue, beach cricket (playing beach cricket... with Courtney Walsh... awesome) and Red Stripe. Except when I and a couple of my fellow rabble rousers started on the booze and offered Courtney one he intimated that he was not particularly keen to imbibe alcoholic beverages with us ever again after that post-match party.

It was a magical day to finish off a turbulent week and the next day saw us on our way to Antigua. It might be the fact that I saw the whole island rather than just the capital city but Antigua was far more what I had in mind when I dreamt of a trip to the Caribbean than Jamaica. It's a great island with a small capital 'city' or town, St John's, that has just enough to keep you interested and there are other points of interest even though you can explore the whole island in a day. Nelson's Dockyard is a restored British colonial naval station named after Horatio, who was the Senior Naval Officer of the Leeward Islands between 1784 and 1787 before going on to win the Battle of Trafalgar 20 years later. And if you fancy a day on the beach you can choose a different one for every day of the year as the island boasts 365 of them.

Not that many people got out and about much as the large majority of accommodation on Antigua is all-inclusive resorts, the like of which repulse me. Personally I can't think of anything worse than going to a resort, eating and drinking there every night, hitting the beach during the day and doing precious little else. You could be anywhere in the world and it's just the same old same old every day. I hated it so much that although I had access to free drinks all the time I found myself more than willing to head elsewhere and pay for the privilege. At the same time I appreciate that's what some people want, although what they might not want is to turn up and find half the Barmy Army in the same hotel. As usual we entertained the majority and upset the occasional person but overall our tenure was a success, I think. Someone sent a letter to the *Daily Mail* insisting we had ruined their holiday and that was immediately countered by a reply from someone who insisted we had made theirs. You win some, you lose some. One girl on holiday certainly enjoyed our visit. She's been in a relationship with the Barmy Boy she met there ever since.

I'd never really got involved in selling merchandising before but from the moment I headed down to breakfast in our hotel and saw my good friend Gilo trying to serve a million people at once I offered to give him a hand

and really got into it during this Test. The love for Barmy Army merchandise and demand for it always staggers me. It's the ultimate cricket tour souvenir for most people and they can't wait to get their hands on it. And chatting to people and selling to them is strangely a lot more enjoyable than it always looked. I wouldn't want to do it all the time and never at the expense of actually watching cricket but the banter and chat really immerses you in the event. There was a point when Gilo and I were locked up in his room counting money as everyone else was partying downstairs when I looked up solemnly at him and asked him 'how the hell did we end up doing this?' But overall it was another good experience and one I would repeat very occasionally afterwards. It felt like the essence of the Barmy Army to me.

Several of us got out of bed early on day one of the Test to head down to the ground to set up and sell Barmy Army merchandise. As we turned up at the entrance we were stopped by security, understandable as only official vehicles were allowed inside. But when we disembarked and started to drag cricket bags stuffed full of T-shirts, caps and hats out of the back of the bus the security guard mistook us for the England cricket team and waved us through. What on earth he thought the England cricket team were doing wearing Barmy Army T-shirts and arriving in a taxi minibus I have no idea but it gave us a good chuckle and saved us carrying our bags too far.

As we ambled round yet another new venue there was reason to be positive. While the ground bearing the name of Antigua's favourite son, Sir Vivian Richards, was also victim to the idea of having two huge stands facing each other, you could at least circumnavigate it and the land between the stands consisted of a tiered grass bank on one side. This looked like a place for the Barmy Army to congregate and watch the game in collective comfort. This grass bank had lots of potential, but it would remain untapped. England's score of 51 in the first Test was appalling, but it was 44 more than they would score in this one. That was not because of the profligacy of our batsmen, it was because the field was more akin to the 365 beaches adorning the island than a Test match venue. Bowlers were running in and losing their run-up because the ground couldn't support their weight properly. The game was abandoned after just ten balls and the only reason the game lasted more than ten minutes is because there was a rain break after eight.

Now I am lucky enough to go to the majority of England's overseas Test matches and you get used to the unexpected so I hung around in a state of bemusement and wondered what would happen next without being too concerned or upset. What would be would be. But can you imagine if this was your big trip, your one Test match, your opportunity to travel the world and see England play international cricket overseas? How livid would you be? There were no announcements and the very notion that it would be possible to play a Test match on what amounted to a beach was ridiculous. To find out just how ridiculous I made use of the shiny photographer's pass round my neck to venture onto the pitch. As I approached the middle it wasn't difficult to see why the major issue had been the bowler's run-up. Such was the lack of binding in the 'soil' that some old guy was pulling up huge chunks of turf covered in sand by hand and putting them into a wheelbarrow. What he was expecting to achieve by this I don't know, but I do know that within half an hour the bowler's run-up was a trench running through the pitch and he hadn't needed a spade to dig it. If he could pull it up by hand then how on earth (no pun intended, but I quite like it now I've put it in) were bowlers expected to put their bodyweight on it without it giving way? It was a shambles.

As the Barmy Army's media liaison guy my phone started going a bit mental and I wandered around giving interviews to radio and television stations back home to explain just what was happening at the ground. Credit must go, as it so often does, to the England players who made an effort to leave the changing room and mingle with all the disgruntled fans who were hanging around wondering what to do with themselves. The players signed autographs, chatted about anything and everything and basically turned what was a rubbish turn of events into an experience of which a lot of people will still have fond memories. And that was the end of the second Test as people gradually dispersed back to their hotels for an afternoon in the pub or on the beach, or in some cases a combination of both. Rumours had already started to do the rounds as to what might happen. Antigua might be a tiny island but it has three top class cricket grounds. There was the beach we had already seen (the joke doing the rounds was that Antigua now had 366 beaches to choose from), Sir Allen Stanford's ground that had been the venue for the previous year's Twenty20 for 20 game and the famous old Antigua Recreation Ground. The only issue was that one of them was a sandpit, one was not really a Test cricket venue and the other was dilapidated and not really in a state to host Test cricket by virtue of the fact that it was now used predominantly for football matches. Not only that, but the upper tier of the famous Oil Drum stand had been condemned by FIFA as unsafe for use in international sport. This was going to be interesting.

The West Indies Cricket Board had to do something. As well as the disgruntled Antiguans there were a few thousand English fans who had travelled rather a long way in the hope of seeing some cricket. What would have happened had there been no alternative grounds I don't know but as Peter Hayter summed up in the *Daily Mail*: 'The authorities at the Antiguan Recreation Ground were yesterday continuing to pull a whole herd of giant rabbits from the maddest of hats in getting the old stadium fit for international cricket, it having been abandoned for that purpose two years ago.'

And so, remarkably, just two days after the débâcle at the ground Sir Viv no longer wanted to be associated with, we were all watching Test cricket. I still love the fact that given two years' preparation they couldn't provide a pitch but given just two days they somehow managed it.

We didn't care how they did it because we were happy. Like Sabina Park, the Antiguan Recreation Ground had magical connotations. This is where Brian Lara had scored 375 and 400 and where Sir Viv had smashed the fastest century in world cricket. That all this had happened against England was somewhat chastening but the Rec had something Sabina Park lacked. Whereas Sabina Park had been renovated, the Rec had been left alone so it retained all of its old character. It was old, shabby, slightly dangerous and absolute bloody brilliant for any cricket fan preferring character over sanitised cleanliness. A quick glance at my match report from that first day summed up the kind of experience it provided:

'This morning I ordered a chicken sandwich and got given a cheese one. Nothing strange about that you may think, but when I said just get me a hot dog if it's easier they came back with... another cheese sandwich. The fact that it took 20 minutes to go through this process was rather annoying, but it's the way things happen round here.'

Want a cricket pitch, here's a sandpit, Want a hot dog, here's a cheese sandwich. That's the way of life it seemed and it was utterly endearing in a mad sort of way. The shenanigans had offered us some interesting possibilities when it came to merchandise, and while the WICB were still trying to sell shirts advertising the other ground we had ordered new versions of ours that had the venue and dates of the second Test crossed out and replaced with the new ones. It's the kind of collector's item you can sell to someone who has already bought the original version without even trying.

If the change of venues had inspired us then it seemed to have had a similar effect on the England players, who batted first and totalled 566 for nine declared. It seemed that the pitch did not contain the demons some feared it would after such a lack of preparation but if the wicket was holding up well the top tier of the Oil Drum stand was struggling. And that's because they had opened it to spectators and that was like a red rag to the Barmy Army bull. While we spent the mornings sunning ourselves on the bleachers, the open air and facing wind meant any singing was ineffective. But as afternoon beckoned we would head over to the other side of the ground where there was a roof to aid acoustics, a prevailing wind and a big group of fans keen to make some noise. This singing at cricket lark gets quite technical you know.

The tier was far from full, but then it was also far from stable. We got in there for a late afternoon session and cracked into some serious singing and a bit of jumping around. Now I'm stupid when it comes to these things and just trust everything in life will be OK rather than worrying about the very real possibility of the whole thing just collapsing, so I figured everything would be fine. Besides, it was the people below us who needed to worry more if it did crumple. It's probably a good thing that I couldn't see what those in the press box directly opposite us could. According to our friends watching at home we were making so much noise they could barely hear the commentators but when they could the fragility of England's batting line-up had ceased to be of concern and had been replaced by a worry about the fragility of the stand we were in, which to them looked as if it was about to fall down at any moment. Not that we cared. We were happy little Barmy Army bunnies doing what we do best in a historical, ramshackle venue that helped us in every way.

I was to get a view from the other side myself when I hit the highest high of my media work with the Barmy Army. By now I was used to appearing on Sky Sports and various other radio and TV channels and my friends were used to seeing me and sending in the obligatory abusive text messages. I had done far too many interviews under the influence and always managed to pull them off but when the call came through to go on *Test Match Special* I wasn't going to take any risks. I stayed sober and when the time came made my way from my seat in the stands to the press box and found my way to the *TMS* position. Squeezing past Geoffrey Boycott (who was later pictured with one of the Barmy Army hats I had taken as presents for the *TMS* crew) I found myself squeezed into a seat and before I knew it I was live on air talking to Aggers on the most famous radio sports show of them all. Apparently I was eloquent enough for them to extend my interview longer than they had originally planned but I don't really remember much of what I said other than the comment about bringing wives and girlfriends out which caused such consternation in the ranks. That's the problem with being in the media – one little slip and people pick up on it. Anyway it was a hugely fulfilling experience and I could only laugh when my time to leave came and I was replaced by Michael Holding. Who would you rather listen to?

The good times kept rolling and later that day my mobile rang. It was Courtney Walsh, who had recovered enough from his Jamaica exertions to fancy a beer with the Barmy boys again. He had a lot of friends and family around so it meant a lot to us that he would make the effort to come and share a few cold ones with us for a couple of hours.

There was a cricket match going on as well and such was Graeme Swann's impact on the game that I had to keep rewriting his song to keep up with events as another Swanny super over saw him take two of his five wickets as England bowled the Windies out for just 285. We'd also come up with something to commemorate the aborted second Test that went to the tune of *Ten Green Bottles*:

There was one ball bowled at the second Test
There was one ball bowled at the second Test
And if one more ball was bowled at the second Test
There'd have been two balls bowled at the second Test

There were two balls bowled...

You can guess the rest until it gets to eleven when it changes to

There were no more balls at the second Test
No more balls at the second Test
Because they played it on a sandpit
At a ground we all detest
There were no more balls
At the second Test

That song will perhaps never see the light of day again, unless someone remembers it when we go back to Antigua. And there was another opportunity for short-term songwriting when we found out that Sir Allen Stanford had been arrested for fraud. We ended up with several songs for him such as this one to the tune of *Hokey Cokey*:

You put your money in
And Stanford takes it out
He flew it down to Lord's
And shook it all about
He had loads of cash
So Giles Clarke kissed his ass
What was it all about?

Ohhhhh Allen Stanford
Ohhhhh Allen Stanford
Ohhhhh Allen Stanford

He's bent (allegedly), long stretch (maybe)
Rah rah rah

It wasn't the first time we'd been inspired to write about him. When the Twenty20 for 20 was played we'd also got our thinking caps on and came up with such never-used classics as this, to the tune of *Money Money Money*:

I bat all night, I bowl all day, to pay the bills I have to pay
Ain't it sad
And then Stanford came along he said
That's too bad
In my dreams I have a plan
It will make you a wealthy man
You won't have to work at all, just turn up and smack the ball

Money, money, money
Must be funny
In a Stanford world
Money, money, money
Always sunny
In a Stanford world
Aha-ahaaa
All the things I could do
If I had a little money
In a Stanford world

A man with so much cash, but still he's got a dodgy tache
Ain't it sad
But his wicket's really slow and his floodlights are too low
That's too bad
And please don't flirt with our players' wives
Cos you don't appreciate their cover drives

They win a fortune in your game, but compared to Tests it's really lame
Repeat chorus

There was also this to the tune of *Big Spender*:

The minute you flew into Lord's
I could see you were a man with a mission
A real big spender
'Tache bristling, not refined
The WAGs are beginning to see what's going on in your mind
So let me get right to the point
We don't want your sort, it's still our game you see?
Hey big spender
Spend... your dosh on baseball, not with me

The minute she sat on his lap
I could see a certain Texan swelling
Around midwicket
All the players, got the hump
She was only supposed to sit on his knee, not his middle stump.
So then he got right to the point:
'All this money, it's for just one thing, that's me!'
Hey big spender
Hey big spender
Hey big spender
Spend... your dosh on baseball, not with me

The Stanford news manifested itself on day four when our numbers had dwindled somewhat for a rather obvious reason. With the Test scheduled to finish on February 17 most people had booked flights home or onward to Barbados on the 18th. That included the Barmy Army tour party but as the official website reporter I felt a heavy sense of duty that forced me to consider alternatives. That and the fact you wouldn't have got me off that island even if you'd tried. I wasn't the only one either. Rearranged flights and accommodation options were the talk of the day as many hardy souls bought new flights, changed existing ones and figured out where to lay their heads for an extra night or two.

I got lucky, or so I thought, when I was chatting to Ian Kerr from Howzat Travel and he mentioned that he had an unused flight available on the evening of the 19th when the Test was due to finish. That would do me nicely thank you very much. The airport is just down the road from the Rec so I would simply leave the ground at the end of play, grab my bag and fly onwards. Gilo and I had a chat to a couple of guys who were staying in cheap accommodation in town and found ourselves a room for the night and we were set to go. What could go wrong? Quite a lot as it happened.

By the end of day four England needed seven wickets to win the game and while the West Indies could win it with 356 runs, little they had done previously suggested that was a realistic possibility. My flight was at 6pm, which was going to be a touch tight but only if it went right down to the last few overs. Or if play was delayed for any reason. So when I awoke on February 19, 2009 to see dark clouds emitting water I was less than impressed. Not only would this put England's victory charge on hold, it would mean the start and finish would be delayed. My only hope was for England to get it over with relatively quickly and not let it go down to the wire. Some bloody hope.

Lunch arrived with no wickets down. But there were still two sessions for England to take the wickets and so we had to give ourselves the opportunity to watch them try. We jumped into a taxi and headed for the airport to check if there was any possibility we could postpone our flights for one more day. There were no seats available on any flight the next day so the only option was to go on standby, an option taken by several people but one I eschewed for reasons I will furnish you with shortly. I headed back to our accommodation and took my backpack to the cricket with me in order to facilitate a quick getaway. Thankfully the security guys didn't insist on searching all of it.

The West Indies got as far as drinks in the afternoon session without losing a wicket. It seemed my ultimate fears were to be unfounded as a draw beckoned. But just four balls later the cat was immediately among the proverbial pigeons as Sarwan lost his wicket and the game was afoot (and I had gone cliché crazy). Six overs later and Sarwan's partner-in-digging-in-crime Chanderpaul had gone as well. Five down, half a day to go. Come on England! Finish this and finish it early so I don't miss anything. Tea arrived with no further wickets and my head was in a whirl. Six o'clock was approaching faster than I wanted, wickets weren't going down quickly enough and the pressure from my friends in the frenzied excitement was immense. 'There's no way you can leave this before it ends,' was the overwhelming opinion.

Now you haven't got this far without realising that I'm not averse to going out of my way to see England play cricket. Just three months previously I had rearranged an itinerary to watch a tour under threat from terrorism. I had been to Pakistan. I had put my entire career, nay life, on hold so I could watch an inordinate amount of cricket at the expense of making decent money or indeed having a permanent address. So what could ever make me leave a game that wasn't finished even if it meant spending a few more quid and the fairly minor inconvenience of a few hours waiting to get on a standby flight? The answer was Klara, the girl who had inadvertently been responsible for me getting to the Caribbean on time and the girl who was due to arrive in Barbados the next day to join me for ten days.

To reiterate, I had known Klara at a rough estimate for about ten weeks. I'd spent four of those weeks overseas watching cricket and another ten days on holiday in

Romania where she had joined me. In between that holiday and me leaving for the West Indies we had decided to move in together. She had to leave her flat, I was homeless, and while we both knew it was a bold move so early in our relationship it made sense. Indeed she was flat-hunting for both of us while I was loving the cricket. She had also decided the night before I left for Jamaica to join me on my next round-the-world backpacking adventure that would begin in a few months time. And she had agreed to come to Barbados despite a complete lack of interest or knowledge of the game I loved so much. Swedish girls are not known for their cricketing appreciation or their understanding of those who love it; indeed she was adamant that had she known about the intensity of my fixation with the sport there would never have been a first date, but here we were planning a lot of things together and the one thing she wasn't anticipating was arriving at Barbados airport to find her other half stranded in Antigua. If we'd been together a long time it's something I might have got away with. In these circumstances it was neither fair to her, nor remotely healthy for me, to not be at the airport the next day (Barbados airport that is, as opposed to Antigua). I would have been fine had I made a morning standby flight but no morning flight, no meeting and I might as well have stayed in Antigua full stop for all the welcome I would receive if I was late in Barbados. Of my two friends who did go on standby one made a morning flight and the other was stuck in Antigua all day, which just sums up the odds.

So I was in something of a ridiculous situation as the tea break went by. Five quick wickets or none at all was the order of my day. The thought of England winning and me not seeing the last wicket was something I was struggling to deal with. Of course I wanted England to win, but I would never live it down if I missed the victory. As I recount those memories it's worth pointing out that Klara is now an ex-girlfriend. We did indeed move in together, into a flat she found for us when she returned home from Barbados. We lived together for eight months before embarking on an epic travelling trip around Africa and Asia. We split up halfway through the Africa leg but continued to travel together and remain good friends. Whether we would have done any of that had I not been there to meet her in Barbados I'm not sure. Whether I could have ever completely got over the fact that I missed an England victory I'm not sure either. Fortunately neither theory was tested.

The atmosphere at the ground was hotting up and the Barmy Army was getting behind its team like only they can. Then in the fourth over after the break Swann struck. A few overs of crazy tension and excitement ensued as I sat in a private bubble with the Windies seven down. Time ticked by, 6pm got ever closer, men round the bat, the drama, the very essence of Test cricket, the excitement of those around me who didn't have to face up to leaving and disbelief from those who knew me so well that I could even contemplate walking away from such a situation.

What happened next is something not clearly marked in my memory bank as it all seems a bit of a daze but as far as I remember it goes like this. As the clock ticked onwards I finally made the move that had seemed almost inevitable since I opened my eyes that morning. I slowly moved to the back of the stand, grabbed my backpack and left the ground. I jumped in a cab where, inevitably, the driver had the cricket on his radio. In the short journey to the airport wicket number eight fell. I got to the airport, checked my bag in and found a couple of guys running a shop who weren't remotely interested in serving people as they were busy listening to the cricket. I joined them and as we listened the ninth wicket fell. Then it was boarding time and I found myself queueing next to one Geoffrey Boycott. I pointed out that surely he of all people should still be at the ground. He muttered something about there being no other flights and I wasn't in the mood to muse on why *TMS* couldn't have sorted him an alternative. Not only was I not at the ground for the culmination but now I didn't know what was happening either. Had we won? Had it finished? If there's one place I didn't want to be at that point it was on a plane with no way of communicating with the ground. But there were people with communication facilities and after a while the pilot came over the intercom in the only sports result service I have ever received while flying. He told the passengers on the plane that the game had been drawn, much to the joy of the few locals and the disgruntlement of the English contingent.

As for me I didn't know whether to laugh or cry. If ever the *Oxford English Dictionary* needs a practical example for the word bitter-sweet I believe I could be the provider. I was upset England hadn't won and yet secretly delighted because I hadn't missed the victory. Then I felt guilty about that so tried to feel upset about it. But I couldn't quite bring myself to do it. I hadn't missed anything, I wouldn't miss Klara and I had done the right thing by her. The episode was over and it was time to move on.

And on it was to Barbados. It's an island with all the attributes to make it a tremendous holiday destination. But they just don't add up. Deep blue skies, deep blue sea, sunshine, beaches. But then there is a long line of towering, ugly hotels, a strip of bars that could be taken from any Brits abroad holiday destination, and St Lawrence Gap, where the majority of holiday makers stay, could be just about anywhere.

To be fair there are many different parts of the island which are a touch more elegant. Indeed our favourite day consisted of hiring a Moke beach buggy and exploring the island, which is beautiful and untouched in most places. Get out of the tourist traps and the people wave at you and are pleased to see you because you've made the effort to do more than just sit on a beach all day for a fortnight before buggering off home. The capital, Bridgetown, is a bustling little metropolis with pleasant waterfront features and the Oistins fish market is always popular with travellers. One of the most endearing aspects of the island is its public transport. The reggae buses are minibuses that play very loud music and fit in as many people as humanly possible and a couple more besides. They are hardly unique but they are a great experience nonetheless and I always think you get a bit more respect from the locals when you use them as opposed to taxis.

With a break from cricket and with my relationship saved by my early departure from Antigua I could leave the tour behind for a while and enjoy some time away from cricket, although I did drag poor Klara to the Barmy Army CC game I felt I should attend. We walked, we swam in the sea, we drank rum, we did what most people do while also saying it was the last place we would think of returning to. If package holidays are your thing then it's probably perfect but they aren't mine. And there are no beach bars... that's wrong.

Cricket caught us up again and it was time to see whether Klara would have any interest in it at all. It's fair to say in retrospect there was none. Actually there's no need for retrospect. I'm not sure how long it was before she called for some rum but I reckon it was before midday. There's no easier place to get drunk at the cricket than the West Indies. When usually you have a choice of beer or wine there's a veritable off-licence inside every Caribbean cricket ground with bottles of spirits freely available for purchase; a dangerous situation. We got steadily drunk together and to be fair I could hardly blame her for not getting excited. It was one of the most boring Test matches I ever saw with just 17 wickets falling in five days of tedium. Not that Klara watched five days, of course, although she did also manage to attend day three but only because that was the day for Dawn Patrol and she reckoned she could get drunk enough to last the day without dying of boredom. So long as I was around to spend the evenings with her she knew what to expect, so it would all be good.

Unless, that is, I turned up back at our apartment too drunk to speak, which is what I did on day two. 'I'll be back about half six and then we'll go for dinner,' I told her as I walked out of the door in the morning. In reality I was back about seven so smashed after an afternoon drinking spirits that I would be of neither use nor ornament to her. To her eternal credit she went out for dinner by herself and when we awoke in the morning and my profuse apologies began she brushed them aside, told me what was done was done and that all was forgiven. I might not have got away with not being in Barbados to meet her but she was clearly the forgiving sort in most circumstances.

The new circumstances of day three were that it was about 6.30am and we were due for Dawn Patrol. Fortunately I'd sobered up and she hadn't had the opportunity to get drunk so we were in finer fettle than many of my colleagues, although it did become a tad scary when I was talking to the owner of the bar who told me about his special Jägerbomb glasses and I insisted on trying them out immediately. I'd drunk an obscene amount of Jägerbombs over the previous 12 months but never for breakfast. Ah well, there's a first time for everything. Besides, I felt like a drink after realising that in my drunken state the previous evening I had mislaid my video camera, passport and various other bits of paraphernalia somewhere on Barbados, never to be seen again.

Another tedious day ensued so I have no real recollections of it. I remember being singularly unimpressed by the Bridgetown Oval, yet another shining example of how to renovate a ground and simultaneously remove any semblance of character and leave it devoid of life. As the most popular destination for the English travelling contingent the ground was reminiscent of an England home ground and, as happens in those, we struggled to create any kind of atmosphere. A quick read through of my daily match reports proves just how dull the game was as I struggled for anything meaningful or interesting to write about, until the final day.

'Today we saw a highly entertaining sports match between two teams of international sportsmen where no one was sure what the end result was going to be. It was ebb and flow, with both sides fairly evenly matched. It was played out in front of a sparse crowd with many people having disappeared to grab a bit of beach action rather than watching the international sport on offer.

'There was a cricket match going on as well, but short of Ally Cook getting his highest ever Test score and first century since a rather more difficult and gritty effort in Galle four tours ago, we decided to bring you a report on the football match between the England team which took place after the Test had been declared a rather inevitable draw.

'Fabio Capello could do worse than look towards Nottinghamshire if he has defensive difficulties as the county provided the defensive backbone of the red team with Graeme Swann and Stuart Broad keeping it tight at the back with Ryan Sidebottom helping out at a fairly orthodox left-back position. Admittedly their defending was helped out by some rather shocking finishing from KP who spurned a host of chances, always blaming a dodgy hamstring for his appalling finishing.

'Tim Ambrose impressed in the middle of midfield for the greens, with Paul Collingwood showing occasional threatening glimpses down the right wing. But Ambrose came up against a determined Steve Harmison playing a deep lying central midfield role for the reds that helped the Notts contingent to keep it tight.

'As you can imagine the game was a fairly non-contact affair as it wouldn't look good if they all started wiping each other out, but there was one dreadful tackle and that was committed by none other than Monty Panesar. And it wasn't on one of the other spinners either.

'We couldn't work out the score if we're honest but it provided a bit of entertainment at the end of a fairly dull and yet quite enjoyable day. Forgive me if I was miserable yesterday. Test cricket is always good, even when it's not that good. But then we do hope it's a lot better in Trinidad.'

Fortunately for us it was better in Trinidad. I can't tell you too much about the island itself although we did go on a day trip the day after the Test and based on that I suspect I would have loved it. Its twin island of Tobago is more of a tourist destination; Trinidad a bit rough and unspoilt which, as you may have guessed by now, is the way I like it. The beach we visited had a tiny cafe and absolutely nothing else to ruin it. It was pure, unadulterated beach life the way nature intended. The last of many games of beach cricket was played in the best environment but before that there was a Test match to watch.

The Queen's Park Oval has the highest capacity of any ground in the West Indies and perhaps that's why they weren't required to renovate it for the 2007 World Cup so there was no concrete hideousness. It is a ground that has evolved gradually and looked very much like a cricket ground should do with numerous different stands and, all the better for us, a grass bank in front of the stand we would mostly occupy.

Not that our use of this grass bank was a given. We're used to random bureaucracy around the world, but as we congregated on said bank on the first morning we were told that we would have to vacate it. Over to the match report for the ensuing shenanigans:

'We were not exactly in the mood to do as he [the steward] said as we couldn't really see why we should have to. It was not exactly a health and safety issue. Then he brought his two mates out. One had a big scary gun and the other was scary enough without a gun. Still, we stood our ground as he didn't really seem to have a reason why we weren't allowed and others around the ground were doing the same thing. Not only that, but when you walked into the lower tier of the stand it actually took you onto the bank before you could get into the stand proper.

'Eventually we moved, but this was not to be the end of it. Bowesy, Becky, Chelsea and H may sound like a weird firm of solicitors, but it was this formidable foursome who decided they would go and see what a bit of girl power would do. After a bit of discussion it was agreed that we could sit on the grass after tea. When everyone took their place after lunch no one batted an eyelid and so the battle was won.'

The battle wasn't completely over as it happened as we went through the same rigmarole the next day only to arrive at an agreement whereby we could have our grass bank every day but only after lunch. I could spend the rest of my days trying to work out the logic of that decision and not get anywhere so I shall try not to waste any of my valuable seconds on this earth doing so.

All of this was played out in front of what we feared it would be played out in front of, another batsman-dominated game where wickets were rarer than people standing up for Allen Stanford. This was not the ideal kind of match in which to make your debut, so you had to feel a bit sorry for Amjad Khan, who will almost certainly end his Test career with figures of 1 for 122 from one match. What I didn't know about him until now was that he was born in Denmark and as such was only the fourth person born in mainland Europe to represent England after Ted Dexter (Italy), Paul Terry (West Germany) and Donald Carr (Germany). If ever there was a stat to file away in 'completely useless information' that would be it, but had I been reading *Cricinfo* that morning I may well have tried to work it into a song. He did manage to have a song written about him though and you'll almost certainly never hear it so here it is for posterity to the tune of *Gold* by Spandau Ballet:

Amjad Khan, Khan
Always believe when you bowl
Wickets are your goal
You're indestructible
Always believe in
Amjad Khan, Khan

Adil Rashid managed to have a song written about him that tour and he has yet to play Test cricket, which is probably a Barmy Army first. It was another *My Old Man's a Dustman* variation:

Adil Rashid's from Bradford
He bowls from leg to off
He'll take us loads of wickets
Just like Darren Gough

Although he's only five foot nine
He's better than Shane Warne
And when he plays the cover drive
He looks like Michael Vaughan

New skipper Andrew Strauss also had a new ditty written for him to Neil Diamond's *Sweet Caroline*:

Strauss
Andrew Strauss
Opening bat
Skipper too
We love you...

Oh Andrew Strauss
Whoah whoah whoah
Scoring runs we knew you would

Oh Andrew Strauss
Whoah whoah whoah
Batting never looked so good

Sadly that never really took off so he remained generally serenaded to the classic Tears for Fears tune *Shout*:

Strauss, Strauss
Never gets out
He plays the shots that we dream about
Come on, we're talking bout you
Come on

Meanwhile Paul Collingwood inspired the following to *Hey Jude*:

Hey Paul
Don't let me down
You're a Mackem
But that don't matter
The moment you step up to the crease,
Our troubles will cease
You'll make things better better better better better....
Na na na na na na na... Collingwood

But again this never really took over from his traditional song *When the Boat Comes In*:

Who will take his wicket
Spinners he will pick it
Never take his wicket
When Collingwood comes in

Drink with the army
Sing with the army
Drink with the army
When Collingwood comes in

Drink with the army
Sing with the army
Drink with the army
Sing with the army
Drink with the army
When Collingwood comes in

Clearly there had been lots of time for songwriting, albeit with no real long-term anthems written, as by the end of day three Chanderpaul and Nash were at the crease on their way to being the fifth and sixth centurions of the match. According to the match report 'we'd already been reduced to investing heavily in rum and having heated debates about what to do on day five to entertain ourselves as the cricket almost certainly won't do it for us.'

And therein lies another reason why this game I love so much is fantastic because the fifth day would actually entertain us immensely. By the time England had finally bowled out the West Indies for 546, two behind England's score, there was an hour and a half left of the fourth day.

The only excitement in the match had been the tension as England went for a world record. In true England style they couldn't quite pull it off though and had to be content with conceding the second highest number of extras in an innings with a stunning 74. It seems ridiculous now that Matt Prior could concede 35 byes in a game, but that's what happened. Indeed byes were the West Indies' fourth highest scorer.

But that was merely a sideshow, giving us something to talk about, and now we had something else. England were 1-0 down in the series and this was their last chance saloon. Their only option was to go, go hard, rack up a few runs and then declare and bowl out the West Indies in quick time. They set about their task in helter-skelter style, lost three wickets, but still managed to score 80 in 15 overs. It was all set up for a potentially cracking last day of an otherwise dull Test match. It could, of course, just be a tedious last day as well, but hope springs eternal and we were to get a belter.

KP did most of the damage with 102 off 92 balls and Matt Prior showed no ill bye effects hitting 61 off 49. The declaration came at lunch with West Indies set 240 to win. That total was eminently gettable, although with Chris Gayle injured and thus depriving them of their impetus at the top of the order we weren't convinced they would really go for it. By tea that was obvious as they eschewed a run-chase to defend their 1-0 series lead. We'd taken three wickets, but it would need something spectacular to force a win. I was happy in the knowledge that whatever happened I could watch all of it without having to leave early. A quick tea-time tactical discussion led to us changing ends so we could sit in a stand with the wind at our backs to make sure our singing could be heard. This was the time when the England players would need us behind them.

It was just the kind of nerve-shredding/jangling/teasing cricket that makes Test matches so great. Four days of tedium had suddenly erupted into a game of tension, excitement and madness. Half of the overs in the West Indian innings were maidens and Graeme Swann ended up with faintly ridiculous figures of 21-13-13-3 but it wasn't enough. The eighth wicket went down with just three overs left and that was that.

So close again, yet so far away again. Such is the nature of Test cricket. But for one innings in the series England had been by far the better team, but that innings was enough and the West Indies had won it.

It's funny to reminisce about that tour in such an affectionate manner as it was perhaps the least edifying tour I have ever been on. I'm not a huge fan of the Caribbean, I didn't like any of the grounds apart from the dilapidated one we weren't supposed to be at and the cricket went from utterly depressing to stultifying.

Somehow though we managed two of the tightest finishes I have ever seen but I had to leave one. The Barmy Army was pretty quiet, struggling to get big enough groups together to make much noise. This has much to do with the demographic of the fans that were there; they tended to be older and in couples. We hadn't come up with any new songs that would stand the test of time. After the phenomenal tours of Sri Lanka, New Zealand and India it was a let down.

All that said, of course it was brilliant. Touring always is. It's just that from my point of view the standards set in those aforementioned tours had been ridiculously high and life can't always match up to expectations. It only goes to show how utterly and completely spoiled I had become. It's not often you get to spend six weeks watching Test cricket, play beach cricket with Courtney Walsh, have your girlfriend join you for a Caribbean jaunt and spend every day with your mates enjoying great weather and good company... and all without paying a cent for it. I needed to get some perspective.

If I really wanted that, a horrific incident happened during that tour to offer it to me. Three days before the final Test started the Sri Lankan cricket team were on their way to the Gaddafi Stadium in Lahore when gunmen opened up and killed several policemen and injured several of the cricketers. The only reason Sri Lanka were even there is because India refused to tour after the Mumbai bombings.

This may not have been my favourite tour but it was still fantastic and I wouldn't have been anywhere else. And at no stage did anyone point a gun at me, which always makes the days less stressful.

Fourteen

Victory in Australia

With Strauss our captain, we'll take the urn home

WHEN I INTERVIEWED ONE of the Barmy Army's longest serving regulars, Nicky King (aka Bagpuss), for the Barmy Army magazine I asked what her biggest ambition as a cricket fan was. When she replied that she wanted to see a Test match at Eden Gardens I was quite surprised. I guess this makes her more of a cricketing purist than me, because had I been interviewing myself I would have had a different answer. My ambition was to see England win the Ashes in Australia.

Bagpuss got the chance to fulfil hers as England were finally awarded a Test at Eden Gardens in 2012 (although knowing the BCCI they'll change that between me writing this and the book going to print). But my wish had already been granted by then.

I didn't think about the significance when I arrived in Brisbane the day before the 2010–11 Ashes series, but I was about to embark on the longest tour I will probably ever do. Five-Test tours are now a thing of the past anywhere other than Australia and the chances of me doing all five again are pretty slim to say the least, but then I had no plans to do all five on this occasion either. (As I am now resident in Australia I might well do them again but that would hardly count as a tour, would it?) I had spent the time between the South Africa tour of 2009–10 and that first Test travelling with Klara who, as we have ascertained, has little interest in cricket. In acknowledgement of that we had planned to do some travelling in Australia before I again immersed myself in the game. My intention was to turn up in time for the third Test in Perth and watch the last three. But before we could get anywhere near Australia Klara and I split up, so I figured I might as well change my plans and get to Adelaide in time for the second Test. Then I realised that wherever I was in the world I would be glued to a TV watching cricket anyway so I might as well just accept the inevitable and go to Brisbane for the opener.

By this time Australia had become about the most expensive place on the planet and as I'd been used to living on about £25 a day as I travelled round developing countries suddenly finding that my £25 a day would struggle to even buy me a round, never mind pay for accommodation and food, was a bit of a shock. As Perth is such a long and expensive flight away from the other venues, I decided for financial reasons to forsake the third Test. But just as I came to grips with the thought of missing it I managed to get a contract with the *Herald Sun* online to write a column for them throughout the Ashes. That meant I could afford to visit Perth, so I booked the whole lot. We may have lost that Test badly but I don't regret going. We won the Ashes and I saw every day of it – the rough and the smooth.

But before we got to Australia there was work to do. Not just for the players, but for us. As Strauss would later recount in a post-match interview, 'I think the fans have put in more preparation than we have.' There was no boot camp, but there was a lot of planning in terms of what we could do in the stands to support England.

A group of us decided that it would do no harm to freshen up our repertoire when travelling down under. The staples were all well and good and would always be amusing but at the same time we had barely come up with anything original for touring this part of the world for a long time so we felt honour bound to change that situation. The emails going back and forth were lengthy. Not for the first time in my life I would find myself on long bus journeys staring out of the window at the passing countryside when a kernel of an idea for a new song would come unbidden into my mind. I would scribble it down and then drop a line to my mates to see what they thought. We shared ideas, suggested improvements and passed judgement on whether things 'scanned well' – a favourite measure of songwriting success.

The almost inevitable outcome was that one classic emerged and the others barely saw the light of day. Australia is the hardest place to get new songs going and Gilo tapped into exactly what was needed whereas the rest of us came up with stuff that would only be successful if we went balls out and stood up to sing it in front of everyone. And few of us have the voice or the chutzpah to do that in front of big crowds. Because of that, none of the following really saw much action, but I'm going to put them here because I spent ages writing them and they'll never get announced to the world any other way.

First up was an attempt to hijack one of Australia's most iconic songs, *Down Under* by Men At Work.

Travelling around convict land
On an Ashes trail, and getting suntanned
Just look at Ricky, he's feeling nervous
He's so scared he can't eat breakfast
And we said

We've come to a land down under
Ashes treasures we will plunder
Strauss's going to steal Ricky's thunder
He'll score more runs, he'll smash it through covers

KP loves an Ashes tussle
He's six foot four and full of muscles

They say Afrikaans is his language
He just smiles and chews his Marmite sandwich
And he said

We've come to a land down under
Ashes treasures we will plunder
Strauss's going to steal Ricky's thunder
He'll score more runs, he'll smash it through covers

We've seen England win in Bombay
Even Shaun Udal got four that day
Now Swanny has them saying 'tempt me'
He's going to end the Ashes with plenty
And he said

We've come to a land down under
Ashes treasures we will plunder
Strauss's going to steal Ricky's thunder
He'll score more runs, he'll smash it through covers

I then hit old favourites Oasis after realising that *Don't Look Back in Anger* is advice Ricky Ponting might need:

Slip inside Ricky Ponting's mind
He's trying to find
Some new players to play
He wants to play his older team
But that's just a dream
They're too old to play
He said he'd start a revolution in his head
But he's been through all the players A to Z
Now there's just a summertime of doom
If he loses the Ashes race
He is going to lose his place
Losing three would simply tear his heart out
So Ricky can wait
Shane Warne is too late

And there's no Glenn McGrath
Gilchrist's had his day
And don't look back to Langer
He cannot play

And on a similar theme I tapped into Ponting missing his old mates to the tune of The Beatles' *Yesterday*:

Yesterday
Ponting's troubles seemed so far away
But Nathan Hauritz is here to stay
McGrath and Warne were Yesterday

Suddenly
They're not half the team they used to be
Will he lose Ashes number three
Yesterday came suddenly

Why Haydos
Had to go I don't know, Langer wouldn't say
Adam Gilchrist's gone, now Ricky longs for Yesterday

Yesterday threatened to take off at one point and probably would had I tried harder but the others were a bit too intricate for a big tour and I'm not the sort to do solos. Neither were the following ever destined to be sung because they're far too complicated. Ever since meeting Chantal in New Zealand I'd been trying to come up with songs for Ian Bell and I came up with this to the tune of *Fairytale of New York:*

He's handsome, he's pretty
His batting is gritty, when he hits a boundary the crowd call out for more
Ian Bell was humdinging and the Army was singing
It was hot as a sauna
The Army drank through the night

And the boys from the Barmy Army choir where singing all the day
And Ian Bell was batting well at Christmas time

And if you think that is overly complicated then just once I would love to hear the following because it's crazy and because we just don't use Meat Loaf enough but this version of *Bat out of Hell* still amuses me.

The Aussies are screaming and the fires are howling
Way down in the Gabba tonight
There's a man in the shadows with a glint in his eye
And his blade shining oh so bright
There's blonde in his hair and there's thunder in the sky
He's ready for amazing feats
Oh and down in the tunnel where the Belly is rising
Oh I swear I saw a young boy
Starting to mutter
He had the Aussies to beat

Belly, you're the only one in this whole world
Who bats pure and good and right
And wherever you are and wherever you go
You're always gonna bat just right
You'll never get out
Please don't get out now
Please just crack another four
So you gotta make the most of putting bat on leather
When it's over they'll know
What we've always known

With his bat Ian Bell
Is going to score tons of runs
He'll stay for loads of overs
With his bat Ian Bell will score runs runs
With his bat Ian Bell will be there when the morning comes

But when the day is done
And the sun goes down
And Belly's shining through
Then like a winner he bats just like heaven
We'll win the Ashes with you
Then like a winner he bats just like heaven
We'll win the Ashes it's true

We did have a song for Belly by now, to the tune of *Ding Dong Merrily on High*, which was a whole lot simpler and easier for people to join in:

Ding Dong Belly is our King
He's England's shortest batsman
Ding Dong Belly is our King
He'll score more runs than Bradman
La la la la la la la la la la
He'll win the urn for England

But while I was writing overly complicated and never-to-be-sung ditties, Gilo had nailed exactly what was required and what would become the anthem of the tour by reworking Doug Mulholland's classic from New Zealand to the tune of *Sloop John B*:

We came over from old Blighty
The Barmy Army and me
Around Sydney town we did roam
Six quid for a pint
A grand for a flight
With Strauss our captain
We'll take the urn home

So hoist up the John B sail
See how the mainsail sails
Call for the captain ashore
We'll take the urn home (take the urn home)

We'll take the urn home (we'll take the urn home)
With Strauss our captain
We'll take the urn home

Ricky Ponting is a broken man
Without Warne he has no plan
He's trying to carry this team
All on his own
He's losing his hair
But we don't care
With Strauss our captain
We'll take the urn home
Repeat chorus

Graeme Swann is a caring guy
He rescues cats in his spare time
Now he's going to tear the Aussies apart
They can't read his spin
So England will win
With Strauss our captain
We'll take the urn home
Repeat chorus

Post-Perth we added a further verse:

Brad Haddin's a simple man
He appeals whenever he can
He even appeals a catch down the leg side (even a wide)
He's rubbish at his job
We think he's a nob
With Strauss our captain
We'll take the urn home

After much tinkering and fine-tuning of the words by email Gilo was ready to go by the first Test. Now all that was needed was for everybody to get there. Arriving in Brisbane the day before the first Test was a strange experience. My year had started with the end of the South Africa series, taken in a trip round Southern and Eastern Africa, the football World Cup and then a tour of Asia. Having not been near a truly developed country for a year it was a culture shock and a half. And having hardly seen a face I knew for a year it was also a shock to be inundated with an avalanche of familiar faces. I was conscious that if I wasn't careful the cricket would immerse me so much that my memories of the epic year I had just experienced would go right out of the window.

At the same time it was great to see everyone again and the excitement that is always bubbling under in the build-up to a new Test series soon came to the surface. There was no time to ease into the tour so the beers flowed and old acquaintances were renewed with gusto.

I awoke on the first morning of the Brisbane Test with the four Aussie guys in my dormitory making a hell of a racket. I felt like shit. I was tired, a bit fuzzy around the edges and all I could think of was that this was not how I wanted to start the series. There would be plenty of time for feeling knackered and rough later but if you start a tour like that then it's going to be a tough haul. When they'd left I got up, had a shower and trotted down to reception to find out what time it was – 7am. I never worked out why they decided to be up so early but I was less than impressed. I went back to bed, grabbed a couple of hours' kip and turned up to the Gabba feeling vaguely human. I picked up my tickets and headed into the ground.

Having arranged my tickets late I was sat well away from the Barmy Army section but alongside my good friend Heather Storry, a Barmy Army trooper whose first experience of the Army had been four years previously when she had witnessed the 5-0 debacle in its entirety. Somehow she had still picked up the Barmy Army bug and despite the fact it took her three years to see England win a Test overseas, she had a lot of touring experience. She shares my childish excitement in the run-up to a tour and on the morning of a Test so was an ideal person to be with on day one. Our enthusiasm was heightened by the fact that we hadn't seen each for ages and had much to catch up on.

That buzz lasted precisely three balls when Strauss cut a Ben Hilfenhaus ball straight to Mike Hussey. Shit. That wasn't supposed to happen. Later in the day Siddle got a hat-trick. It's amazing just how easy cricket can knock the optimism out of you.

It seemed at that point we would not get to use one of my favourite songs from the 2009 Ashes constructed by one of Southgate's friends to the tune of the Oasis song *Little by Little*:

Siddle by Siddle
You bowl us everything we ever dreamed of
Siddle by Siddle
The wheels of your team are slowly falling off
Siddle by Siddle
You always bowl a ball that goes for four
And all the time
Ponting asks himself why
Are you really here?

Why are you really here?
Why are you really here?
Why are you really here?

As it turned out we would have excuse to dust that one off in the future but after three days of the series it seemed that any songs about the relative quality of this Australia side would be consigned to the scrapheap for that tour as they were utterly dominant.

I never used to understand people who travel overseas and sit and watch cricket in a pub but when you are on a long tour the occasional afternoon session can be a nice change and you get more of an idea of what is actually happening in the middle. I usually pick one afternoon per Test to engage in TV watching and day three seemed the perfect time to do that as we saw Hussey and Haddin taking the game away from England. This tour of Australia was supposed to be different and yet as their lead grew and grew it all seemed so familiar. To take our minds off the bad situation on the pitch we started getting heavily involved in credit card roulette. While usually rounds of Jägerbombs are bought by whoever is in the mood, they were so expensive in Australia that we stole an idea from the players. Everyone puts their credit card in the hat and the last one drawn out pays for the round. All good fun, unless you lose... and one of our number lost four out of five that afternoon. Ouch.

By tea Australia were 436 for five in reply to England's 260 all out, the roulette loser was $400 poorer and we were well on the way to being drunk. In the third session we started to take some wickets though, mainly thanks to Steven Finn, who had my fellow credit card rouletters singing the song they had come up with for him in Bangladesh to Manfred Mann's *The Mighty Quinn*:

He swings it out
Comes steaming in
He's gonna knock 'em over
He's Steven Finn

All of a sudden Australia were all out and England were fighting to save the Test. And so we went into day four with hazy heads, a horrible feeling that we had been here before and that already our hopes, dreams and expectations for the tour were in danger of going down the drain faster than Mitchell Johnson loses his action. And that's exactly what he did because this time the hopes, dreams and expectations fought back in style. England's 517 for 1 still doesn't look right even as I write it. Did I really witness that? All of a sudden England were on top, Mitchell was struggling, Hilfenhaus was getting stick, their only wicket was taken by a part-time bowler who couldn't actually fulfil his primary role of batting. We had been right, this England team were better... and this Australian team were worse.

By day five we were in jubilant mood. It wasn't a win but it was an amazing fightback and all of a sudden those songs we had about the Australians not being as good as they used to be seemed very relevant. Peter Siddle's song no longer seemed inappropriate. And that third-ball wicket must have seemed an age ago to Ben Hilfenhaus who ended the Test as Barmy Army enemy number one. He fielded in front of us on that final morning and steadfastly refused to sign a young kid's bat despite many polite requests to do so. We sang 'Sign the kiddie's bat' relentlessly and why he chose not to just sign it and shut us up I will never know. He was shown up by his captain Ricky Ponting, who actually gave us a wave at one point as we intimated that he might want to come and help Hilfy with the spelling of his name.

He had no support from his own fans as they were noticeable only by their absence. The Gabba was almost devoid of Australians on the final day so we made it our home. The Test had been a topsy-turvy affair but it ended with England on top on the field and the Barmy Army making an away ground their own off it. This was more akin to the plan. But if we thought that was good, we hadn't seen anything yet.

When I was writing my column for the *Herald Sun* at the end of the tour I had to come up with a favourite moment of the series. Four years previously there wouldn't have been any to choose from, but this time there was a plethora of options. But watching Australia reduced to 2 for 3 on the first morning of the second Test at Adelaide, with Katich out for a Diamond Duck and Ponting for a Golden has to be one of the best things ever. Ever. Ever. Someone pointed out to me that I was physically shaking after that third wicket. Now that is not a unique sight early on in a day's cricket but it usually has to do with the cumulative effects of too much drinking and not enough sleep. This time it was purely a reaction to over-excitement and adrenaline as we witnessed something that simply doesn't happen. The celebrations for the third wicket were almost muted as we waited for the umpire to signal a no-ball or for us to wake up and realise it was all just a dream. Because this was dreamland. Utopia. Elysium. Call it what you want, we had achieved it. If you'd have asked us before play would we be happy bowling out the Aussies for 245 we would have bitten your hands off. After that explosive, mental start it was almost a disappointment they got so many.

We needn't have worried. Cook, Trott and KP went about ensuring Australia were never in the game for a second. Cook and Trott accumulated another mammoth stand to add to the one in Brisbane as KP waited yet again in the wings. The joke doing the rounds was that Australia had brought in a left-arm spinner with a plan to get KP out but they hadn't yet come up with a plan to get him in. When he did get in their plan worked. He got out to the left-arm spinner, but only after he had continued to wreak destruction with 227. I think that was the inspiration behind his new song to the tune of *Let It Be*:

When we find ourselves in times of trouble
Andy Flower says to me
We need a batting hero, get KP
Get KP, get KP, get KP
Smashing fours and sixes get KP
Get KP, get KP, get KP

Not that KP was happy just batting. To rub it in he took the vital wicket of Michael Clarke at the end of the fourth day, which meant that for once it was the Aussies looking to the skies for rain to save them. England still needed six wickets and we expected the Aussies to fight hard. As it was they scored around 70 runs before the final wicket fell and we had just enough time to watch the ceremonies and get to the pub before the heavens opened in spectacular style. We had won. Away. By an innings. In Australia. In a competitive game. We were so surprised we barely knew what to do with ourselves. We had a sing-song and a lot of beers obviously but there was a sense of unreality about it. It was time for a breather.

The Barmy Army dispersed around Australia for some time away from cricket and to explore this vast country. For me that involved going to see friends in Melbourne, which coincidentally gave me the opportunity to watch England again, in a warm-up match with Victoria. Some might question whether I wasn't taking this whole cricket love thing a bit too far and in an empty MCG with weather cold enough to make me shiver I probably did myself at times. If the phrase 'after the Lord Mayor's show' was invented for something, it had to be that day.

And then to Perth and a feeling that was alien to us. Before we could settle in Australia were 69 for 5 and any fears we had about Tremlett were dispatched quicker than the Aussie batsman he dismissed with three early wickets. The alien feeling is that we were actually expecting this to happen. After the sheer madness of that first morning in Adelaide this was now becoming business as usual. Another day, another dominant session for England. We'd barely lost a session since day three of the first Test. This was the new status quo and all we had to do was sit back and relax as England dismantled Australia. In the meantime we had to come up with a song for Tremlett and we hit upon a seasonal theme, utilising Slade's *Merry Christmas Everybody*:

So here he is, Chrissy Tremlett
Bowling fast for England
He's got a future now
The convicts on the run

Unfortunately they weren't on the run for very long because we should have known better than to be lulled into that ridiculously false sense of security. It went wrong. Spectacularly wrong. England were bowled out for 187 on day two as Mitchell Johnson did what we knew he could do but didn't seem to be able to do very often. It was all over in four days as England were bowled out in the second innings for just 123 and lost by 267 runs. Oops.

The ironic thing about that defeat is that we found it easier to take than we had victory in Adelaide. Being in the Barmy Army is about gallows humour, about being happy even when your team is losing heavily. After the 2005 Ashes victory Paul Burnham had told me 'we know how to lose well, now we need to learn how to win well'. With our post-2005 demise we hadn't had to learn for long so we were still much more used to losing with a smile on our faces. As the game ended we chirped at a few cheeky Australians, sang songs for them and even sang *Happy Birthday* to Ricky Ponting. We had a traditional end of Test piss-up and went on our merry way.

And it was a very merry way on the occasions that we were allowed to get merry. While the cricketers had been doing battle around Australia we had been fighting our own against the Australian hospitality industry, which seemed intent on ruining some of our fun. It's fair to say we don't get on with Australia's Responsible Service of Alcohol (RSA) laws. The Barmy Army has drunk together all around the world and never had any serious issues. Until then.

Firstly there were some strange rules about how many drinks you could buy at once in a cricket ground. One afternoon four of us decided to have a glass of wine or two. This entailed two people going to get wine because after a certain time you were only allowed to buy two wines per person. This, of course, lengthened the queue somewhat. We spied a young girl sporting an RSA badge and holding a clipboard and politely asked what was the purpose of rationing drinks when the only effect was that two people had to miss the match and clog up more of the stadium with queues that were twice as big. She replied that it was so they could keep an eye on how much we drank and to ensure, and this still staggers me, that more people left their seats to buy alcohol. Firstly I pointed out that there were numerous bars around and that she had absolutely no way of knowing how much I had already drunk. Secondly I intimated that as I had paid good money for my ticket it might be nice if I was allowed to actually watch the cricket rather than spending my time queueing unnecessarily for wine. Faced with cold logic she had no reply other than reiterating that she could keep an eye on how much I was drinking. I never saw her again.

Later that day two of us returned to a different bar at the ground only to be told that now we could only buy one wine per person. Knowing that argument was pointless, Jock returned to our seats to deliver the first two glasses while I rejoined the queue at the back to buy the second two. He rejoined me and as luck would have it we ended up with the same barmaid again. She asked whether we had just necked the wines we had just bought and I patiently explained that we had taken them to our friends. I also pointed out that if we had necked them she would have no way of knowing and would sell us some more so the plan to slow down our drinking would actually have had the opposite effect. To be fair to her she did actually acknowledge the logic. They weren't her rules but whoever made them up hadn't really thought it through.

However much we were rationed it evidently wasn't enough as getting kicked out of pubs became an occupational hazard on that trip. Now if someone is absolutely hammered then fair enough, kick them out. But it seems that being mildly tipsy is enough in many of the pubs of Australia. On our final night in Perth we turned up to a club and strolled in past the bouncers. Twenty minutes later the girl who had facilitated our entry by talking to the bouncers came to the bar with me and we were both out of the door within five minutes. We ordered beer, got given water and the same bouncers who had just let us in were ordered to kick us out. In a short space of time we had gone from being acceptable to inebriated past the point of acceptability. Brilliant. But I shouldn't have been overly surprised; four years previously I had been refused entry to a pub in Sydney before I had even had a drink only to return six pints later and walk straight in. It's the arbitrary nature and the difficulty of keeping a group together that frustrates.

One person who couldn't really complain about being refused entry to the club we were turfed out of was one of our more inebriated number. Upon being refused entry he decided to take a breathalyser test and registered a reading of 4.0. 'Is that good,' he asked? 'Sir, that is the highest reading we have ever had,' replied the bouncer. 'You are eight times over the legal limit.' 'Yeah,' he said, 'but I don't want to drive, I just want to come in for a beer.'

So after a fairly disastrous Test a handful of us ended the evening sat around a table outside a shop opposite the club from which we had been ejected in which our equally drunken (or should that be equally sober) friends who had not had to run the gauntlet of going to the bar were still enjoying themselves. At least the early finish to the Test meant we would have a day to explore Perth. But any plans for that were wrecked as one of the country's driest cities decided to use up one of its meagre rations of rainy days. It was time to move on.

After celebrating Christmas in Melbourne, thoughts again turned to cricket and our faith was still evident. We still thought we had the better side and that Perth was an anomaly. We're generally good at blind optimism but we really believed this and we were proved right. I have to watch that first day in Melbourne on DVD to prove that it wasn't just a dream. Even seeing it on a TV screen there is an air of unreality about it. Australia 98 all out. Nope, still doesn't sound right. Even in the years when Australia were so much better than us they struggled to dismantle our batting line-up in the same calculating, destructive way we did theirs that day. And to top it off we casually scored 157 without losing a wicket. I can't really complain about being kicked out of the pub that night if I am honest. I was drunk on delirium before a beer had passed my lips.

The introduction of Tim Bresnan to the England side gave us the opportunity for the Bangladesh veterans to bring out another of the songs that had come out of that tour to the tune of *Those Were The Days*:

> *We've had a garlic naan*
> *We've had a butter naan*
> *We've had a plain, we've had a keema too*
> *But our favourite naan, is Tim Bresnan*
> *All because he hates the convicts too*

It's just as tenuous as the Tim Ambrose/Ambrosia connection, faintly ridiculous and as such is obviously one of my favourites. It was particularly relevant in Australia's second innings when his 4-50 played a huge part in finishing the job off. Those four days were like some kind of dream as the blip that was Perth was eradicated by a performance of such dominance it was hard to believe that Australia could ever have matched us, never mind beaten us, in the previous game.

Such was the dreamlike quality of the occasion that I went to the fourth morning with mixed feelings. Yet again we took over an Australian cricket ground and made it a corner of England as the Australians stayed at home. It was such an amazing atmosphere I found myself willing the Australian batsmen to stay in for a while so we could enjoy it a bit longer, while simultaneously wanting to see wickets fall for the victory to be confirmed. As it is we got about 20 overs which was probably the right balance.

Before the Melbourne Test I wrote the following for my column in the *Herald Sun*:

'With a lot of relatively new faces we were at a loss of what to make of this [Australian] team, but now we have reasons to dislike Brad Haddin for his ridiculous appealing (here's a clue Brad: just because you catch the ball doesn't mean it's out) and there's a mutual dislike forming with Mitchell Johnson as well.

'We have come up with songs for both players, but not ones I would publish here. We have rules on decency and these definitely push the barriers, but if they continue to wind us up then no doubt we will use them. We like to be polite to players generally, but if they upset us then the game becomes fair...

'Hopefully we'll be too busy winning in Melbourne to worry about Aussie players.'

We were obviously busy winning in Melbourne but not so much as to let the Aussie players off the hook. A few of them had been annoying us, Hilfenhaus with his refusal to sign bats in Brisbane and Bollinger chirping at us in Adelaide. Bollinger got some good-natured ribbing about his 'rug' in Adelaide and responded by telling some of my mates to 'get f*cked' while chirping that we'd paid for his second house. Haddin had also incurred our wrath by his incessant appealing but Mitchell Johnson somehow stood head and shoulders above everyone as a potential target. I think partly it's a sign of respect. Despite his sometimes awful bowling we also knew he was the only one who was capable of world-class performances. And there was the fact that his girlfriend and mother had had such a public spat that led us to sing, to the theme from the TV show *The Addams Family*:

His mother hates his missus
His missus hates his mother

They all hate each other
The Johnson Family
De le la le de le la le de le la le

Johnson had responded to that in Perth by gesticulating towards the scoreboard when Australia were winning and there was little doubt in our mind that a few expletives accented *à la* Bollinger would have come our way had he been near enough. But it was his otherwise wayward bowling that inspired the chant of the tour and one of the most amazing crowd scenes seen at cricket.

The fourth morning saw several thousand England cricket fans waving from left to right as they chanted:

He bowls to the left
He bowls to the right
That Mitchell Johnson
His bowling is shite

The England players were clearly pissing themselves laughing when they worked it out and we were all laughing in the stands as we could tell what it must have looked like and we certainly knew what it sounded like. Meanwhile Michael Vaughan was laughing on *TMS* so the only one who probably didn't see the funny side was Mitchell himself.

It always helps when the man you're singing about plays into your hands. As England chased the four wickets they needed for victory he was out to the 11th ball of the day. This came on top of a duck in the first innings and 2 for 134 at an economy rate of 4.62 during England's knock that meant he was giving us real opportunity to sing the song. It was hard to believe that this was the guy who had smashed us up in Perth, who had looked in our direction and pointed angrily at the scoreboard in reaction to our singing. Much easier to believe he was the man who was dropped for the second Test and bowled one of the worst balls in Ashes history for five wides in the first Test.

But worse was to come for Mitchell. Now that we had the bit between our teeth he was always going to get more of that song in Sydney. He hit a decent half century in the first innings and took four wickets in England's 644, but with another horribly high economy rate of 4.66. Then came the zenith, or nadir depending on which side of the fence you were on. As he strolled out to bat in Australia's second innings Australia were still 193 runs behind with four wickets left and facing defeat. As thousands of Englishmen and women started waving and singing again one of my mates turned to me and said 'Can you imagine if he gets out first ball here?' I didn't say anything but just nodded. Within 60 seconds Tremlett had bowled him for a golden duck, we jumped on each other and if the singing of that song was loud before then the next few verses were thunderous.

There are occasions when I have felt a bit sorry for Johnson. Surely no cricketer in history has got that kind of chirp. The fact that it's not abusive means there is no real moral high ground for him. It's nothing compared to what most footballers have received at some time or other but it must be a bit tough. You have to assume that any cricketer worth his salt would sing it to him in the middle now. I hope he has a sense of humour and sings it to himself as Shaun Pollock does with his song. He was, at least, responsible for Cricket Australia shifting more merchandise as Mitchell Johnson pin badges became the must have Barmy Army accessory. Going into the SCG on day five a steward asked why so many England fans were wearing these. When I explained that Mitchell was one of our best players, he replied 'but he's Australian'. Clearly irony was lost on him.

But I have fast-forwarded somewhat in the quest to fulfil that particular strand of history. We were still in Melbourne I believe. Mitchell had just been caught out and England were three wickets away from a 2-1 series lead. There was a bit of a delay as the tail smashed a few runs but it was short-lived and then it was time for the celebrations all the way and they were led by the England players. They did the expected lap of honour before returning to the main Barmy Army section. We wondered what they had in mind before Swanny led the team in the Sprinkler dance routine they had shown off in his online diary. The bonding between players and fans was growing ever closer and this was another example. And if that wasn't, then what happened later definitely was.

As the English hordes gradually streamed out of the MCG to go and put a hell of a lot of English pounds sterling behind the bars of Melbourne we headed to the Barmy Army HQ, PJ O'Brien's, to embark on a session. After the Adelaide Test had finished early we had taken our drinking relatively slowly, conscious of the fact that there was a long night ahead of us, but if there's one thing we don't usually lack it's stamina, so on this occasion we had decided on a shit or bust tactic. Go out, have fun, drink, be merry and deal with whatever life throws at us. Ironically, although we drank all day no one got kicked out of a pub and we were all out till the very late hours of the morning. A Barmy Army drinking session lasts a lot longer than Australia's first innings had.

There was an incident that afternoon that shows how difficult it can be to get the regulars and occasional Barmy Army members singing from the same hymn sheet. While the Mitchell Johnson song was funny, singing it what seemed like hundreds of times that afternoon diluted it. Indeed merely repeating a few of the same few songs everyone knew got repetitive. At one point the old hands decided to spice things up by going through the whole repertoire. You're always going to have a lot who don't know the words at this point, but then that's how we learned them – by listening to others sing first. And most of them had been included on the freely available

Barmy Army songsheets. But one guy took someone aside and complained that they felt left out as we sang songs they didn't know. I know it can be frustrating when you don't know the songs, we've all been through that stage, but you just have to make an effort to learn. We never want to turn it into a clique – the more people know more songs the better it is for everyone but you have to meet us halfway.

There was a bit of a clique that night, however, because there was another smaller party in a different bar and not everyone was invited. This may sound hypocritical but when numbers are limited at a venue you have to draw a line somewhere and besides we would be allowed to sing a bigger variety of songs as everyone attending would know them. There was also the advantage that the players had been invited. So we shifted off to the new venue and sure enough after a few beers were joined by several of our on-field heroes intent on sharing the evening's festivities with those who had backed them. And it wasn't long before I was to end up the object of every pair of eyes in the pub as I had in Sydney 12 years earlier, but in dramatically different circumstances.

I was chatting to Swanny and he demanded, as only Swanny can, that I sing his song for him. I told him that if he wanted to sing it he could do it with me. This led to something of a Mexican stand-off, but unbeknown to me Jock had overheard the exchange, high-tailed it to the DJ and demanded he put *Champagne Supernova* on. Upon hearing the opening strains Swanny, Millers and myself donned our sunglasses, stood on a table and sang the Swanny version we'd concocted in Chennai (albeit I had to whisper in his ears some of the words as he admitted he'd never got round to learning them). Now I ask you dear reader, is there anything better that could happen to you as a sports fan? You've just seen a team you have supported through thick and thin for several years beat their biggest rivals in their own backyard to retain the

Ashes. And then you find yourself stood on a table with one of the best players in the world, arm-in-arm, singing the song that you had the major part in writing for him back on his first day of international Test cricket. It was a moment of moments and when I watch the video footage I get a warm, tingly feeling.

The rest of the evening was a blur of exchanges with different players singing and partying; another of those great occasions where everyone was inhabiting the same headspace and proof if proof were needed that while they were the ones doing the business on the pitch they truly appreciated our support, and we were all in this together.

There was an Ashes series still to win, however, and while the Australian press was saying that they had lost the Ashes it was patently obvious to us that they hadn't, yet. Yes, we'd retained them, but we hadn't won them outright. A defeat at Sydney would mean the series was only drawn. Even a draw would knock off the gloss. If the players had got a taste for victory on Australian soil then so had we and by god we wanted more. And while we had learned never to expect (OK, we had expected in Perth and look what happened) we still went into this with a level of, erm, expectancy. We were better. And the best team wins five-Test series. But, of course, who were we kidding that we weren't nervous too? This could be the biggest comedown we'd ever known. I just hoped after that night in Melbourne that the players had a quieter New Year period than I did.

As the scene of my first ever day of overseas Test cricket and my first ever overseas Test victory, Sydney has special relevance for me. It's the Test ground I have spent the most time at outside of the UK. And I used to quite like it. That was until they redeveloped Yabba's Hill and stand and replaced it with the Doug Walters stand, which is an affront to modern sporting facilities. Not to put too fine a point on it, it's shit. Getting into the ground is a horrible experience. Getting out of the ground is a horrible experience. Everything in between, except watching England win a Test match, is a horrible experience. This is exacerbated by the fact that Sydney remains, to my knowledge, the only ground in the world where patrons cannot obtain passouts. If you want to leave the SCG you are welcome. If you want to come back in again you're not. You become a prisoner inside the ground. Which would just about be OK if there were enough catering facilities of a reasonable standard, enough bars and enough space to mingle when you want to stretch your legs. There's none of that. Nowhere in world cricket are supporters treated so shabbily – and this in a so-called modern country. Just to top it off they charge around double every other ground in Australia to get in. Pah!

Fortunately what unfolded in front of us over five days made up for this dislike of the venue in which we were contained. There were no real scares and while there were no immense highs such as those in Adelaide or Melbourne a succession of great occurrences kept us happy. Another Cook ton, Bell, who had looked majestic and only suffered from everyone else piling on so many runs before he got in, finally got his three figures. Matt Prior got the fastest England Ashes century since Botham in 1981. Michael Beer took what he thought was his first Test wicket but it turned out to be a no-ball. Australia suffered a comedy run out when their openers were looking comfortable in the second innings. Johnson got that golden duck. Everything that could go right did go right.

The SCG (I appreciate that it is an inanimate object and I am glorifying it with a personality here, but run with it) clawed back some respect by allowing everyone in for free on day five and 'everyone' meant every English person in Sydney who didn't have to go to work. According to the gospel that is *Cricinfo* the attendance that day was 19,274. That must have been a guess because they weren't measuring the crowd, and while there was an English invasion it didn't number that many. The only Australians were the team and staff. Not for the first time that series the team had come, seen and conquered and we fans had taken over an Australian cricket ground as our own.

Another innings victory was concluded and the series was won 3-1. Inevitably another party was in order and the players had obviously sussed out that if there was a party to be had then we were the ones to have it with. I heard one story that the team management had arranged a special meal with a private chef who would cook anything the players desired, only for the players to intimate that actually they'd rather go and have a few beers with those lads and lasses who had spent so much money travelling to the other side of the world to support them through thick and thin. For those who had not had the privilege of partying with them in Melbourne this was obviously an amazing experience. Not that it wasn't for us; it was gratifying to know they appreciated our support enough to share their celebrations with us and it always will be, but nothing would quite replicate that Melbourne night for me.

And then another tour was over. That's always a sad time, but this time the end felt different. There was a definite feeling of finality. A peak had been reached. There was also a realisation that this was about as good as it would ever get. Winning a series in India would perhaps be a bigger sporting achievement as this was not a great Australian side, but to go to the country of the old enemy, full of inhabitants who love nothing better than to shove their sporting dominance down your throat at every opportunity and had been able to do so for years and to batter them... well we might do it again but it will never be as good as the first time.

To appreciate something like that again we would have to endure another fallow period of 20-odd years and I'm not prepared to go through that just to reinvent that feeling. To put that series into some kind of context I'd seen England play in 12 different overseas series and this was only the third England victory. In those 12 tours I had been witness to eight Test match wins and three had come in this series. After years of famine this was a feast. England were now the best side in the world. There were other targets for the team to focus on and we would always be there to support as they tried to achieve them. But I remember feeling a tad detached from the euphoria at the end of the Australian series as I realised that my biggest ambition as a cricket fan had been fulfilled. It felt like my comedown had kicked in before I could even really enjoy the high. And if that truly was as good as it will ever get it seems I will be destined to chase the cricketing dragon round the world for many years to come.

Postscript

Back to Australia, back to Sri Lanka, back to reality

Unawatuna here we come

IF THE ASHES 2011–12 was the aforementioned feast, then what followed was another famine, albeit of a different nature. That Sydney Test match was the last England played overseas in the calendar year and considering it finished on January 7 that made for an unusually fallow period. Normally such a lengthy spell of cricketing cold turkey would be a source of consternation to the travelling regulars but from a personal point of view such a gap could not have come at a better time. Not only had I spent pretty much all my money wandering around the world, my 2011 was another year of personal transition. You might now be thinking that I am always in transition and never actually getting anywhere and you would have a point. But whatever the relative merits of that argument I wasn't really in a position to go gallivanting abroad to watch cricket that year.

As everyone else flew back to Blighty basking in the glory of an overseas Ashes win, I hung around with my Aussie mates and pondered what to do with the rest of my life. I had no real desire to return home to the UK even after 14 months away but then I didn't really have a desire to do much other than carry on travelling, and a lack of funds prohibited that as a course of action. Sooner or later I was going to have to pay my dues and no matter how much I tried to pretend otherwise the reality was that it would have to be sooner.

The problem was I didn't really know how I wanted to pay them. I placed blind faith in the fact that something would turn up and decided to spend what little cash I had left on a return to Sri Lanka for a couple of weeks before heading to the UK to see what life had in store for me there.

I arrived back in the UK on March 2, 2011, 443 days after leaving. Forty-eight days later I was on a plane to Australia to move in with a girl I barely knew. I met Rae on my final weekend in Melbourne, spent a couple of days with her and then said goodbye. Then somehow I managed to entice her to join me on my Sri Lanka jaunt, at the end of which we said goodbye again. If it wasn't for the magic of Skype the rest of this chapter would be very different. But after our trip we spoke every day and so I took the sensible, logical decision to fly all the way around the planet again to move in with her.

Somewhat unlikely as it may seem, this actually transpired to be inspired and it all worked out rather well but there was a slight hitch in my masterplan/instinctive madness. I was penniless, and Australia is not overly keen on letting people just waltz into the country and earn an honest living. It took most of the year to rectify that situation and get myself a work visa, so in a classic cliché Rae worked and earned all the money while I sat at home writing a book. This one. Money was a bit tight and certainly would not have supported my international cricketing globetrotting so it's probably good there wasn't any trotting to do.

I must point out here that Rae had cable TV installed within two weeks of my arrival despite a complete lack of interest in sport. And so, bizarrely, I ended up watching more cricket than ever. With a ridiculous amount of time on my hands I saw everything going. England's home games were never missed: Champions League T20? Check. Pro40? You bet. At one point in December I watched an Australia Test match all day, a Big Bash game for dessert and then Sri Lanka v South Africa for supper.

Because of England's lack of touring my next dose of live international cricket did not involve them. As I took my seat at the MCG on Boxing Day 2011 to watch Australia v India several things occurred to me. First, that I would quite like to transport myself back 365 days and watch England roll over the Aussies for 98 again. Second, that this was the first time I had seen international cricket that did not involve England. Third, that the people I was with couldn't have been more different from my England supporting cricket nuts brethren. Rae knew precious little about cricket when I met her. Thanks to the fact it was on incessantly at home I had educated her to a reasonable standard but it was now time to throw the theory out of the window and get into some practical stuff. Her friend, Molly, knew less than she did. I prepared myself for a long day of explanation and continual questioning.

It was worse than I feared, but that had nothing to do with the girls because, amazingly, they weren't the least informed people in the ground that day. Out of a crowd of 70,068 I managed to attract the one person who knew less than they did. The guy in front turned round with Australia on 11-0 and explained in halting English that he was from Italy and he was confused that Australia had got 11 points but that India hadn't got any. I tried to explain to him the concept of getting wickets but I could sense it was not really going in. He turned round again with Australia on 30-odd and asked a variation on the same question, one that I again failed to answer to his satisfaction. With 20 minutes to go before lunch he stood up, grabbed his bag, turned to me and uttered 'it's boring' and left the ground. Safe to say that will be his first and last cricketing experience. After that educating the girls was simple.

By this stage I had managed to get a work visa but it was taking time to make the Aussies realise they had an understated literary genius in their midst, so while I may have been willing and able I was still pretty much unemployed except for odd bits of freelance writing. Fortunately some of that revolved around the Big Bash T20 competition and while I don't usually indulge in T20 I did get to see Shane Warne play again, although to be brutally honest I was more excited to see Paul Collingwood. Pick the bones out of that if you can.

But funds were still thin on the ground and England had twin tours to the United Arab Emirates (to play Pakistan) and Sri Lanka on the horizon. Something would obviously have to give and it wasn't difficult to work out what. While it would have been nice to watch cricket in a new country, I dislike the UAE and a trip to Sri Lanka was not only more affordable, it also offered the chance for Rae to join me and see how the reality compared to what she had read going through this manuscript. Not that she had any desire to see much cricket but as Galle, and therefore Unawatuna beach, was again on our agenda, she could happily while away her days while we were at the game.

When we booked the trip we didn't really know where the money was going to come from (blind faith being my standard modus operandi as always), but thankfully I managed to get a job in time for us to enjoy the trip without worrying about the rupees. The job was similar to that I had carried out in a freelance capacity for the Barmy Army in terms of magazine editing, website editing, social media, PR and marketing. The employer was Bowls Victoria – and bowls has a lot of similarities to cricket. Not on the pitch but it's the kind of sport you either love completely or don't understand at all, and if you love it you are fiercely protective of it. It could have been tiddlywinks for all I cared by then but it's turned out to be a rewarding role. My start coincided with the UAE series, so I contented myself with watching that on TV safe in the knowledge I now had spending money for Sri Lanka. Life was coming back together just in time to do my favourite thing again.

The last time I had gone this long without touring overseas was between the 2002–03 Ashes series and 2004–05 South Africa jaunt. Clearly it was going to be a big reunion for me with all my Barmy buddies, and to top it off my brother Darren and his wife, Jane, also decided to pop their overseas cricket-watching cherry. And then my great friend Phil, of whom you first heard failing to buy beer, pies and tickets back in Australia 2002, decided he would join in the fun. If that wasn't enough another great friend and perhaps most dangerous of drinking partners, Paul Gaston, also announced his intention to experience some Barmy Army madness. As Jock would later term it, this was becoming the Paul Winslow reunion tour. How I was going to fit everyone in and spend time with all the people I wanted to I had no idea but there was only one way to find out.

Rae and I landed at 7am and were on Unawatuna beach by midday. I'm lucky enough to have some great friends in Australia but to see so many familiar faces from home in one deluge was akin to the feeling I had had in Australia after travelling for a year. Barely a minute went by without bumping into someone I hadn't seen for a year, or sometimes two and sometimes more. And as that included my family and non-Barmy Army friends it was a bit of a crazy time.

A Barmy Army tour wouldn't be a Barmy Army tour if it didn't have some drama, and much of this one had happened long before anyone got a grain of sand between their toes. An old contact of mine from my Barmy Army working days had emailed a few of us to say he knew a guy who could organise cheap flights, so obviously I spread the word. A couple of hundred people booked, many of them because of my introduction. It became apparent after some time that the guy behind it was not what he seemed. I'm not sure of the legal situation here so I won't say too much but suffice it to say that nobody ever got on a plane booked through him, and while the majority of people involved managed to get their money back thanks to the joys of the consumer credit act and went on to book more legit flights, many lost their cash as they had paid via bank transfer. That so many people had been stitched up thanks to a deal I had brought to their attention made me feel sick to the stomach – writing that phrase makes me wonder exactly where else anyone would ever feel sick to so I'll leave that in as a rhetorical question.

Once most people had got to Sri Lanka it occurred that being ripped off would be the theme of the tour. On our last visit you could get a ground pass for 20p. While no one was expecting that still to be the case, no one had budgeted for paying £25 per day, the figure the Sri Lankan cricketing authorities had decided was fair. That's a lot of inflation. Considering the Aussies had recently been in town and paid just £2.50 it seemed that Sri Lanka Cricket had spied a quick and easy way to get rid of some of the debts they had accrued building new and largely useless stadia for the 2011 World Cup.

Our initial reaction was that they could go and stuff themselves but there were several factors that would come into play. In 2007 there were a few hundred England fans on the tour to Sri Lanka. Had there been the same number now and we'd made a concerted effort to boycott the games we might have been able to affect the prices. But now there were thousands of fans, many on official tours who had been promised tickets as part of their package. If a few of us decided not to pay the price it wasn't going to make a whole lot of difference because the majority of people had already paid or would pay without really caring about the price because they weren't going to come all this way without seeing the cricket and, after all, it wasn't prohibitively expensive to relatively rich Brits.

You could argue, and many did, that this was just a case

of someone working out the going rate for the product they were putting on and that maybe it was about time they sussed that out. But then there was a huge argument that it would price the locals out of the games. The answer to that was to have cheaper tickets for locals but then surely the whole thing becomes an issue of discrimination. And there's also a wider question of biting the hand that feeds you. No one else ploughs money into Sri Lanka's economy like England cricket fans so why get so greedy?

The other issue was that we couldn't help but wonder where the money would end up. Sri Lanka cricketing authorities are hardly famed for their transparency and the players were so used to not getting paid that captain Mahela Jayawardene had joked in a press conference after being fined part of his match fee in an ODI against Australia, 'If I get paid then I don't mind paying 10 per cent.' There was a huge feeling that even if we did pay, cricket in that country would not benefit from the cash.

In the scheme of things £25 is not a terrible price to pay for a cricket match. It's certainly cheaper than going to a game in England. But I've spoken elsewhere about England cricket fans propping up world cricket with their travelling habits so while ripping them off might seem a good idea in the short term what effect will it have in the long term? It will be interesting to see how many travel the next time Sri Lanka beckons. But enough of the moralising; that was the decision that had been made and we had to live with it and pay the price. Or did we?

It quickly became apparent there might not be enough room in the ground for everyone who wanted to get in. But then we also worked out that we wouldn't necessarily have to go into the ground. You may remember on my previous visit to Galle I had spent the morning sessions watching the game from the famous Galle Fort Wall. It didn't take us long to realise that if they wanted to rip us off we didn't have to let them. And so I found myself watching an entire Test match without deigning to go in the stadium. Those who did go in generally had little good to say about it anyway so I didn't feel as though I was missing out on much, although we were obviously quite a long way from the action, with no replay screen and we needed zoom lenses to read the scoreboard.

The other negative is that everyone was scattered around the ground, or along the wall, and that made it difficult to get much of an atmosphere going. All of which was a shame as we had a new song within 15 minutes of the start of play. It didn't take long for Raffill, Wellington and Winslow to rejig our 2007 version of *Another Brick in the Wall* to the following:

We don't need no stands to sit on
We don't need no seats at all
No getting fleeced to watch the cricket
We'll just sit up on the wall
Oi Ranatunga, we won't pay that at all
All in all it's just another Test match in Galle

Being on the wall was a great and different cricket-watching experience. The local entrepreneurs soon cottoned on that it was the ideal place to sell cold water and cold beer. One chap in particular became something of a mascot in the same way Hotdog, the star of the previous tour, had been. Apparently Hotdog was in evidence as well although I never saw him. There was a sense of solidarity among us as we roasted our nuts off in stupid heat described by one Sri Lankan newspaper as 'appalling conditions'. But while it might not have been comfortable I'm not sure being in the ground would have been any better. We had drinks brought to us, we had a top class hotel just behind us which was ideal for lunches and also provided awesome toilet facilities, and while our view was somewhat distant at least we had a breeze to knock the edge off the heat, which is more than most in the ground did.

While there may have only been a few of us anxious to get some singing going, I did manage to get my new song for Jimmy Anderson off the ground on a couple of occasions. I'd sworn myself to nail something and had come up with the following to the tune of *Can't Take My Eyes Off You:*

James you're too good to be true
You bowl so fast and so true
Batting line-ups you will run through
I can't take my eyes off of you

James when you make it swing
The Barmy Army will sing
You're our nightwatchman too
The Burnley Lara are you

Der de, der de, der de de de etc

Oh Jimmy Anderson
When you bowl right arm fast
Oh Jimmy Anderson
The batsmen never last
Oh Jimmy Anderson
Take a wicket for me

Oh Jimmy Anderson
When you get the ball
Oh Jimmy Anderson
The wickets start to fall
Oh take a wicket Jimmy
Take a wicket

We only sang it about four times in the series but Jimmy has given it his official seal of approval so we need to make an effort to sing something he likes for once. While we were still struggling to get one off the ground for him after umpteen years of Test cricket, Jonny Trott had another by the end of that first Test, inspired by a particularly gritty century. Gaz 'Dingle' Thomas utilised the tune of *You Can't Hurry Love:*

You can't hurry Trott
No you just have to wait
(She said) tons don't come east
It's a game of 'Yes, no, wait
You can't hurry Trott
No you just have to wait
Just trust in his batting
No matter how long it takes...
Now wait!

But as England slipped to defeat on day four the consolation was that if you're going to lose in four days there are few better places in the world than Galle to do it. And it meant we could have an extra day on the beach, where Giles Wellington led us in the following variation on an old classic:

Unawatuna here we come
On the beach and in the sun
When we draw the series
This is what we'll sing
We are England, we are England
Swimming in the sea

Giles was to lead us again that night in one of the more random Barmy Army sing-songs. Giles had organised a Charity Barmy Army party that raised £6,500 for the local 'Their future today' charity and 'Chance to Shine'. In total the Barmy Army raised nearly £10k for those charities throughout the tour. It was a massive night that literally went with a bang early doors when the fireworks that should have been heading out to sea shot back into the alcove in the front of the bar from which they were supposed to have been fired. Considering it was full of fans at the time it's frankly unbelievable that no one was hurt. My friend Paul spent 18 months in Afghanistan and quipped that he thought he had left that all behind.

We had decided not to have a Dawn Patrol on this tour, but that was ultimately revoked when someone decided that as a fair few of the hardcore were still at the coalface at 6am we could have a reverse Dawn Patrol. The next thing we knew Bill was stood in the sea playing the last post as the sun rose over the ocean. It didn't take long for us all to join him for a swim and we spent a good period of time swimming around while going through the usual repertoire of songs in what as far as I know was a unique Barmy Army aquatic singing session. My apologies to those whose balconies were close to us – the last thing anyone needs to be woken up by is a bunch of tuneless idiots singing songs about Ally Cook at seven in the morning. It was certainly the last thing the wife of one of those singing needed and one errant husband was soon beating a hasty retreat.

The rest of us went for breakfast (pina coladas apparently being a crucial part of your five-a-day). For several this signalled the end of the night's festivities; for four hardy, stupid souls (inevitably I was one) there seemed little point in stopping now so we headed to a bar that had now reopened for a couple of, erm, daycaps. Rae discovered me there on her way to do a cooking course, shrugged her shoulders and went on her way. It was behaviour she had come to expect. As I finally wandered down the beach to bed at midday I had several conversations with people who had had a good night's sleep and were now approaching the new day with vigour.

Strangely I managed to show some vigour of my own. After three hours' sleep I woke up, which was annoying as I really should have been catching up on kip, and headed down the beach and into the sea to join other Army members. We found a tennis ball and started throwing it around in the sea. Then we procured a bat and spent the next two hours playing a brilliant game of beach cricket. After the night I had just had, running around in 40-degree heat was possibly the last thing I should have been doing but while I basically knocked myself out for the rest of the day, and was the least entertaining dinner companion ever, I'm glad I did it. To be there and not play cricket would have been wrong. However, it took what little energy I had and I lay on my bed on the edge of sunstroke wondering if one day I might become a little bit more sensible.

A much needed rest day was spent in Bentota staying at one of the most beautiful hotels I've ever been in. Rae is the opposite of a backpacker and while we had gone budget in Unawatuna she insisted on having at least one night of luxury. As she offered to pay for said night I was unlikely to say no. And so, refreshed and reinvigorated, we set off to Colombo. There was no beach and no fort wall here so tactics would have to change both at and away from the cricket.

There are four international cricket grounds in Colombo. According to *Cricinfo,* the Sinhalese Sports Club holds 10,000 people, the Premadasa has a capacity of 35,000, and the Colombo Cricket Club can take 6,000. The site doesn't have a figure for the P Sara Oval, but I can tell you now it's around 4,000. So if you're playing against the one Test nation in the world renowned for bringing thousands of fans overseas which ground would you choose to host the game? No prizes for that one I'm afraid, so the P Sara Oval readied itself to try to fit in everything the England fans could throw at it. As we had arrived in Colombo the night before we didn't have tickets and there was a real concern that there wouldn't be any. So by 8am we were queuing to get tickets that we weren't even sure would be available. Fortunately for us there were 200 to be had on the gate so the early start was worth it. If there hadn't been any I reckon we'd have been on the first bus back to Unawatuna to watch it on the beach.

The benefit of the smaller venue was that a ground filled to capacity is always more exciting to be in than one that's half empty. Some chose to blag their way in rather than pay the cash but however we got in there was enough room and leeway that we could actually congregate, have some fun and get a bunch of likely suspects together to do a bit of singing. There was nothing remarkable about this Test – it was just a classic example of everything this book has been about. Good banter, good camaraderie, good atmosphere, good singing and an England victory to add the cherry on the icing on the cake. Old friends, new friends, great times.

I had, as always, slightly overdone it on occasions, especially on day four which was Poya – a Buddhist holiday that takes place every full moon when no alcohol is sold. I worked on the basis that a day off would be a good thing but evidently just because they didn't sell it didn't mean we couldn't drink it. Several bottles of duty-free spirits made their way into the ground and it was, if anything, worse than ever. Thankfully England didn't win that day – it would have been an interesting celebration to go out and not be able to buy a beer.

But victory was achieved on day five, and that evening we partied in the Taj Samudra hotel and although the players were due to fly out at 2am that night they still found time to come and join us for an hour or two in what is now becoming an accepted part of any tour. I had the opportunity to catch up with Swanny before he got on stage to belt out a rather good rendition of *Mustang Sally,* sought approval from Jimmy Anderson for his new song and had time to discuss beards with Matty Prior when he was kind enough to compliment me on mine.

And then it was all over again. During the tour it felt as though it was lasting forever, but as always it ended far too abruptly leaving a gaping chasm in my life where cricket watching and everything associated with it had been. This special group of people who mean so much to each other had congregated once again and almost before we knew it dissipated to their homes until the next time. And inevitably as it drew to a close, talk turned to the 'next time' – a four-Test tour of India and the possibility of a visit to Eden Gardens, the mecca of cricket, the number one ground at which we all wanted to watch Test cricket. And this is when reality really hit me. For so long cricket had consumed my life and become my *raison d'être.* I had put myself in a situation where I rarely missed out on anything to do with England and cricket. As a self-employed journo working for the Barmy Army I had engineered a lifestyle where I had gone where I wanted when I wanted and seen an inordinate amount of cricket. I had missed nothing. I was the one who was always where everyone else wanted to be.

But now the reality was different. A combination of travelling and the desire to experience living in another country had required sacrifices, the main one being I was now employed. And being employed meant limited holiday. Limited holiday meant limited touring. No longer was I at liberty to just sod off every time I wanted. The reality was I had already suffered from this. Every time my hardcore mates reminisced about the Bangladesh tour in 2010 or the UAE tour of 2012 something inside of me hurt at the fact I had missed out. Now it looks like I will miss out again… although as I write this the only two words that are really active in my brain are 'unpaid' and 'leave'.

Was going on every tour a temporary odyssey that was bound to end, or is the fact that I can no longer go on every tour a temporary hiatus? The desire is still very much there so I will keep my powder dry, safe in the knowledge that after India we tour New Zealand and Australia, both of which should be easy options for me. After that it's probable that I will be in some other stage of transition, hopefully one that accommodates perennial touring. Because while most elements of my life are prone to sudden and dramatic paradigm shifts, cricket is my one reassuring constant.

Other cricket books from SportsBooks

Arthur Milton – Last of the Double Internationals
by Mike Vockins
Hardback, published May 12 2011
ISBN: 9781907524035
£18.99

Arthur Milton was surely the last of that rare breed – a man good enough to play cricket and football for England. Twelve have had that rare distinction but the all-year-round nature of both sports makes it impossible that the feat will happen again. Milton had played 12 games for Arsenal when he was called up to play against Austria in 1951 because one legend, Tom Finney, was unavailable and another, Stanley Matthews was dropped. Milton decided to concentrate on cricket at the relatively young age of 29 in 1955 and Arsenal sold him to his home town club, Bristol City, for whom he made 14 appearances. He had played 84 times for Arsenal, scoring 21 times.

But if his football career was all too short his cricket career extended far beyond most of his contemporaries. He finished his six-Test career with 204 runs at 25.50 but he played for Gloucestershire from 1948 until 1974. He finished with more than 32,000 runs and 56 hundreds in first-class cricket. He was also outstanding in the field with 758 catches.

Duckworth Lewis – The Method and the Men Behind it
by Frank Duckworth and Tony Lewis
Hardback, published Apr 16 2011
ISBN: 9781907524004
£12.99

Name cricket's most famous partnership nowadays and you can forget Hobbs and Sutcliffe, Statham and Trueman or Lillee and Thomson. Instead you have to turn to Duckworth and Lewis, the two statisticians who brought order to the one-day game when rain interfered.

These days almost every weather-truncated one-day match throughout the world is decided by the Duckworth Lewis method; this book tells the story behind it; how it came into being and how the two were sometimes pilloried in the media after commentators and correspondents failed to understand the logic behind it.

The Victory Tests – England v Australia 1945
by Mark Rowe
Hardback, published Sep 16 2010
ISBN: 9781899807949
£10.00

One minute before 7pm on Tuesday, May 22, 1945 a packed Lord's roared as Australia beat England in the last over of the first Victory Test. A fortnight after Victory in Europe, the result did not matter – only the cricket.

The five matches between a near full-strength England and Australian servicemen, at least one of whom had just been released from a PoW camp, drew huge crowds. Great cricketers played on both sides: Len Hutton, Wally Hammond, Keith Miller, Lindsay Hassett. Everyone hailed the spirit of sportsmanship. Even the result - a 2-2 draw – was satisfying.

Yet this story is forgotten today. The only history of the series is a limited-edition Australian book on the subject.

The story has characters - besides the stars, men such as the Australian Dambusters Squadron pilot Ross Stanford; the quiet un-Australian Australian spin bowler Reg Ellis; and the English teenagers Donald Carr and John Dewes, who were on the wrong end of Keith Miller discovering that he was the fastest bowler in the world.